De-/Anti-/Post-colonial Feminisms

in Contemporary Art and Textile Crafts

Edited by Katy Deepwell

KT press publishes books and *n.paradoxa: international feminist art journal*
to promote understanding of women artists and their work

De-/Anti-/Post-colonial Feminisms in Contemporary Art and Textile Crafts
Katy Deepwell (editor)

ISBN: 978-0-9926934-7-3

Publisher: KT press, 38 Bellot Street, London, SE10 0AQ, UK
Website: https://www.ktpress.co.uk

Book series editor: Katy Deepwell
To report errors, please email: ktpress@ktpress.co.uk

1. Theory of art: Contemporary art 2. Feminist theory 3. Postcolonial Studies
I. Deepwell, Katy (editor). II. Title.

Acknowledgements

This book has its origins in four online seminars (June/July 2022) with the same title, organised by Katy Deepwell, Neelam Raina and Neda Mohamadi at Middlesex University, with support from the Faculty of Arts and Creative Industries' Research Funds. These seminars were organised by the Create/Feminisms cluster for academics and PhD students, which, since 2014, has a history of holding events, conferences and panel discussions on feminisms and art. A previous conference resulted in the publication, Katy Deepwell (ed.), *Feminist Art Activisms and Artivisms*, Amsterdam: Valiz, 2020.

The 2022 seminars were organised around four themes: Feminist Futures, Aesthetics, Textile Crafts and Pedagogies, which mirror the sections and themes in the current book. The production costs of this book were financially supported by Faculty of Arts and Creative Industries' Research Funds, Middlesex University.

The editor would like to thank all the authors for their contributions, with special thanks to Melissa Thackway for her translation from French to English of Françoise Vergès; to *Afterall* for permission to reproduce Madina Tlostanova's text; and to Nancy Hynes for proof-reading this book.

Contents

Inter-related and Divergent Paths

Katy Deepwell

This book explores theoretical ideas and practical strategies pursued in de-/
anti-/post-colonial research projects in contemporary art and textile crafts. This
book was conceived with the idea that there are important differences across and
between these three hyphenated approaches within feminism that need to be
discussed in terms other than a liberal celebration of decoloniality as diversity,
multi-culturalism or intersectionality in the West, and that represent more than a
"banal refrain" or an "affective promise".[1] Each essay offers distinct configurations
of the stakes for feminist politics in de-/anti-/post-colonial approaches in relation
to gender, class, racial and ethnic differences within interpretations, practices
or education in contemporary art and textiles crafts. These differences matter
and they produce conflicting accounts. Only when considered as a whole, do
they represent a (non-exhaustive) pluri-versality of lines of enquiry to criticising
coloniality in feminist terms within and across these hyphenated approaches.

The essays encompass art historical, political and sociological research,
including PhDs, about art and experimental film; artists' reflection on art
practice; active educational projects and public education programmes and
work in development initiatives around craft and employment in rural areas
affected by conflict. As the contributors argue de-/anti-/post-colonial feminism(s)
have provided a means to consider both feminism(s) and art/textile crafts in
developing and developed countries, through their divergent economies, social
organisation and histories in relation to global politics, without reinforcing
colonial forms of anthropology (us and Them), centre/periphery forms of Area
Studies or a cultural/political dominant West vs. the Rest. These essays do not
move easily from one paradigm to another from calls for anti-colonial struggle to
postcolonial analysis, or from a critique of postcolonialism to decolonial options,
and vice versa, from decolonial ontology/epistemology to a postcolonial future.
They attempt to articulate a feminist case for the activities/praxis they discuss,
through the means of discussion itself, and aim to do more than offer arguments
for greater recognition of women as creative producers from ethnic and sexual
minorities in different parts of the world, or for those whose voices are rarely
heard or whose contribution has not been recognised – the sub-altern, the
"minoritised"/ "racialised" or the dispossessed.

A commonly understood distinction between decolonial and postcolonial scholarship has been drawn according to Latin American scholars' dominance in the former (Mignolo, Quinjano, Lugones, Anzaldúa), and South Asian scholars' in the latter (Bhabha, Said, Spivak), but this distinction has shifted with the widespread use of these terms in academic thought globally. Colonialism developed many forms of organisation and administration, under different Empires, with impacts in the West and the East as well as North and South: "settler colonialism" continues for many Indigenous peoples and the extraction of resources or the impact of plantation slavery systems were not exclusive to one Colony or colonial power. Feminism (as a plural) has emphasised how all knowledge has a politics of location – as both an intellectual and physical/geographical place from which to see the world, and a moment in time, but what is the relation of this emphasis on standpoint and localised struggle to postcolonial claims for universality or decoloniality's emphasis on specificities or anti-colonial struggles?

As Aarti Kalwra shows in her essay on women's involvement in education and promotion of craft practices in India, use of these terms has more than a temporal dimension over the last 150 years when traced across colonial/anti-colonial, postcolonial and decolonial positions. Her essay draws attention to the 1960s decolonial arguments around crafts by Kamaladevi, that actively link Asia and Africa, and highlight her role in setting up new institutions to promote craft in India. Madina Tlostanova in her essay suggests the difference should be drawn in the following terms: 'The postcolonial is meant here as an objective condition, the geopolitical and geo-historical situation of those who were born and raised in ex-colonial societies. The decolonial is different as it is an option, a choice of how to interpret reality and act upon it' (p.27). She expands what the decolonial option as an aestheSis (not an aesthetic) might be in relation to the work of three women artists from post-Soviet Republics. In education, as Michelle Williams Gamaker writes, the decolonial became the framework for A Particular Reality's (APR's) work foregrounding the experiences and work of BiPOC students in the UK (whether born or based in Europe or those paying international fees in Europe). The re-imagining elements of decolonial praxis (where thought and practice are conceived together) offered the potential to develop alternative proposals for anti-racist/anti-sexist curricula, when neo-liberal celebrations of "diversity" in the student population have led to some very superficial changes, given the hard facts of minimal BiPOC employment amongst academics. By contrast, Françoise Vergès' critique of the situation in France proposes "a" decolonial feminism that 'accepts the existence of other feminisms; it does not wish to become *the* theory, but [to] facilitate transborder and international alliances' and names her proposal for anti-racist entanglements as a form of 'maroon feminism'.[2] Her critique of capitalism and coloniality, (following Maria Mies), where heteropatriarchy is central to its construction, leads her to argue for a feminist future positioned against the dominance of 'civilizational feminism' as a neoliberalism bringing white Xenophobic and extreme right values (as forms of femo-nationalisms, femo-Imperialism) to bear on all parts of the world while promoting capitalism and the free market as the only options for everyone's future. In solidarity with feminists from the Global South, she argues that we should take a 'stance against a temporality that describes liberation only in terms of a unilateral "victory" against the reactionary' in a linear model of struggle or appeasement. She advocates instead a broad, transnational, pluralist, decolonial politics in which only a 'multidimensional analysis of oppression that refuses to divide race, sexuality and class into mutually exclusive categories' can challenge the erasure or non-existence of women in the global Majority.

These readings of the decolonial are contested by Shanna Ketchum-Heap of Birds who uses the decolonial, rather than the postcolonial, to discuss First Nation artists' approach to indigenous issues, rights and agendas in the US. She focuses on the performances of Spiderwoman Theatre about missing and murdered indigenous women, which exemplify the extreme violence indigenous women have received. She draws on Eve Tuck and K.Wayne Yang's point that 'Decolonisation is not a metaphor'[3] for indigenous people living under "settler colonialism" or for how indigenous knowledge is valued, and takes up Bolivian feminist Silvia Rivera Cusicanqui's argument that 'there can be no discourse of decolonisation, no theory of decolonisation, without a decolonising practice'.[4] Dalida María Benfield describes her own work as a decolonising practice across several decades, in a series of episodic essays about time and place, from her birth in Panama, and working in the US to a residency organised in Kenya. Her collaborative works – first with María Lugones on *Mujeres de Pilsen,* then Video Machete and the Center for Arts, Design + Social Research – are discussed.

How to produce decolonial outcomes for research on women craft producers in rural areas affected by conflict is the subject of Neelam Raina's and Fatima Hussain's essays. Neelam Raina discusses how these women are not considered by either the UN's postcolonial development policy or its post-conflict reconstruction policy, and in addition how their contribution to the history of craft-making is poorly recorded. The 'Culture and Conflict' project, which she leads, examines what is at stake for women who become heads of households, when they turn toward or return to crafts to earn a living (in conflict areas like Sri Lanka, Afghanistan, Pakistan and Indian Kashmir). She examines what it means for these women to work from home. Fatima Hussain, in her examination of women's craft activities in the Upper Chitral Valley in Pakistan, offers insights into how postcolonial development's emphasis on commercialization and bringing goods to market, might disrupt the location of craft-making in daily life and the cycle of seasons, for rural women working in a mountainous and conflict-ridden region. Her research focuses on how the decolonial might offer intra-relational perspectives emphasising how craft is valued as a shared practice of making between women.

Focusing on blackwomen's creative practice in experimental film in the US and UK, Ayanna Dozier develops a trait, first identified by Caribbean writer Sylvia Wynter, called 'mnemonic aberrations'. This provides the means to examine a corpus of works by experimental women filmmakers as positive expressions of women's creativity, in contrast to how the legacy of plantation systems of slavery continues to function as a negative in anti-blackness and racism today. Dozier argues that mnemonic aberration is 'a tactic for destabilizing linear or colonial temporalities', but it is not a claim for an 'ethno-aesthetic': nor is it about representation, representational politics and identity politics. 'Mnemonic aberrations" is central to an ethic-aesthetic politics of care, contesting how colonialism and anti-blackness has rendered invisible and mis-read black women's creative production.

The value of postcolonial approaches to discussions of art or craft has not diminished and is often referred to throughout this book. Jean Fisher, who was Emeritus Professor at Middlesex, former editor of *Third Text* and an art critic, wrote about the revival of 'dialogic aesthetics' as a reconciliation of the 'aesthetic, the social and the ethical in ways that may at least form conditions of possibility for a new thought of the political.'[5] Her words were formed in relation to the postcolonial work of Stuart Hall and Edward Said. Highlighting how 'the psycho-social dimensions of identification' are fraught with ambivalence and contradiction, she argued that a 'dislocated subject' – often the basis of artistic practice – has roots which are 'already rhizomatic and multi-lingual; the self is already doubly or even multiply inscribed with the other' imposed by forces outside the self. Is this postmodern understanding of dislocation – not identity politics and representation – applicable to all discussion of many women artists' practices, when they are born in one country but working in another, or for the themes and issues they tackle which do not just return to their personal subjectivity, but are issue-based, polemical or aimed to produce social/political awareness of racism, the continuing impact of coloniality or ethnic conflicts.

Visibility and recognition of the contribution of women artists from the Global Majority in these debates, not just in Europe, the Caribbean or USA, but also internationally for artists from South America, Asia or Africa, remains a key issue for many feminist initiatives, but this is not centred on questions of Otherness to a dominant (national) culture or simply their lack of visibility in a mainstream internationalist art world or popular culture in general. Feminism, as a politics and across many disciplines in academia, has argued by, with and on behalf of women for the end of social, political and economic discrimination against women, not only based on their sex/ gender, but also on women's sexuality, race, religion and creed. A strong emphasis in feminist theory/history/politics has been on the value in women learning from previous generations of other women or from female role models. This emphasis in feminisms is present throughout this book. The South African project, Art on My Mind, described by Sharlene Khan, offers a positive example of resistant feminist self-organisation within a University context, for students to listen to different artists who are women of colour, and learn from their experiences. Inspired by bell hooks' work, the value of listening to women artists from a wide range of backgrounds and ethnic groups with very different experiences in art practice, education and life developed into a major research project and website and alongside other initiatives – conferences and reading groups to profile the creativity of women of colour in South Africa. Do we see here a decolonial anti-racist call for recognition of alternative ways of being and doing?

Two educators, from opposite sides of the Atlantic, offer their very different experiences in developing significant initiatives in/outside formal art education institutions. In one, APR, the black arts movement from the 1980s in the UK provides inspiration; in the other, for Leslie Sotomayor, it is the writings of Gloria Anzaldúa and the Chicano/x movement. The influence of Paulo Freire's *Pedagogy of the Oppressed* and Ivan Illich's anti-institutional thought have played a major role in critical forms of arts education since the 1970s, but there are many other models circulating in art schools. Feminism has developed both separatist and consciousness-raising approaches to art education, as well as collective and collaborative group projects and practices, and taken part in teach-ins, protests and occupations. Self-education, however, outside the sanction of educational institutions, has taken priority where there were few women teachers or no women artists discussed in the curriculum. At the heart of all critical models of art education is the notion of questioning what is already established as canon or curriculum: its limits according to gender/ race/ class/ nation/ ethnicity are well documented but so too are critiques of multi-culturalism for their token interventions towards diversity or representationalism. It has been the reproduction of rote learning, or pre-digested packages of knowledge as a transmission from (male) "master" to (junior) student, which is most criticised by feminisms in both art practice and textile crafts. While it has been a criticism of postcolonial cultural studies that it analysed discourses, rather than produced models for change, what does decoloniality as a praxis now offer in its links between the realities of coloniality and systems of knowledge production for women? Sotomayor explores how *auto-consciencia* or self-awareness may offer a decolonising approach to education through *visual platicas*. As a method for student-led learning about everything from caste to the crit, APR's extra-curricular activities remain focused on what students bring to the class in terms of their own knowledges and expectations of learning, while Sotomayor highlights how this attention must also include awareness of their experiences of pain, trauma and racism. Both educators ask, are we flexing what is possible in the system or only allowing questions to be raised in isolated initiatives?

Both postcolonial and decolonial theory have argued against Eurocentric constructions of knowledge and the devaluation of other ways of knowing, but given growing awareness and greater acknowledgment of the global distribution of knowledges and their uneven development, what will "going global" as an institutional goal for academic research mean in these debates, if women's knowledge, voice and experiences are not heard? While this book explores the potential and possibilities of some de-/anti-/post-colonial theories, there remain many more to explore, for example, a "planetary consciousness" in the humanities, as envisaged by Gayatri Chakravorty Spivak,[6] or Chandra Mohanty's proposal for *Feminism without Borders* (2003) or Sylvia Wynter's models[7] for rethinking the basis of human praxis. This book is a feminist contribution to these debates.

Notes

1. S.C. Persard, 'The Radical Limits of Decolonising Feminism', *Feminist Review*, vol. 128 no. 1 (2021), pp.13-27.

2. Francoise Verges, *A Decolonial Feminism*, London: Pluto, 2021, quotes from p. 17, p. 22, p. 4, p. 5 and p. 20.

3. Eve Tuck and K.Wayne Yang, 'Decolonisation is Not a Metaphor', *Decolonisation: Indigeniety, Education and Society*, vol. 1 no. 1 (2012).

4. Silvia Rivera Cusicanqui, 'Ch'ixinakax utxiwa: A Reflection on the Practices and Discourses of Decolonization', *South Atlantic Quarterly*, vol. 111 no. 1 (2012), p. 100.

5. Jean Fisher, 'Where here is elsewhere' in Kamal Boullata (ed.), *Belonging and Globalisation*, London: Saqi, 2008, pp.61-74

6. Gayatri Chakravorty Spivak, *An Aesthetic Education in the Era of Globalization*, Boston: Harvard University Press, 2012, Chapter 12.

7. Katherine McKittrick (ed.), *Sylvia Wynter: On Being Human as Praxis*, Durham: Duke University Press, 2013.

   De-/Anti-/Post-colonial Feminisms

Decolonial Antiracist Feminism

Françoise Vergès

Since the 1990s, State feminism, femo-nationalism, "civilising feminism", universalist feminism and femo-imperialism have turned gender equality into national and international policy. After the International Women's Year in 1975, the United Nations Decade for Women (1975-1985) helped officialise the linking of women's rights and universalist policymaking. Declaring, in her closing speech at the 1995 UN Fourth World Conference on Women in Beijing, that 'human rights are women's rights and women's rights are human rights', Hillary Clinton summed up this type of feminism's prevailing ideology. Yet she was inventing nothing new. In 1965, powerful US foundations like the Ford Foundation made gender equality one of their primary fields of intervention. Progressively, gender equality became the cornerstone of international and State policy. Have these demands to include women's rights in governmental policies helped overcome social, economic, and cultural inequalities between women? Between women of the Global South and the Global North? Between racialised women and non-racialised women?[1] What decolonial analysis can be developed in this context? How can we make visible the entanglement of class, age, racialisation, gender, sexuality, public health and conditions?

Who is the Subject of Feminism?

At the very heart of universalist discourses on women's rights, the homogenising category of "women" has helped mask the differences between women and their conditions of existence. It has also invisibilised the processes of racialisation, class difference, and other forms of discrimination and inequality that might impact them (ageism or ableism, to cite but two), and which are inherent to the regime of capitalism. Accordingly, universalist women's rights policies implemented by countries of the North have proved to be complicit with the very structures that perpetuate inequalities and exploitation. How can gender equality contribute to liberation processes in societies that engendered racism, capitalism and imperialism? And in what ways is the goal of gender equality promoted through racist, capitalist, imperialist policies? Black, racialised feminists, and feminists of the Global South already responded to this contradiction back in the 1960s, calling into question the very category of "women" articulated in such universalist policies. Far from covering all situations potentially experienced by these people, this category was constructed from the referent of the white, bourgeoise woman. The feminists who developed this critique thus indicated that this "human rights" discourse depoliticised the history of women's struggles against slavery, colonialism, imperialism, and capitalism. These tensions between universalist feminism and the forms of feminism that articulate questions of class, age, and gender with those of sexuality, racialisation, imperialism, the fight against environmental destruction, land rights, indigenous peoples' rights and so on, are irresolvable. Divergent, or even opposing, in their analyses of relations of domination, the connections between patriarchy and capitalism, and racialising processes in the oppression of women from minorities or the Global South, these forms of feminism do not share the same goals.

Taking the situation in France as my starting point, I shall first examine the context in which Western feminism and neoliberalism gradually found a common ground in the 1980s, before going on to consider decolonial feminism. This short text will inevitably skip over many of the feminist debates, developments, or propositions in France (both mainland and the French "Overseas" Territories). It will not draw up a detailed cartography of feminist groups either, which have multiplied over the past few years, nor of the different ecofeminist or indigenous feminism currents, nor feminism in the arts and sciences. Here, I will simply pose the question of the intertwining of a certain feminism and the upheavals heralded by neoliberalism.

Integrating Racialised Women into the Global Market

The phenomenon commonly referred to as "second-wave" feminism emerged when women massively entered the paid labour market.[2] In France, they very soon began taking action in sectors where women were highly present (notably in the factories manufacturing Chantelle textiles, Wonder batteries and Moulinex household appliances),[3] in a context in which the colonial wars in

    De-/Anti-/Post-colonial Feminisms

Algeria and Cameroon were coming to an end, feminist, antiracist and anti-imperial struggles were multiplying all over the world, but also one in which neoliberalism and State feminism were emerging, notably in Europe and the United States.

In the 1980s, neoliberals presented capitalism as "blind" to gender, capable of eliminating hierarchies between men and women, and enabling the latter not only to gain autonomy, but also to be competitive on the international labour market, while at the same time perpetuating the gendered division of labour.[4] Frantz Fanon's famous observation with regard to colonial policy – 'Let's win over the women and the rest will follow' – was re-actualised.[5] When Fanon wrote these words at the height of the Algerian War, he was commenting on the French policy that aimed to thwart the National Liberation Front's struggle; to keep control of the colony, start by "saving" its women. This process helps understand how, in the late twentieth century, policies sought to separate women's rights struggles from anti-capitalist and antiracist struggles. Racialised women's education, training, and integration into the International Labour Organisation were ardently defended by foundations, NGOs, international organisations, Western governments and feminists. Presented as economic, social and sexual emancipation for all women,[6] the demand for their entry into the labour market eclipsed the fact that racialised women have always worked and have always been exploited. For the latter, the labour market represents insecure, devalued, and very poorly paid work; they are the majority in nannying, serving, cashiering, cleaning and care activies. Transforming "women's rights feminism" into a movement bereft of an emancipatory dimension, a weapon in the hands of imperialists and neoliberals, this turn informed a whole series of decisions and declarations from the late twentieth cenutry on. In 2006 the then United Nations General Secretary Kofi Annan asserted that 'empowering women and girls is key to development'; he also considered that the recognition of women's rights was the condition for so-called developing countries' entry into the international economic system.[7] He made no mention, however, of global capitalism's racial and class structures. Racialised women of the North and women of the South became a highly valuable labour force in the wake of policies that historically transformed their wombs and bodies into capital. Gender equality was thus integrated into a dominant cultural system and became a target only attainable on the condition that women be extricated from their societies and cultures, demanding their assimilation into Western norms. According to Christine Delphy:

the instrumentalising of feminist discourse by defenders of the law demonstrates how the general principle of "women's rights" is put at the service of specific measures taken against a specific population.

Delphy continues:

> The opposition between antiracism and anti-sexism is based on beliefs that, on the one hand, presuppose the radically other nature of this population relative to "normal" French society, and, on the other, that it is only possible on the condition that the women are "extracted" from this population affected by racism.[8]

Today gender equality remains a powerful ideological tool; any obstacle to or denial of it is met with emotion and indignation, notably when it comes to crimes committed against young girls or women from minorities or from the Global South, yet without the politico/cultural/economic context of North/South relations ever being evoked, nor the colonial past that criminalised sexualities, imposed a family model, "acceptable" sexual norms, and neo-colonial paternalism. Gender equality is not only deemed good for global society and culture; it is so too for the neoliberal economy, as attested by the World Bank's "gender equality as smart economics" initiative.[9] Goldman Sachs, Nike, the Bill and Melinda Gates Foundation, the Levi-Strauss Foundation, Unilever, and investment funds have all adopted international programmes destined to integrate women into the neoliberal world.[10] OPIC2X, a US government fund, thus deployed concepts of empowerment, capacity building, and women's leadership to launch its investment programme guaranteeing investors significant returns. According to the elements it provided, women of the Global South are set to represent nearly 15 trillion US dollars of world consumption and will thus constitute a market double the size of that of China and India combined. All these investments are correlated with controlling the birthrate of women of the Global South. It must be understood that the connections between governments' and foundations' policies to control women's bodies and those of capital investments have no intention of overthrowing the capitalist system, of course. Both exploit women's needs and desires in their own interests. The example of the Bill and Melinda Gates Foundation, which is highly active in Africa, is particularly enlightening in this respect.

Focused on gender equality, universalist feminism is mobilised to safeguard a capitalism whose logic is to spread and to colonise the entire planet. French President Emmanuel Macron launched into his own gender equality "civilising mission" using the same references: birth control and promoting microcredits and individual entrepreneurship. He accordingly deployed an old racist argument

De-/Anti-/Post-colonial Feminisms

according to which African women are responsible for poverty and under-development. On 8 July 2018 during a G20 summit meeting, he declared: 'When there are still countries with seven or eight children per woman, you may well decide to spend billions of euros, but you won't stabilize a thing.'[11] On 29 September 2018, he repeated the same argument, claiming in English this time: 'Present me the woman who decided, being perfectly educated, to have seven, eight or nine children.'[12] Controlling African women's wombs is concomitant with the policy to invest in African women's economic activities, guaranteeing 'highly beneficial returns for the whole economy.'[13] This discourse concerning African women positions them as victims to be saved, their rescue remaining firmly in the hands of forces from the North.

A Colonial History of Feminism

This rapid summary helps better understand the ideological climate of our times. French State or political party feminism cannot be artificially separated from a long racist colonial history, and some of its components cannot be exonerated from their complicity with colonial and postcolonial crimes. There is no excuse for its ignorance of women's struggles in the colonies and the French "Overseas" Territories. It is not for lack of references. In the 1970s, reading the texts of the Coordination des femmes noires (Coordination of Black Women) set up in 1978 would have helped understand how Black women analysed their oppressions.[14] European feminism has yet to undertake a radical decolonisation and deracialisation process, re-reading its major texts and actions: what are its blind spots? Its denials? What allowed the conviction that, in theory, feminism escaped structural and cultural racism, colonial and postcolonial representations, and the intimate connections between family history and colonial history? What role was played by feminists from the French Socialist Party, which, after coming to power several times, embraced a conservative and neoliberal turn?[15] The feminist movements' policies have too long been studied from the perspective of a reaction to patriarchal and heterosexist policies, as if the ideological and economic transformations that racialisation produces never had any impact on the evolution of European feminist movements, and as if the women's rights struggle was by nature immune from racism and neoliberalism. It is important, for example, to understand the way in which the record privatisations undertaken by the 1997-2002 Lionel Jospin government, State-facilitated delocalisation, and the increasing flexibility of the workforce, movements of capital, free-trade agreements, and financialisation of the economy all led to greater precarity for racialised people.[16] The conception of women's rights defended by the French Socialist Party does not differ radically to that of the neoliberal Right and the reforms it has adopted.[17] Laws introduced to protect women (notably legislation concerning night work, dangerous jobs and women's health) certainly came in response to demands, but they were adopted at a time when economic decisions were already leading to the abandonment of public services, when women were massively affected by the ever greater roll-out of part-time work, when racism, Islamophobia and the silences concerning the colonial past increasingly weighed on racialised people. Racialised feminists in the North and feminists in the Global South have highlighted the fact that white women in the North's comfort and their access to the labour market are rendered possible not only by the exploitation of racialised women in their countries and women of the South, but also by that of racialised men. This is the case in France, where French women have gained from the new international division of labour. Indeed, as Silvia Federici writes:

> A vehicle for a ferociously antifeminist political project in that, far from being a means of female emancipation, the expansion of capitalist relations accentuates the exploitation of women. Moreover, it yet again offers the image of the female sexual and reproductive object. It exacerbates division among women through a specialising and a fixing of tasks that reduce our life possibilities and introduce new hierarchies and stratifications among us that undermine the possibility of common struggle.[18]

In the years that saw the rise of neoliberalism, which were rich in theoretical debates on the entanglement of economics, gender and racialisation, few white French feminists embarked on a process to decolonise and deracialise their theories and praxis – which is not the same as denouncing racism and imperialism. Feminist groups admittedly denounced class exploitation and racism, but, on the whole, French feminism nonetheless remained indifferent to the boomerang effect of the slave trade and colonialism as regards its own theories. The "boomerang effect" is how in *Discourse on Colonialism*, Aimé Césaire described what he saw as the inevitable fact that colonising societies cannot escape the spirit and the logic of the laws and racial practices that their own governments imposed in the colonies.[19] This process of decolonisation and deracialisation could not be undertaken by State feminism as its aim is not to overthrow racial capitalism, but rather to reform it. By making male/female opposition the foundation of women's oppression worldwide, so-called universalist feminism occulted the consequences

  De-/Anti-/Post-colonial Feminisms

of neoliberal economics and racial capitalism for the situation of racialised people and for women's social rights. African-American feminist Barbara Christian's essay, 'The Race for Theory', remains fundamental in understanding how bourgeoise feminism became subsumed into neoliberalism.[20] Playing on the dual meaning of race, the author reveals the ruses of power. Her warning continues to resonate today in a context of increasing repression of all that is labelled "decolonial",[21] and of the instrumentalising of feminist concepts. That 'theory has become a commodity', as Barbara Christian writes, gives even racialised people the hope that they might be recruited or promoted in an academic institution and finally heard.[22] This takeover of theory, she continues, has succeeded in influencing racialised women and women from the Global South to the extent of getting them to adopt a lexicon divorced from the needs and objectives of their communities. Freeing ourselves from this hold is one of the major tasks of antiracist feminism.

Letting Women Define Their Struggles

There are clearly, then, different *types* of feminism. Several currents can be discerned, but to resume, admittedly somewhat schematically yet not unfoundedly, I distinguish: a current that is complicit with racial capitalism; a reformist current that contests the economic and social system but seeks to improve the situation of women through institutions; and finally, a current that, more wary of those institutions, advocates women's liberation and the liberation from macho, sexist, racist and capitalist society in one and the same movement. This latter current forms alliances with the second reformist camp as it recognises the urgency of obtaining measures that limit the abuses of employers and institutions. But its objective remains liberation and decolonisation of the self, and of the self with others. In a recent publication, I advocated a "decolonial feminism" within this third field of struggle. It does not seek to impose a doctrine nor to be prescriptive. Its aim is to start from the voices and struggles of women, and of all those in the most vulnerable and insecure positions: sex workers, queer people, trans people, people in migration, refugees, indigenous peoples. As for the refusal of working-class women or those from the Global South to call themselves feminists, this is not a sign of being behind or of alienation, but rather one of resistance to what is perceived as an imperialist and bourgeois ideology.

The 17 March 2020 lockdown decreed by the French government in response to the Covid-19 pandemic is one example that helps illustrate the methodology of decolonial feminism. A decolonial feminist analysis of the lockdown helps understand what, from a political perspective, the difference in treatment put in place between different groups revealed: a simple ticking off for the white bourgeois who did not respect the lockdown rules, on the one hand; repression and police violence in poor neighbourhoods on the other. Decolonial feminism visibilises what underlies summary hearings, State lies, the destruction of the hospital system, and adds to it the taking into account of State feminism – the very same that was expressed on 4 April 2020 by the good grace of the members of the G7 Gender Equality Advisory Council:

> Because of deep-rooted gender inequality, girls and women worldwide will … experience the COVID-19 pandemic differently. We … urgently call on G7 member states for joint emergency action to respond to the particular challenges facing women and to prevent the deterioration of gender equality and women's rights worldwide.[23]

It continued,

> [women represent] seventy percent of healthcare and social service workers worldwide, putting them at the forefront of the crisis and at greater risk of exposure. They also hold the majority of low-paid and shut-down retail and service jobs.

In conclusion, the signatories called on the G7 leaders to increase the protection of girls and women.[24]   On this specific and fundamental point, the objectives of the text were in contradiction with the policies that these very governments instigated: surveillance, increased insecurity, militarisation and control – not to mention the lack of compensation given to these women (cashiers, hospital cleaning staff, day nursery workers, sex workers, etc.), who had to continue working during the lockdown and thus put their health and that of their families at risk. By exacerbating injustice and racial, class, and gender inequalities, lockdown policies once again highlighted the racial structure of capitalism and the fact that its notion of protection is based on the age-old division between lives that matter and lives that do not. A decolonial feminist politics of protection differs from such approaches by taking as its starting point the situation of those rendered the most vulnerable, of racialised women massively working in so-called "key" jobs but who are underpaid and underqualified, by taking as its starting point the fabrication of their invisibilisation and their being confronted with the institutionalised violence of patriarchal capitalism. It is on the terrain of their struggles that new feminist theories and practices are emerging.

This essay was translated from French to English by Melissa Thackway for this publication. It was first published as'Féminisme décolonial et antiraciste' in Omar Slaouti, Olivier Le Cour Grandmaison (eds.), *Dans Racismes de France* (La Découverte/Cairn.info, 2020), pp. 325-338. Reproduced with permission of the author.

Further Reading

The following references are necessarily incomplete and do not suffice considering that there has been intense debate within the different types of feminism for decades now. But these works need reading, and as widely as possible: Johanna Brenner and María Ramas, 'Repenser l'oppression des femmes. Capitalisme, reproduction biologique, travail industriel structures familiales, État-providence. Un débat avec Michèle Barrett', Europe.solidaire.org, 1 March 1984; Paolina Caro-Astorga, 'Quand le Nord s'inspire du Sud', *Ballast*, 19 September 2016; Collectif, *Pour un féminisme de la totalité*, Paris: Éditions Amsterdam, 2017; Silvia Federici, *Le Capitalisme patriarcal*, Paris: La Fabrique, 2020; 'Le féminisme contre la famille: Entretien avec Sophie Lewis', *Acta-Zone*, 24 August 2019; 'Cross-border Feminist Manifesto. To emerge from the pandemic together and change the system', eng-crossborderfeministmanifesto.pdf; Jennifer Nash, *Black Feminism Reimagined. After Intersectionnality*, Durham NC: Duke University Press, 2019; Françoise Vergès, *Un féminisme décolonial*, La Fabrique, Paris, 2019 / *A Decolonial Feminism*, trans. Ashley J. Bohrer with the author, London: Pluto Press, 2021.

Notes

1. Even though white women are also racialised in the sense that they are not exempt from the racial hierarchies that structure Western societies, the process of racialisation in terms of skin colour has made theirs a "non-colour". They are thus not considered "racialised" – so much so, even, that talking about "white women" can be perceived as stigmatising. In this text, I use the term "racialised" to refer to people who are disadvantageously racialised (i.e., non-white people).
2. In the early 1970s, half of white French women aged 25 to 59 worked. Today, three-quarters work, but, in the space of thirty-five years, women's unemployment levels have risen from 3% to 12%, and the share of part-time work has risen from 13% to 30%. Cédric Afsa Essafi and Sophie Buffeteau, 'L'activité féminine en France: quelles évolutions récentes, quelles tendances pour l'avenir?', *Économie et Statistiques*, no. 398-399 (2006), pp. 86-95; Margaret Maruani, *Travail et emploi des femmes*, La Découverte, Collection "Repères", Paris, 2006.
3. Ève Meuret-Campfort, 'Luttes de classes, conflits de genre: les ouvrières de Chantelle à Nantes', *Savoir/Agir*, vol. 12 no. 2 (2010), pp. 43-50. See also Hervé Le Roux's film about the post-strike return to work at the Wonder factory in 1968, *Reprise du travail aux usines Wonder.*
4. 'Based on the observation that patriarchy and accumulation at an international level constitute the ideological framework in which women's current reality is inscribed, the feminist movement throughout the world has no choice but to challenge this framework at the same time as it does the sexual and international division of labour relating to it,' wrote Maria Mies in 1986. Cited in Silvia

Federici, 'Reproduction et lutte féministe dans la nouvelle division internationale du travail', *Cahiers genre et développement*, no. 3 *"Genre, mondialisation et pauvreté"* (2002), pp. 45-69, p. 45.

5. Frantz Fanon, *A Dying Colonialism*, trans. Haakon Chevalier, New York: Grove Press, 1965, p. 37.

6. The ties between exploitation on the one hand, and the promise of emancipation on the other have been analysed with regard to North/South relations, but more rarely with regard to France. Already in the 1960s, however, women from the "Overseas" Territories were recruited as servants or in subaltern public service positions, enabling white women to rise up the labour market ladder, notably by entrusting childcare and housework to other racialised and precarious women. Racialisation processes continued with the arrival of women from the African and Asian continents. On the contradictions of class, race, and gender, see: Sabine Masson, 'Sexe/genre, classe, race : décoloniser le féminisme dans un contexte mondialisé. Réflexions à partir de la lutte des femmes indiennes au Chiapas', *Nouvelles Questions féministes*, vol. 25 no. 3 (2006), pp.56-75. On race, gender, class, see: Houria Bouteldja, Christine Delphy and Christelle Hamel, 'Sexisme et racisme: le cas français', *Nouvelles Questions féministes*, vol. 25 no. 1 (2006).

7. Cited in Hester Einsenstein, 'Hegemonic feminism, neoliberalism and womeno- mics: empowerment instead of liberation?', *New Formations*, no. 91 (February 2017), pp. 35-49, p. 36.

8. Natalie Benelli, Ellen Hertz, Christine Delphy, Christelle Hamel, Patricia Roux and Jules Falquet, 'De l'affaire du voile à l'imbrication du sexisme et du racisme', *Nouvelles Questions féministes*, vol. 25 no. 1 (2006), pp. 4-11, p. 10; see also: Patricia Roux, Lavinia Gianettoni and Céline Perrin, 'L'instrumentalisation du genre : une nouvelle forme de racisme et de sexisme', *Nouvelles Questions féministes*, vol. 26 no. 2 (2007), pp. 92-108.

9. In 2019, the Umbrella Facility for Gender Equality programme continued to defend this initiative. Bringing together fourteen States and international foundations, it is a 'multi-donor trust fund dedicated solely to strengthening awareness, knowledge, and capacity building' and generating 'pilot programs, innovative interventions, and impact evaluations…to close gaps between women and men.' https://www.worldbank.org/en/programs/umbrellafacilityforgenderequality/about [accessed 13 February 2023].

10. Hester Einsenstein, 'Hegemonic feminism, neoliberalism and womeno- mics', *New Formations*, no. 91 (February 2017), pp. 39-40. Also see: Sara Farris and Catherine Rottenberg, "Introduction: Righting Feminism", *New Formations*, no. 91 (February 2017), pp. 5-15; Alison Winch, Kirsten Forkert and Sally Davison, 'Neoliberalism, feminism and transnationalism', *Soundings*, no. 71 (2019), pp. 4-10. Female scholars from the Global South have produced very many critiques of the consequences of development and birth control policies, neoliberalism, and microcredits on women from the Global South.

11. ' "7 à 8 enfants par femme" en Afrique, les propos de Macron qui passent mal', Ouest-France.fr, 11 July 2017.

12. Cited in Jacques Pezet, 'Emmanuel Macron a-t-il vraiment dit 'Montrez-moi une femme parfaitement éduquée, qui décide d'avoir 7, 8, 9 enfants?', https://www.liberation.fr/. *Check News*, 10 October 2018.

13. 'G7 Biarritz: Conférence de presse conjointe consacrée au programme Afawa', https://www.

De-/Anti-/Post-colonial Feminisms

elysee.fr/, 26 August 2019.

14. For more on the Coordination des femmes noires, see: Emmanuelle Brunel and Tauana Olivia Gomez Silva, 'Paroles de femmes noires. Circulations médiatiques et enjeux politiques', *Réseaux*, vol. 201 no. 1 (2017), pp. 59-85; and on female immigrant movements, Nadia Châabane, 'Diversité des mouvements de "femmes dans l'immigration" ', *Les Cahiers du Cedref*, no. 16 (2008), pp. 231-250.

15. Serge Audier, 'La gauche réformiste et le libéralisme', *L'Économie politique*, vol. 48 no. 4 (2008), pp. 83-100; Pierre-Nicolas Baudot, 'Hégémonie néolibérale, conquête du désir et crise de la gauche', *Le vent se lève*, 20 November 2019.

16. Didier Fassin, 'Priorité à l'ordre et obsession sécuritaire: les causes perdues des socialistes', *Le Monde*, 25 September 2012. On neoliberal ideology in France, see: Henri Lepage, *Demain le Capitalisme,* Le Livre de poche, Paris, 1978; Luc Boltanski and Ève Chiapello, *Le Nouvel Esprit du capitalisme*, Gallimard, Paris, 1990; on the spread of the theory and its European rooting, see: Arnaud Brennetot, 'Géohistoire du néolibéralisme. Retour sur une étiquette malléable et mouvante', *Cybergeo. European Journal of Geography*, doc. 155 (2013) pp. 1-30.

17. In January 1975, the Veil law legalised abortion in France under certain conditions; in July 1975, divorce was no longer only obtainable on the grounds of fault, but also by mutual agreement; 1980 saw a ban on making pregnant women redundant.

18. Silvia Federici, 'Reproduction et lutte féministe dans la nouvelle division du travail', *Période*, 17 April 2014.

19. Aimé Césaire, *Discourse On Colonialism*, trans. Joan Pinkham, NY: Monthly Review Press, 2000 (1950), p. 36.

20. Barbara Christian, 'The Race for Theory', *Feminist Studies*, vol. 14 no. 1 (1988), pp. 67-79.

21. See, for example: 'La pensée 'décoloniale' renforce le narcissime des petites différences', a tribune signed by eighty French psychoanalysts, LeMonde.fr, 25 September. 2019. 'Le 'décolonialisme', une stratégie hégémonique: l'appel de 80 intellectuels', *Le Point*, 13 September 2018.

22. Barbara Christian, 'The Race for Theory', p. 67.

23. 'Step it up G7: An extraordinary time requires extraordinary solidarity', tribune by members of the 2018 and 2019 G7 Gender Equality Advisory Councils, 6 April 2020, https://www.unwomen.org/en/news/stories/2020/4/op-ed-joint-step-it-up-g7, [Accessed 17 June 2023]. Set up in 2018 by Canadian Prime Minister Justin Trudeau during the Canadian presidency of the G7, this council was renewed by the President of the French Republic Emmanuel Macron in 2019, who nominated new members to it.

24. Ibid.

Decolonial AestheSis and the Post-Soviet Art

Madina Tlostanova

One certainly cannot speak of a well-shaped 'decolonial art movement', so to speak, in the post-Soviet context.[1] However, artists are increasingly developing self-conscious critical practices of subversion and corporeal emancipation grounded in decolonial agendas. What I will refer to here as 'post-Soviet decolonial art' – and as is the case with other examples of decolonial creativity – seeks to engage with forgotten native sounds, tastes and odours. Decolonial artists often aim at reinstating geo-body storytelling and disqualified ideals of beauty. In fact, works by such artists in the post-Soviet space are often ironic, at times grotesque; they include parody, mimicry, chiasmus, overlay, exaggerated nostalgia, deconstruction and creolisation of the previous official aesthetic norms and rules of Soviet modernity. These artists strive to restore human dignity by reclaiming memories and histories, as well as by reviving and reimagining native cultures in tension with Soviet, post-Soviet, national and global neoliberal modernities. These artists value the resurgence of native cosmologies and local histories vis-à-vis modernity. Instead of positioning native cultures in the modern/ colonial sense of going back to something dead and frozen, artists negate progressivist temporality and the translation of exotic spaces into lagging behind times, thus advancing a complex interpenetration of traditional and contemporary features.[2]

In addition to the characteristics mentioned above, among the most recognisable decolonial themes in post-Soviet art is the problematisation of the museum as a euro-modern site for knowledge production and of modern/ colonial, man/woman, human/animal or natural/cultural binaries. It will become clear throughout the text that such a decolonial drive in this context mainly affects those artists who belong to ethnic-national minorities and to colonised and indigenous groups within the post-Soviet space. In what follows, I discuss the work of post-Soviet artists such as Kazakh Saule Suleimenova, Chechen Aslan Gaisumov and Dagestanian Taus Makhacheva, as either in conscious or intuitive dialogue with decolonial aesthesis. Such framing becomes significant as it allows for the identification of one of the many challenges some of these artists face today: is it possible to exist between the devil of the state and the deep blue sea of the market? On the one hand, the international art market seems not yet to have a separate space for artistic practices of this kind. With such space lacking, decolonial post-Soviet works are categorised as ethnic, ornamental, decorative or in a trendier language – multicultural. These categories blur any specificity and works are drowned within the larger category of contemporary art, causing decolonial elements to be rendered invisible or irrelevant. Archival work on coloniality and decoloniality of sensing has become a central goal, in opposition to many post-Soviet artists who continue to concentrate on ideology through replaying the (post)avant-garde models or blending in with the larger fashionable trends in contemporary global art. Additionally, decolonial post-Soviet artists are actively criticised by their leftist underground peers with their predictable progressivist neglect of any ethnic-national agendas such as ancestral bodies and memories, non-linear temporal paradigms and re-existence modes of being, while the postcolonial post-Soviet states have rediscovered the commercial value of national art and actively engage in its appropriation and depoliticisation.[3]

Contextualising the Post-Soviet Experience Through a Decolonial Lens
The decolonial thought that originated at the end of the Cold War allowed to consider the experience and history of the so called 'second-rate' empires. The Czarist Russia and the subsequent Soviet modernity/coloniality, for example, have been the zones of external imperial difference, bound to "catch-up". Decolonial thought humbles the mostly anglophone field of postcolonial studies – downsizing it to a mere reflection of its specific geopolitical and corpo-political experiences.[4] In decolonial interpretations, the Soviet past and post-Soviet present are seen as complex intersectional conglomerates of ideology, ethnic-racial, gender, religious, colonial, indigenous and other factors instead of homogenous ideological constructs. The end of the Cold War generated both the dominant neoliberal 'end of history' narrative and decolonial thinking with its central concepts of coloniality and decoloniality. These concepts came to replace previous ones, such as colonialism (as a historical and descriptive term) and decolonisation (as a political process), focusing on knowledge production instead. The collapse of state socialist modernity, which allowed neoliberal globalisation to take centre stage, became the proverbial elephant in the room as it changed the global geopolitics of knowledge that remained unnoticed. Western liberal and neoliberal thought interprets post-socialism in an exclusively temporal sense, as after socialism, ignoring the spatial and, what is most important, the human dimensions. Likewise, decolonial thought initially largely ignores both the experience of state socialism and what has come after it. The actual lives of those who were told to forget about their socialist experience, to go back to the end of modernity's queue and start from scratch in a different paradigm, were not considered relevant on either side of the decolonial/neoliberal equation.

Starting from the mid-2000s, a number of decolonial and post-socialist thinkers have begun to establish connections that allowed the post-socialist discourse to enrich decolonial thought with certain ideas linked to our specific experience.[5] Art plays a central part in such cross-fertilisation. In many post-Soviet countries art remains the only provisionally allowed form of critical thinking and venue for designing an alternative image of the future. Metaphorical artistic expressions are also strangely more effective than bare facts, as they call directly to our emotions and sensibilities, thus launching a painful process of existential liberation.

Walter D. Mignolo and Rolando Vázquez present the concept decolonial aestheSis in opposition to aestheTics, which they associate to the colonial matrix of power.[6] AestheSis is here understood within the context of its original meaning: an ability to perceive through the senses, and the process of sensual perception itself. Decolonial aesthesis originates, then, in the affective experience of those who have never been given a voice before or have been seen as dangerous or noble savages and native informants. It acts as a mechanism of producing and regulating sensations, and hence is inevitably linked with the body as an instrument of perception that mediates our cognition. Decolonial aesthesis proves to be a useful interpretative tool when discussing post-Soviet artists coming mostly from the non-European ex-colonies of the USSR. These artists were weary of the prescribed Soviet aesthetic models, including those created specifically for the ethnic-national others, and uneasy about simply emulating Western trends. They attempted to decolonise their aesthesis in turning to forgotten native models of perception censored during the Soviet time, and dismissed as outdated in the only remaining global neoliberal modernity after 1989. Decolonial impulses are often the only source of re-existence[7] as another way of being in spite of coloniality and beyond modernity. Decolonial aesthesis plays a key role in strategies of regenerating and re-futuring, found in the darker colonial side of the post-Soviet existence. Its immediate (though not only) sphere of realisation is art. The outcome of decolonial aesthesis is the 'decolonial sublime'.[8] This special optic is triggered by the audience's recognition of the enormity of global coloniality, and through a process of learning to identify it in various phenomena, people, events, institutions and artworks, including one's own self-reflexive positioning in relation to coloniality.

Zooming In: Decolonial Artistic Practices in the Works of Saule Suleimenova, Aslan Gaisumov and Taus Makhacheva

Ironically Russia is increasingly represented at international art biennials by non-Russian artists who have little to do with its imperial culture, history, language and imagery. In fact, some of them come from the former and present colonies of this empire. Artists with postcolonial origins – for the purposes of this essay, meaning ethnically and culturally belonging to non-European Soviet ex-colonies – and decolonial in their political, ethical and aesthetic stance, are involved in prestigious exhibitions.[9] 'Focus Kazakhstan' (2018), an international series of exhibitions of Central Asian art, included strong decolonial voices like Saule Suleimenova, Almagul Menlibayeva and Said Atabekov. Suleimenova strives to decolonise and reinvent Kazakh national identity and self-esteem in her collage series *Kazakh Chronicle* (2018), *I am Kazakh* (2010), *Aruahs* (*Ancestors Spirits*, 2017) and *No Cultural Value* (2014). Moving from wax engraving to painting superimposed onto archival and contemporary photographs to collages of plastic bags, the artist uses photographs as a more sincere and less embellished way to reflect the times. Suleimenova tries to cure the persistent inferiority complexes and coloniality of perception typical of contemporary Kazakhstan, urging her compatriots to unlearn someone else's artificial ideas of the beautiful and sublime: Western, Russian or local. In the project Cellophane Painting (2014–ongoing), the artist turns the used plastic bags into art, striving to show that contemporary Kazakh reality is 'awful and beautiful at once', and people must learn how to appreciate this complexity, this symphony of life.[10] Art should not take this reality to flat images and stereotypes, to rosy prettiness or stylized archaism. The artist links ethnic-national stereotypes to a more global, ecological dimension and a reflection on colonial forms of consumer society and second-rate modernity. For example, one of the collages in this series depicts the primordial blooming steppe (the main symbol of Kazakh national identity). The artist ironically refers to the fact that staunch patriots are proud of the steppe yet continue to profusely litter it with the very plastic bags the work is made of. The bags themselves are indicators of how Kazakhstan's postcolonial/post-Soviet consumerist boom goes hand-in-hand with its indifference to environmental responsibility. As with her scraperboard collages, Suleimenova invents her own technique for the cellophane paintings, using a hot glue gun and silicon sticks to attach multicoloured plastic bags. The artist refuses to depict people in this series according to Western aesthetic conventions, Russian orientalist representations of the exotic or demonic other, or the recently reconstructed Kazakh canon of beauty that has nothing to do with past ethnic-cultural patterns and values. Instead, she recreates unadorned faces of ordinary people, often children and the elderly, whose low-key beauty manifests in a feeling of unity with the native land and a joy of life.

The exhibition *Residual Memory* (2019) is entirely devoted to the decolonisation of collective and personal memories through an act of collective mourning and commemoration. Suleimenova's cellophane collages are based on rare archival media, and revisit the erased, forgotten or distorted pages of Kazakh history, such as the genocidal famine or the political repressions and massacres, censored both from official textbooks and memory. She investigates periods of history recorded in rare, residual photos and video documents; she depicts these scenes of historical trauma in collages of plastic bags, which are as difficult to destroy as memory, performing a ritual of purification and acceptance.[11] A particularly striking work from this series is Kazakhian Exodus, a collage in which there is a reproduction of an old photograph of Kazakhs migrating from their devastated native homeland in the hopes of physical survival.[12] Significantly, Suleimenova made this collage out of plastic packaging for tea, chocolate and bread – trying to pay homage to the victims of famine with the very food they were deprived of, and at the same time stressing that the empty food packaging won't bring those lives back. The exhibition encourages the audiences to revisit and set free their suppressed memories, to reconnect with their forgotten ancestors, to reject the sanctioned versions of the past, and through reliving these dark histories anew, to critically rethink the present and themselves as contemporary Kazakhs.

Soviet national republics were put through a contradictory, accelerated and forced modernisation, which, among other things, prescribed particular models of making national art according to the infamous formula 'socialist in its content, national in its form'. After this grand experiment was over, people who longed to reconnect with their forgotten roots realised that any return would have to take into account the experience of Russian/ Soviet/ post-Soviet modernity. Decolonial post-Soviet art partly emerges out of the painful yet fruitful transculturation of the local and the imperial/ global, as it critically reflects on both ethnic national traditions and Russian and Western canons. However, in the case of post-Soviet artists coming from originally Muslim societies, the revival of the 'Islamic aesthetics' that has become possible after the end of the USSR often acts as a decolonial lens through which they engage in their critical dialogues with modernity and with modern and contemporary art.

Since individual artists in all Muslim regions of Russia, Central Asia and the Caucasus were forced by the Soviet powers into a decidedly secular (Eurocentric) aesthetic system, today we mostly find creolised forms of secular/ Western/ Russian (post-Soviet) and native/ Muslim sensibilities ironically seen through the prism of modernist and postmodernist art. For example, works resembling Western abstract painting – often automatically tagged as second-rate, lag-behind imitations – in reality have little or nothing to do with the genealogies of Western abstract art. Instead they contain elements that link them to the textures of indigenous and Muslim art, its symbolism, semiotic system, rhythmic and compositional patterns. These works are abstract not because they wish to enter the global contemporary art market, but rather because they perform a radical return to multiple cosmologies and aesthetics grounded in non-figurative, symbolic, ornamental and esoteric elements.[13] One interesting example is Dagestanian Oleg Pirbudagov's series *Structures* (2008-13), which seem completely abstract. On closer inspection, the shapes resemble mountains, and there are elements of anthropomorphic and zoomorphic figures and human-made objects – all similar to ornaments one can find in traditional local crafts (jewellery, weapons, carpets). Such art, informed by diverse global influences, refuses to remain within the singular prescribed Russian/Soviet realistic tradition (a pale copy of the Western original), and longs to re-enter and remake its own native epistemic and aesthetic sphere in a dynamic dialogue and debate with modernity/coloniality.

Decolonising memories through art entails a restoration of agency: the right and the ability to finally make our own choices and decide what to remember and how. The cathartic power of such art is realised through resisting and re-existing acts as forms of embodied memories, evoking the most primal senses – sonic, visual, olfactory, tactile – causing uncontrollable avalanches of previously censored remembrances. Some decolonial post-Soviet artists, reflecting on troubled relations with the past, strive to fix the rupture in the texture of memory connected with violence, trauma and humiliation in order to force the audience

De-/Anti-/Post-colonial Feminisms

to self-critically face ugly truths. For instance, Aslan Gaisumov's *The Household* (2016) consists of a big, tightly closed crate. Inside are everyday objects, such as utensils and clothes, that had been used by the artist's family during a long period living as refugees during the post-Soviet Russian-Chechen wars of the 1990s through 2000s. Made specifically for Gaisumov's solo exhibition at M HKA (Museum of Contemporary Art Antwerp) in the summer of 2016 and subsequently bought for their permanent collection, this installation materialises a past, carefully packed and stored in a Western museum. In 1944, deported Chechens were sent to Central Asia in cargo and cattle cars; this work is then historically relational – an act of 'sending back' to the centre.[14] Gaisumov makes a reciprocal gesture of sending the meagre objects collected from his family's homeless past to a museum, ridding himself of memories through making this past public and preventing further disembodiment of its palpable materiality. This is an act of decolonial radical return.[15] The artist recalls his ancestors' similar destiny, commemorating the negative lineage capable of triggering emancipating drives, through the parcel containing the embodied past. It is sent to the museum for permanent storage to mark the end of refugee existence and deposit the processed past, which he wants to let go, but not erase.

Gaisumov keeps returning to decolonial readings of silence and overcoming it. The short film *Keicheyuhea* (2017) shows the artist's grandmother talking about her deportation from her village, and her return after 70 years. The work closely traces her trip, taking the audience with it. A car slowly climbs an abandoned mountain road. One can look out the windows at the depopulated planes and hills, sharing in Gaisumov's grandmother's emotional and physical difficulty as she gets out of the vehicle and walks to the edge of the road. She looks down on her birthplace below, finding only a deserted landscape and the last traces of human presence barely visible. Gaisumov is a silent interlocutor, a humble recorder of his grandmother's looks, reactions, words, movements, terrifying stories, prayers and songs – of her potent decolonial coming back to speech and memory. The affective power of the decolonial sublime is too strong for the long-suffering woman. In the end it's unbearable. The film concludes with her bursting into tears and asking her grandson to stop filming and go back. The artist focuses on a painful struggle to take back the right to find the words to narrate her mournful testimony. Putting memories into words runs the risk of trivialising a cycle of exile and abjection. It aches for an act of exorcism and healing that is not necessarily verbal. Indeed, 'some things can be left unsaid' and not just because it is painful to talk about them, but also because of the inadequacy of language to represent this suffering.[16]

Decolonial post-Soviet art can take less traumatic forms. Dagestanian artist Taus Makhacheva deals with the decolonisation of museums in complex performances such as *Tightrope* (2015) and *The Way of an Object* (2013). In the latter, the artist questions the disciplinary role of the museum as an imperial/national institution that provides one legitimised historical or aesthetic truth. Instead, the artist narrates multiple histories, putting museum objects – mute after being torn away from their original contexts – in unfamiliar contexts outside the institution to give their voices back to them. In *Tightrope*, the central figure, a funambulist, crosses a tightrope strung between one mountain and another, balancing himself by holding paintings, which he then places in improvised storage. The fragility of art in the face of humanity's responsibility to preserve it amid changing times is exemplified by Dagestan's history. The funambulist is a fifth-generation representative of a famous local dynasty (tightrope walking being a venerable tradition in the region) and the paintings he carries are twentieth-century examples of Dagestanian art, a peculiar mix of stubborn local tradition and forceful Soviet modernity with its predominant realist aesthetics. Makhacheva regards artists as custodians of continuity – risk-taking acrobats for art's sake. The project muses on the complex transfer of ethnic-national traditions, and the precarity in artists' works that end up in museums as easily as the abyss of a crevasse. In this work the museum becomes movable, and the art, hanging in the balance, becomes more alive, part of the de-canonised present, not yet or no longer framed by institutional restraints.

I have discussed three different forms that decolonial post-Soviet art has taken in the works of three artists: Suleimenova, Makhacheva and Gaisumov. Each comes from the ruins of the Soviet empire. Decolonial artworks are less straightforward than artivism – open instead to various interpretations and grounded in different temporalities, unfixed in the actionist metaphysics of presence, reflecting on multiple pasts, without which there is no present or future.[17] In repressed societies such as most of the post-Soviet states, decolonial transcendence of modernity/coloniality through the medium of art is one of the few remaining paths to re-futuring.

'Decolonial AestheSis and the Post-Soviet Art' was first published in *Afterall* (London), vol.48 no. 1 (July 2019). https://www.afterall.org/article/decolonial-aesthesis-and-the-post-soviet-art [Accessed, 17 June 2023]

De-/Anti-/Post-colonial Feminisms

Notes

1. The post-Soviet people, including myself, understand the term post-Soviet spatially, temporally and existentially, focussing on the countries, and the millions of people there who struggle to survive in and as the aftermath of state socialist regimes.

2. It is important to clarify that it is not the case that decolonial post-Soviet artists exoticise their own culture. Instead, they move towards forgotten models and ways of artistic thinking. They rely on means no longer restricted by exclusively local sources. During the Perestroika years artists turned to various neo-mythological ways of representation by using recurrent leitmotivs and symbols. As in other countries, this was a realisation of ethnic renaissances and efforts to reinstate the remaining elements of indigenous, colonised and suppressed cultures outside the prescribed official multiculturalist forms. See Patimat Gamzatova, 'Aktualniye Problemy Iskusstva v Musulmanskom Areale Stran SNG v Nachale 21 Veka' /'Topical problems of art in the Muslim area of CIS countries in the early 21st century', in Patimat Sultanova (ed.), *Iskusstvo Turkskogo Mira. Istoki i Evolutsija Khudozhestvennoi Kulturi Turkskikh Narodov /The Art of the Turkic World. Sources and Evolution of the Artistic Culture of the Turkic People*, Kazan: Zaman, 2009, pp. 56-67.

3. See Madina Tlostanova, *What Does It Mean to Be Post-Soviet? Decolonial Art from the Ruins of the Soviet Empire*, Durham, NC: Duke University Press, 2018.

4. See M. Tlostanova, *Postcolonialism and Postsocialism in Fiction and Art: Resistance and Re-existence*, Cham, Switzerland: Palgrave Macmillan, 2017.

5. See, for example, M. Tlostanova and Walter D. Mignolo, *Learning to Unlearn: Decolonial Reflections from Eurasia and the Americas*, Columbus: Ohio State University Press, 2012; W. D. Mignolo and Rolando Vázquez, 'The Decolonial AestheSis Dossier', *Social Text* Online, 15 July 2013, available at https://socialtextjournal.org/periscope_article/the-decolonial-aesthesis-dossier/ (last accessed on 13 June 2023); and W. D. Mignolo and Pablo Gomez (eds.), *Esteticas y Opcion Decolonial*, Bogota: UD Editorial Creaciones, Bogota, 2012. Along with many artistic, academic and activist projects, the annual Decolonial Summer School in Middelburg for the last decade has always included post-socialist thinkers and artists such as Ovidiu Tichendeleanu, Manuela Boatça, Tanja Ostojić and myself.

6. Colonial matrix of power (coloniality of power) is a central decolonial concept meaning a naturalised world order that emerged with the colonisation of the Americas and was subsequently extended to the rest of the world through four interrelated spheres of social organisation: economic control, control of authority, control of gender and sexuality, and control of knowledge and subjectivity. See M. Tlostanova and W. D. Mignolo, *Learning to Unlearn,* 2012, pp. 44-45.

7. See Adolfo Albán Achinte, 'Artistas Indígenas y Afrocolombianos: Entre las Memorias y las Cosmovisiones. Estéticas de la Re-Existencia', *Arte y Estética en la Encrucijada Descolonial* (Zulma Palermo), Buenos Aires: Del Siglo, 2009, pp. 83-112.

8. See M. Tlostanova, 'La aesthesis trans-moderna en la zona fronteriza eurasiática y el anti-sublime decolonial', *Esteticas y Opcion Decolonial* (2012), pp. 49-89.

9. The postcolonial is meant here as an objective condition, the geopolitical and geo-historical situation of those who were born and raised in ex-colonial societies. The decolonial is different as it is an option, a choice of how to interpret reality and act upon it. See M. Tlostanova, *Postcolonialism and Postsocialism in Fiction and Art,* 2017, p.19.

10. Email from the artist, 5 November 2010.

11. Samira Satieva, 'Saule Suleimenova vossozdayet nepafosnuju istoriju Kazakhstana iz nepafosnikh materialov' (Saule Suleimenova creates a non-pretentious history of Kazakhstan out of non-pretentious materials), *Express K*, 4 February 2019 [former online journal]. https://saulesuleimenova.com/

12. According to independent historians at least 1.5 million Kazakhs died due to the famine in the early 1930s as a result of Stalin's collectivisation policy. See also Robert Kindler, *Stalin's Nomads. Power and Famine in Kazakhstan*, Pittsburgh: Pittsburgh University Press, 2018.

13. See M. Tlostanova, 'A Museum between Heaven and Earth', in Vladislav Shapovalov (ed.), *Taus Makhacheva. Tightrope*, Milan: Mousse Publishing, 2017, pp. 75-96.

14. In 1944–57 Chechens, similar to several other ethnicities residing in the North Caucasus, were forcefully deported by the Soviet authorities from their native lands to Central Asia (many of them to Kazakhstan). Gaisumov's works often make a connection between the deportations of the Stalin's époque and the post-Soviet Chechen campaigns that plunged the people once again into death, homelessness, exile and humiliation. The negative refugee experience is what at least three generations of Chechens share.

15. See Rolando Vázquez, 'Decolonial Aesthesis Overcoming the Post/Human', *The Human Condition: International Interdisciplinary Project*, National Center for Contemporary Art, Moscow, 27 November 2015, available at https://www.youtube.com/watch?v=RKEzFaunz0g (last accessed on 13 June 2023).

16. Aslan Gaisumov, *Keicheyuhea*, HD video, colour, sound, Chechen with English subtitles, 26h, 2017.

17. Anton Nikolayev, 'The Chronicles of Virtual Revolt. Artivism and Actionism', *Bombila.* [blog], 6 June 2011, available at http://halfaman.livejournal.com/510998.html (last accessed on 13 June 2023).

     De-/Anti-/Post-colonial Feminisms

Other Originalities:
Collective Pedagogies of Epistemic Disobedience

Dalida María Benfield

The processes of creation in contemporary arts education, formal and informal, no matter the locale, are often situated in narratives of modernity/coloniality and the capitalist world-system. Delinking them requires the re- and de-narration of the origin stories of human cultural practices, along with the redefining of education as a collective process of epistemic disobedience. Collectivity, in this instance, requires the co-construction of relationalities across difference, or what María C. Lugones calls "world"-travelling.[1] Travelling to each other's "worlds" positions us within other originalities; other origin points from which to conceive and narrate our creativity. The creations that result are the tools and artifacts – old and new – of our re-existence.

In this essay, organized episodically as four stories and image sequences spanning three decades, I narrate moments of my personal/political life next to collective pedagogical projects. Onto that history, I map theoretical and praxical languages and questions. The stories and the questions they raise unfold towards a collective understanding of what it means to co-construct relationalities across difference and de-link from the origin myths of the human and other-than-human constructed by the modern/ colonial/ capitalist world-system.

First story: On 20 November

I am a child born of colonialities; the spaces, times, embodiments, cultural and material flows emanating from global colonialism. "The Land Divided, the World United" is the phrase that adorns the seal of the Panama Canal. The Panama Canal is a space constructed by the colonialism of the US and Europe. It is the first route for the extraction of gold from Latin America, and the site of the US expansion of its hemispheric role in the modern/ colonial/ capitalist world-system. The US creates the nation-state of Panama, to contain the cut, the canal, that crosses the isthmus and connects the Atlantic to the Pacific. The canal allows the US to further control global maritime economies and warfare. My mother leaves the highlands of Chiriquí province to work in the homes of American military families in the Canal Zone, a one-mile wide strip of land bordering the canal, occupied by the US during and after the construction of the canal. She eventually migrates north, to the US, where I am born. Is my body, then, the land divided, and the world united?

On the day I was born, 20 November 1964, Dmitri Shostakovich premiered his String Quartets Nos. 9 and 10 in Moscow. No. 9 is in E-Flat Major, and No. 10 in A-Flat Major. I listen closely to No. 9, Opus 117: 1, *Moderato con Moto*. I hear my birth. The sounds anxiously circle, seek each other out, resonate across now negative fields. A new timbre is found, in-between, encountered in the middle. Given the time difference between the hemispheres, it seems likely that the crowd was applauding these works as my mother struggled with labor. In both Moscow and Ann Arbor, a light snow falls. It would be my mother's last birth. My Catholic godparents, the first to greet me upon my birth in Ann Arbor, Michigan, were exiles from Poland. Both had tattoos of numbers on their arms from the Nazi concentration camps in which they had been imprisoned in the 1940s.

In Frida Kahlo's home in Mexico City, there hangs an unfinished portrait of Stalin. Hers was not Shostakovich's Stalin. Her painting de-territorializes Stalin. This picture mapped her revolutionary project, not his. It operated as one component of a regime of signs in a time-space that was specific to her ancestralities and futures, comprising Mexican, Germanic, and Mayan imaginaries along with cosmopolitan modernities and global communisms. Kahlo was and was not a Stalinist. Shostakovich was and was not a Stalinist. He troubled Stalin as he developed his minor language, as he made neo-romantic classical music stammer. In January 1936, *Pravda* published a review of his opera, Lady Macbeth of Mtsesk. The article, entitled 'Muddle Instead of Music', included the following assessment:

> The listener from the very first minute is stunned by the opera's intentionally unharmonious muddled flow of sounds. Snatches of melody, embryos of musical phrases drown, escape, and once again vanish in rumbling, creaking, and squealing. To follow this 'music' is difficult, to remember it impossible…This is music intentionally made inside-out, so that there would be nothing to resemble classical music, nothing in common with symphonic sounds, with simple, accessible musical speech…This is leftist muddle instead of natural, human music.[2]

It may be that Stalin himself wrote 'Muddle Instead of Music' and that he perceived the eroticism of the opera as a threat to the communist order.[3] It is noise, not music.

Shostakovich's enunciation, with its 'rumblings, creakings and squealings', introduced variables into a regime of signs that destabilized the Stalinist cultural

De-/Anti-/Post-colonial Feminisms

project. But it would be a mistake to call this a new music, and not only because Shostakovich would later denounce the atonal movements of Schoenberg and others. Rather, Shostakovich's innovations should be understood as a 'widened chromaticism', the presence of which creates a new relationship between all the variables of the signifying machine, 'a new amalgamation' to use Deleuze and Guattari's terms.[4] But the Shostakovich of 20 November 1964, my Shostakovich, is not the Shostakovich of 1936. In 1964, the sounds of the Nos. 9 and 10 had different resonances: the composer, nearing the end of his life; Stalin dead; Kahlo dead and I, being born. I listen. I hear discontent, and permanently unfinished, dissonant revolutions.

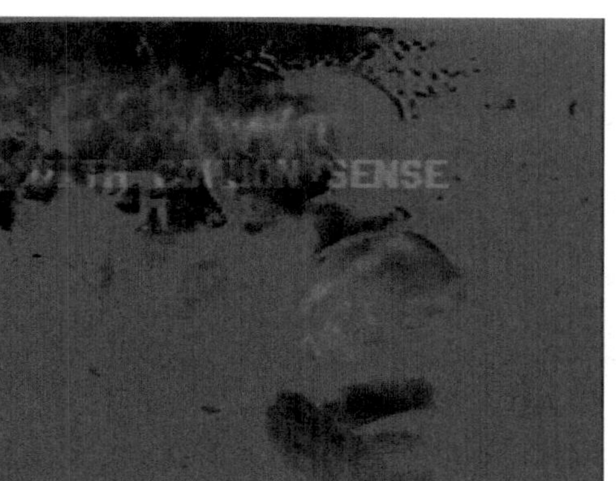
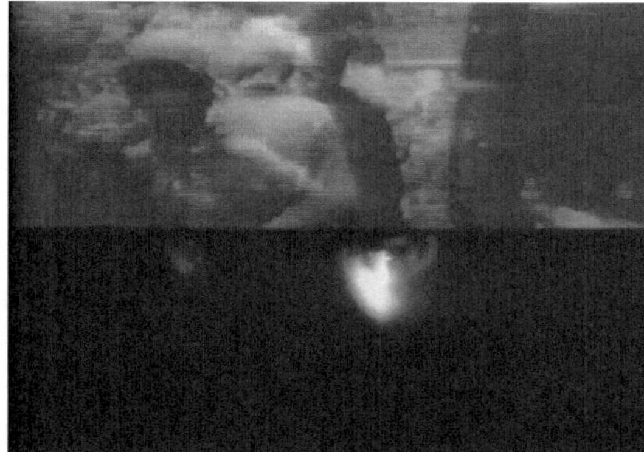

Dalida María Benfield, stills from *Refuge/es* (1988) original 16mm film and public domain newsreel. Sandin Image Processor to U-Matic SPA 60, 14 min.
School of the Art Institute of Chicago Digital Collections, https://digitalcollections.saic.edu/

My film, *Canal Zone/La Zona del Canal*, articulates the colonial history of the US in Panama through my family's memories.[5] Narrated from below, from the south, these include migration and settlement in the US, and the experiences of my family in Panama during the US invasion of 1989. The film allowed me to dwell upon family histories that had never been openly discussed; Panama was my secret language, my minor tongue. This resonated across the invasion of Panama in 1989 and enacted the formation of a new assemblage of media representations of the place. The film was indebted to a conversation that I had with the Chilean artist Juan Downey in 1988. He gave me a single piece of advice about my work-in-progress, *Refuge/es*: 'You should put yourself in it.'

It took me five years to understand the meaning of these words. My body is the multiple temporalities and spatialities that are not only the 'Third World,' but everywhere, always. Downey's own work suggests this. He imagines the invisible energy of Chile playing a concert in New York via satellite in his piece, *Invisible Energy in Chile Plays a Concert in New York, 1969*.[6] In the drawing, a map, he writes 'music' along lines that connect a satellite from Santiago to New York City. The movement of Salvador Allende is in ascendance. There are new variations being introduced. The testimonio of political torture and execution has not yet become the central signifying machine of Chilean culture or, for that matter, of Latin America. Nelly Richard suggests that the dictatorship in Chile used testimonio as the discursive vehicle for consolidating its power.[7] The General appears twice, in the question and in the answer.[8] Downey does not give such testimonio in 1969. Downey insists on the presence of inaudible sounds, invisible energies, or 'music,' in Santiago that must travel to, and be listened to, in New York. Santiago's 'music' is not a variation of a constant but a new amalgamation, that will be transformed by its journey and in its listening in New York.

On 20 November 1923, another collective assemblage of enunciation was produced.[9] This is the date that the Reichstag abandoned the papiermark and created a new system of money: the rentenmark. The inflation created by Germany's debts from World War I was resolved by the institution of a new semiotic machine, which paved the way for another one, a war machine, with awesome power. Also on 20 November 1923, Garrett Morgan patented the traffic light. A Cleveland, Ohio-based Black American entrepreneur and businessman, Morgan also invented another US standard, the gas mask.

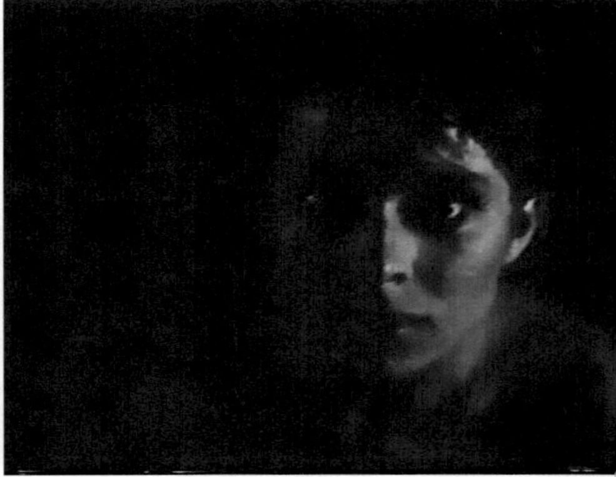

Dalida María Benfield, stills from *The Phantom World of the Lost Continent* (1989),
a re-mix of *The Bounty* (Orion Pictures, 1984), Cat People (Universal Studios, 1982),
and John Lloyd Stephens, *Incidents of Travel in Central America, Chiapas, and the Yucatan* (1841).
VHS video/U-Matic SPA 60, 7 min.
School of the Art Institute of Chicago Digital Collections, https://digitalcollections.saic.edu/

De-/Anti-/Post-colonial Feminisms

**Story Two: Intersectionality, Trans-modernity,
Living Art as Dialogue or 'Lugones, Dussel, Anzaldúa'**

María C. Lugones describes the imbrication of race, gender, class and other terms of analysis in theorizing the oppression and resistance of women of color in 'capitalist Eurocentered modernity:'

> Intersectionality reveals what is not seen when categories such as gender and race are conceptualized as separate from each other. The move to intersect the categories has been motivated by the difficulties in making visible those who are dominated and victimized in terms of both categories. Though everyone in capitalist Eurocentered modernity is both raced and gendered, not everyone is dominated or victimized in terms of their race and gender...It is only when we perceive gender and race as intermeshed or fused that we actually see women of color.[10]

In previous works, Lugones has used the term 'multiple oppressions' and 'interlocking oppressions.'[11] These terms emphasize the simultaneous and multiple character of oppressions. Lugones offers, 'Race is no more mythical and fictional than gender – both are powerful fictions.'[12] Consonant with the colonial/modern project, gender serves to define humanity according to naturalized lines of domination and subordination. Colonized women were not always gendered as 'women,' they were only gendered as 'women' when it suited the needs of Eurocentered capitalism. Lugones reveals the fiction of 'reproductive biology' and shows its 'dimorphism' to be socially constructed, even as its marks or recodes biological signs. Sex as a binary construction is consonant with the 'light side' of the modern/colonial gender system as she theorizes it. The 'light side' is the system of binary gender definitions and relations that are determined by and for the colonizers and supported by the bourgeois family; the 'dark side' is characterized by understandings of gender that are not dimorphic and reserved for the colonized. For the colonizers, 'indigenous people of the Americas [were imagined as] as hermaphrodites or intersexed, with large penises and breasts with flowing milk.'[13] Yet, the understandings of gender for many Indigenous peoples are not dimorphic. There are multiple understandings of gender within and against colonial heterarchies, Lugones argues. As heterosexualism is imposed along with gender dimorphism, Lugones proposes gender plurality and a rejection of compulsory heterosexuality as strategies of resistance. Emerging from positions of exteriority, these practices enable other worlds of sense and ways of being.

Enrique Dussel offers another image of these spaces of exteriority, 'trans'-modernity:

> This modernity's technical and economic globality is far from being a cultural globalization of everyday life that valorizes the majority of humanity. From this omitted potentiality and altering 'exteriority' emerges a project of 'trans'-modernity, a 'beyond' that transcends Western modernity (since the West has never adopted it but,

rather, has scorned it and valued it as 'nothing') and that will have a creative function of great significance in the twenty-first century.[14]

'Trans'-modernity is not simply a given condition; it is also a moment in which struggle is being constantly waged. While it is nourished by ways and practices of Indigenous and non-Western peoples, it is also a practice that is available to all who engage in the struggle to inhabit what has been the 'omitted potentiality' of cultural globalization. Dialogue is a central moment in the construction of 'trans'-modernity for Dussel:

> for the Philosophy of Liberation, which emerges from Alterity, from the excluded, (the culturally dominated and exploited), from the historico-concrete, it is possible to demonstrate the conditions of dialogue, from the affirmation of this alterity, and at the same time, from absence, from its empirical concrete impossibility, except as a point of departure, from which 'the excluded Other' and the 'dominated' can effectively intervene.[15]

Our subjectivities are transformed within this fundamental and necessary dialogue. We must travel between the worlds of Eurocentrism and those of the excluded; a voyage between times, spaces, and epistemologies, forms of art, media and technology, confronting the being and the non-being that our bodies inhabit.

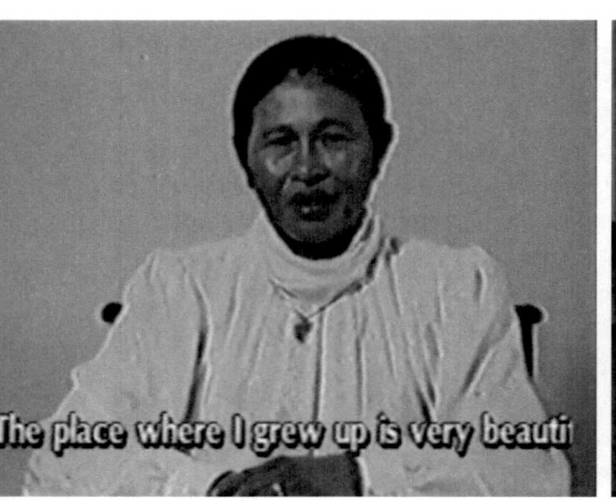

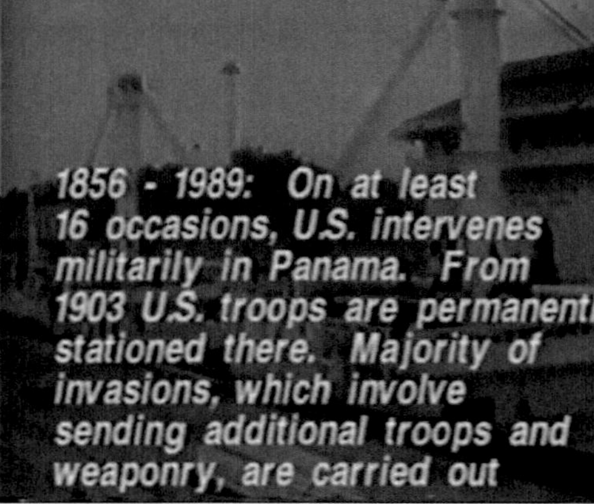

Dalida María Benfield, stills from *Canal Zone/La Zona del Canal*,
16mm film, Super-8 film, and Hi-8 video, edited and mastered on U-Matic SP 60, 1994.
Stanford University Library, Women in the Director's Chair Archive.

                                    De-/Anti-/Post-colonial Feminisms

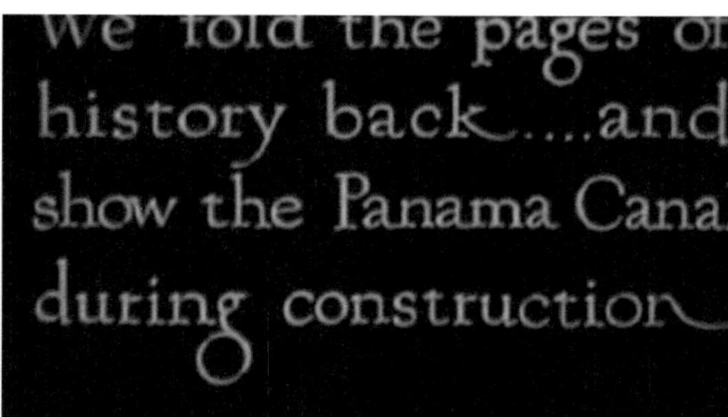

Dalida María Benfield, stills from *Hotel Panamá*, single channel digital video and video installation, 2011-2017. Access at https://vimeo.com/130814058.

Third Story: Video Machete and *Mujeres de Pilsen* (*Women of Pilsen*)

Beginning in 1992, the quincentenary of the 'discovery' of the Americas, I began working with a group of artists, intellectuals, filmmakers and activists to create a project of interventions that 'discovered' and articulated our multiple selves in the peripheralized interiors of Chicago, the global city. This project, which we called Video Machete, worked in schools, community organizations and other cultural institutions, and developed a public presence and dialogue that offered spaces for the collective engagements that were not available in the worlds of art or popular culture. On the streets, making videos, conversing with people from all parts of the world, who were struggling with police, immigration, struggling for their very survival, I was confronted with many diverse dimensions of the realities that exist beyond the horizon of Eurocentrism. Even more powerfully, I was confronted with the fundamental mix of many diverse histories of struggle, continually crossing the border of the being and the non-being. Unforeseen possibilities of transformation have emerged from these dialogues.

Mujeres de Pilsen (*Women of Pilsen*) (1992), a video produced by myself and María C. Lugones, was a starting point for this line of pedagogical and ontological intervention. It is defined by an insistence on the heterogeneity of the women speaking in and through it. It is a radically open-ended text that foregrounds multiplicity through a series of interviews with ten women. The project initiated an on-going inquiry for me into the politics of dialogue, conversation and their cinematic recording. The reader is invited into an experience of "world"-travelling that goes against the grain of documentary conventions of oral history, which is Lugones' term for a process of personal and social transformation effected by crossing into an/other's world. She describes this as a necessity for women of color:

> As Women of Color, we cannot stand on any ground that is not also a crossing.
> To enter playfully into each other's 'worlds' of subjective affirmation also risks those

aspects of resistance that have kept us riveted on constructions of ourselves that have kept us from seeing multiply, from understanding the interconnects in our historico-spatialities. Playful "world"-travel is thus not assimilable to the middle-class leisurely journey nor the colonial or imperialist journeys. None of these involve risking one's ground.[16]

In the making of *Mujeres de Pilsen*, which began in 1989, our concerns were those of "world"- travelers. The speculative nature of our questions rejected a rigid adherence to the confessional mode of the testimonio/testimonial, creating instead a dynamic and creative relation between interior and exterior experience, action and speculation. The creative space of the questions we asked also refutes the normative rules of oral history construction that minimize cultural hybridity and creativity. Our engagement with each woman took on the quality of a performative intervention as well. Developing deep and substantial conversations with women across many different positionalities required relationship building. The site of the videotaping became a transformative space, fixing our gazes upon each other, each constructed very differently, inhabiting different worlds, but focusing solely on each other. The power of this performance transforms the apparatus of representation. The camera becomes an inter-subjective agent; we construct a world of sense together that crosses our historico-spatial specificities. We produce an other timespace, recorded 30 frames per second, within a classroom, within a school, within a community that has legislated in acute ways against our attention to each other.

The video, three hours in length, was recorded at an alternative high school at which we were both teaching. The school had a US Latina/o/x/Chicano/a/x focused curriculum and was located on the southside of Chicago, in a neighborhood known as Pilsen, which is a crossing ground for recent arrivals from Mexico and Central America, as well as longtime Chicagoans from all parts of the world, including Eastern Europe. It is a center of the Spanish-speaking community, with its most important community and cultural centers. The school was founded by activists who were committed to creating a space for high school students who were dropouts, and many of whom were gang-affiliated, to pursue their GED, an alternative degree to the high school diploma. Within that space, women were present as leaders, but the school was dominated by a nationalist male voice that was challenged by the voices of *Mujeres de Pilsen*.

The women recruited for the project occupied a wide range of positions: mothers, gang members, social workers, activists. But they were not recruited as 'representatives' of different positions. Rather, they were recruited through a months-long, complex process of popular education and organizing that occurred across multiple social domains, including the street, grocery stores, exercise classes, and community centers. Women were invited through individual conversations and

　　　　　　　　　　　　　　　　　　　De-/Anti-/Post-colonial Feminisms

the development of relationships. This process re-mapped Pilsen, putting women in contact with each other who otherwise would not have been, and mobilizing a rationale for women's conversations.

The speaking subject of oral history is supposed to be speaking truth. At the originary moment of spontaneous speech, what emerges is thought to be pure, natural, essential expression, unadulterated by artificial writing. The resemblance to reality of the speaker's words is taken for granted and forms the very basis of the logic of oral history. The reality that is referred to is normative reality, the time-space of modernity. The heterarchies of modernity encode the stories of the speakers within already determined narratives. This ability to speak oneself is considered to represent an essential, stable subject. Subjectivity is located precisely in the subjects' self-referentiality. The normative practice of oral history is ethnographically-derived and centered on the informant, the culturally inside speaking subject. These stories are positioned as non-analytical, 'alternative' micro-histories that provide an entry into the 'real lives' of the sub-altern, oppressed people whose experiences have not been represented in official histories. Commonly, oppression itself – as marked by racialization, poverty, gender performance, nationhood, rurality, underdevelopment – is the official 'subject' of oral history projects. Oral history as a method also claims to thicken the description of the experiences and lives of subjects who have been ideologically flattened by official histories.

Against these conventions, we proposed a conversation, in the manner Trinh T. Minh-ha suggests as: 'a chance of breaking the codes of negation, capable of exposing a side-track of thought neglected in the right to speak.'[17] Our questions invited a transformation in the speakers and our own modes of self-narration. The questions also represent an interventionist strategy of 'realist' documentary, undoing the audio-visual conventions of oral history and documentary practices. The questions produced an experience of "world"-travelling in conversations that enabled the elaborate knowing of each woman's world. The speculative nature of the questions rejected a rigid adherence to a mode of confessional, self-reflexive autobiography, creating instead a dynamic and creative relation between the narration of various aspects of interior and exterior experience. Questions, for example, asked the women to elaborate their relationships to other women in their family, to critique relationships with men, to consider their plans for their lives, and to articulate hopes for the future: If they had a magic wand, how would they change their community?

Power is present in the camera, but in this complex encounter with the lens, the apparatus is transformed. I look directly at the subject and only occasionally through the lens. I am an inter-subjective agent. We are constructing a world of sense together, one that crosses our historico-spatial specificities. Oral historians who create moving image or sound recordings of the oral histories of women and sub-altern peoples often lay claim to the 'real story' of oppressed, even as they fail to acknowledge their own roles as possible re-producers of always already constructed realities, as Trinh explains:

> 'giving voice' – literally meaning that those who are/need to be given an opportunity to speak up never had a voice before. Without their benefactors, they are bound to remain non-admitted, non-incorporated, therefore, unheard.[18]

At the same time, it is presumed that the subject will not be able to provide an adequate account; that his/her subjectivity as an oppressed person will be always limited and partial:

> Making a film on/about the 'others' consists of allowing them paternalistically 'to speak for themselves' and, since this proves insufficient in most cases, of completing their speech with the insertion of commentary that will objectively describe/interpret the images according to a scientific-humanistic rationale.[19]

The political positing of the speaking subject as provider of a 'real' account of history over-determines the speaker, resulting in the editing out (throughout the process of recording) of anything that interferes with this narrative of truth. The positioning of the speaker as a 'talking head' de-emphasizes complexity in the negative visual and aural space surrounding him/her, and the tyranny of voice in relation to both sound and visual elements. Rather than reflecting complexity, the speaker is re-flattened out as deemed necessary by the political paradigm, which needs the speaker to verify its claims of veracity and its solutions as correct.

The framing of the women in *Mujeres de Pilsen* does impose a fixed presence. The women are portrayed as stable talking heads, using the fiction of 'realist' documentary strategy. The conventions of documentary framing, which dictate the position of the eyes at approximately the upper third of the screen, imposed themselves upon my eye. Despite this, my eye did and does wander away, whenever the tape is replayed, revealing other aspects of the *mise en scene*. As a reader/ viewer/ listener moves through the sequential ordering of the ten interviews, sustaining the memory/ imprint of each woman, a montage of multiple stories emerges. Multiple talking heads; a multiplicity of possible locations within and outside the frame, and multiple voices echoing simultaneously. The multiple stories move toward a collectivity. When screening the video, we invited the viewers/listeners/readers to find points of contact with the stories but also to attend to the distances and gaps and to re-imagine one world from the perspective of the speaker, to see the distance between the 'I' and the 'we.' This was an invitation towards "world"-travelling, deep coalition, mapping the distance between 'I' and 'we' as a threshold, a crossing.

Lugones' notions of tactical strategies, developed in conversation with the ideas of Michel de Certeau, and of the streetwalker and active subjectivity, are helpful here:

> I propose the concept of active subjectivity for the activity of those who disturb the abstract spatiality of social fragmentation. As I look at lived spaces with an eye

    De-/Anti-/Post-colonial Feminisms

for more than ephemeral refigurements of spatialities and possibilities ordered by institutions and mechanisms of repression, I explore the possibilities opened by a depth of inhabitation and understanding of the social, more enduring inhabitations than 'making do.' In proposing the notion of active subjectivity coupled with that of tactical-strategies and renewed understanding of intentionality, I am exploring the opening of logical paths in order to refigure the possibilities of the oppressed from which the complexities of the social.[20]

Locating active subjectivity – from within a street-walking multitude – is an act of radical multiple conversation-making, and a way of making interventions in modes of visual and aural representation that privilege the commonly "seen" and "heard". In this sense, a silent position is not the same as a non-speaking position, although the two positions may intersect. The formulation of sentences, the crafting of the self through speech, are all acts of production that are privileged in oral history. The production of silence, the active inhabiting of the negative space of the frame, challenges the centrality of these forms. As I consider these questions in relation to *Mujeres de Pilsen*, I am hopeful about the possibility of making a radically open text – open to an internal and external re-ordering of its signs. Taking up again Lugones' discussion of tactical strategies, her discussion of de Certeau's operational combinations of the consumer as producer, I would posit the viewer/listener/reader as a street walker. Mujeres de Pilsen offers a possibility for the 'microbe like operation …an art of combination that cannot be dissociated from an art of using.'[21] I link this to the possibility of the different movements of the times and spaces of 'trans'-modernity. A world begins anew each time the video is screened.

Gloria Anzaldúa's thinking offers a sensibility that might be collectively invoked and constituted relationally in such acts of world-creation. In *Borderlands/ La Frontera: The New Mestiza* (1987), Anzaldúa discusses the difference between dead art and living art. She argues that: 'Tribal cultures keep art works in honored and sacred places in the home and elsewhere. They attend them by making sacrifices of blood (goat or chicken), libations of wine. They bathe, feed, and clothe them. The works are treated not just as objects, but also as persons.'[22] Art that is dead is contained by colonial systems of power: 'An Indian mask in an American museum is transposed into an alien aesthetic system where what is missing is the presence of power invoked through performance ritual. It has become a conquered thing, a dead 'thing' separated from nature and therefore, its power.'[23] Anzaldúa suggests that placing the object back into community and context, beyond the realm of the 'cultural' institution, would enable it to create life, meaning, and interrelation. She reminds us, then, that there is a porous space beyond the Western/colonial binary of culture and nature. Living art, for Anzaldúa, is art that is invoked through creative rituals outside the bounds of 'culture' as it is rigidly understood within the modern/colonial/capitalist world system. Anzaldúa's work suggests that we can create and affirm ancestral, and new, amalgamations of identities, meanings, and social possibilities, redefining both the natural and the cultural, and the human and more-than-human, when we situate works of art as living beings.

Story 3 continued…Video Machete: The Gang as/and Cultural Production: Collective Video Production and Political Education in the Early Work of Video Machete

Who am I?
What am I?
Was I born to die?
Was I born with a gun in my hand,
A needle up my arm?

Crying for hope, crying for
Salvation,
Walking down a lonely path
With a lonely hurt
Only meant for me.[24]

Excerpt from 'Nightmare,' a poem by Ramiro Rodriguez

We live in a society that fears youth: It fears the energy, ideas, and potential of youth to disrupt the status quo and dominant social order. In response to this fear, American society has created a social image of that fear and a variety of systems of social control through the police as a response to this image. This poem, written by an early member of the Video Machete collective, is the expression of the anger and creative resistance of many of the youth in Chicago who have organized around youth issues and attempted to create, through their own words and images, an alternative cultural presence for themselves.

Video Machete was initiated by a group of artists, activists and youth because of our collective anger at growing incarceration rates, media propaganda criminalizing youth of color, and the inadequacy of both social service and alternative arts programs in addressing the urgency of the situation of inner-city youth. In our earliest formation, we were dedicated to working almost exclusively with gang members. This work was formed through extensive deliberation and study with a small group of artists and activists who formed a reading and activist group on race. This group, affiliated with the Escuela Popular Nortena, a popular education collective, was the birthing ground for the ideas that later became Video Machete.

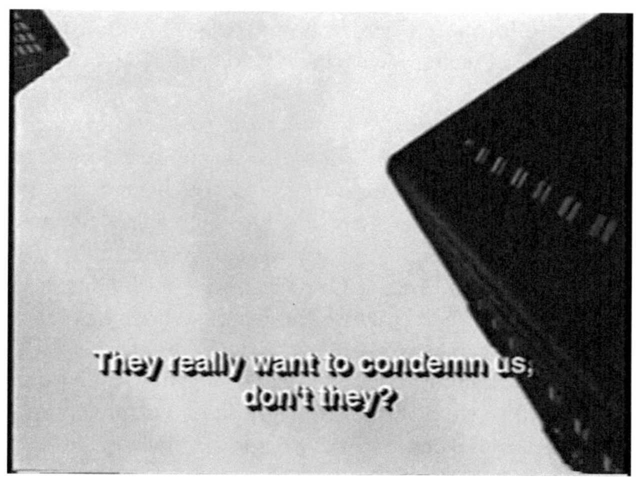

Video Machete, stills from *Division 11 Diary*, Hi-8 video edited and
mastered on U-Matic SP 60 video, 1993.
Access at https://vimeo.com/158076201.

In a public screening of Video Machete works in Chicago, in 1999, the
following statement was collectively read:

They are the people who keep you off the streets, in school, and if that fails, they
are the people who lock you up. Adults see youth as a problem, and we as society have
used the police as the solution. I'd like to remind every adult here that:

Youth did not create schools that are monuments to boredom and irrelevancy,
adults did that.

Youth do not manufacture guns and profit mightily by selling them; adults do that.

Youth do not run the international drug trade; adults, business people and even
governments do that.

Youth aren't responsible for the economic poverty of their communities.

Youth didn't have a say in making cities where there are no places to gather and
meet and be together except places where we spend money. We as adults created – and
continue to accept – these kind of cities.

Finally, youth don't build prisons and jails. We do... so many, in fact, that we now
call it a prison industry. We as adults did that and we use them to lock up the young
and the poor, Latinos, African Americans, and Native Americans.[25]

This manifesto continues to echo across my recent theoretical and praxical
work, concerned with the unfinished project of Third Cinemas, which offers not
just cinematic practices, but also pedagogies 'outside of and against' modernity/
coloniality and the capitalist world-system. In this work, I also understand
María C. Lugones' contribution to be central and particularly her theorization

of complex communication, which, echoing our work in *Mujeres de Pilsen*, insists on the capacity of seeing each other outside of how we are constructed by multiple oppressions.

This means stepping outside of colonial archives of knowledge that would deem our knowledges as worthless. This also means practices of critique and acknowledgements of colonial wounds; that is to say, these are not simply spaces of anger, joy, or imagination. They are spaces for rigorous study of our conditions, as well as spaces of reckoning. They are also, fundamentally, spaces for the construction of inter-relation. And, as Linda Tuhiwai Smith offers in *Decolonizing Methodologies* (1999), it is crucial that we construct methodologies of research and cultural creativity that are in conversation with the forms of accountability that we forge with the multiple communities with whom we work.[26] That is, rather than allowing colonial archives to determine our priorities, we forge other genealogies and alliances that determine our senses of what is worthwhile.

This is made even more difficult by the contemporary global conditions of the neo-liberalization of creativity. As discussed by Ollie Mould in *Against Creativity* (2018)[27], the usurpation of the terms 'creative' and 'creativity,' along with a limited set of practices adjacent to art, design, and craft practice, towards the neo-liberal occupation of our imaginations, is ubiquitous. This constitutes a sustained and institutionalized project of valorizing capitalist creativity over other forms of creativity that insist on alternative genealogies and futures. Creativity is understood as the engine of capitalism, including corporate 'disruption' and art world commodity production, rather than the condition for solutions to the climate crisis, rampant racisms and misogyny, endless wars, and the continued extraction and impoverishment of the many. Resisting this definition of creativity, and insisting on the other infinite potentialities of creation, is imperative. Capitalist creativity is simply not the only means of creating and sustaining livelihoods – other forms of co-sustenance, nourishment of the human and more-than-human, and the commoning of our resources are what we must believe in and seek out as alternatives.

In the context of education, resistance against narratives of development and progress, which are products of the modern/colonial/capitalist world-system (with very few exceptions), is also resistance against the very rationale of education in the twenty-first century. This includes, of course, art education, which is embedded in the Darwinian developmentalist schemes that infuse compulsory schooling. As Ivan Illich, and others teach us, compulsory schooling de-skills people and thereby creates dependencies on the service industries as organized by capitalism. What should we learn to make? Paintings and sculptures in quadrangles? Or baskets and cave drawings, drawn with our hands as we lay on our backs, with dust? In the context of de-schooling, with infinite human knowledges forming the archive of

De-/Anti-/Post-colonial Feminisms

knowledges with which we might answer this question, what is known as 'art' is an unnecessarily limited arrangement of practices and hierarchies resulting from the structures of power of modernity/coloniality.

As I found in making *Mujeres de Pilsen* and working with Video Machete, the de-linking that it engaged is multi-dimensional, recognizing knowledge where there previously was understood to be only experience; developing relationalities that undergird our belief in each other's experience as knowledge; and subsequently the re- and de-narration of our senses of the origin point of our cultural practices. The result is a redefinition of education as a collective process of epistemic disobedience to modernity/coloniality's and capitalism's narratives of education, knowledge, and cultural production – disobediently centering other worlds of sense, the ways of knowing and doing that sustain us and that may be original tactics of creation and survival; while also, possibly, continuing legacies of making, knowing, and doing that are whispered to us by our ancestors and the living artifacts and sensory domains granted to us by them.

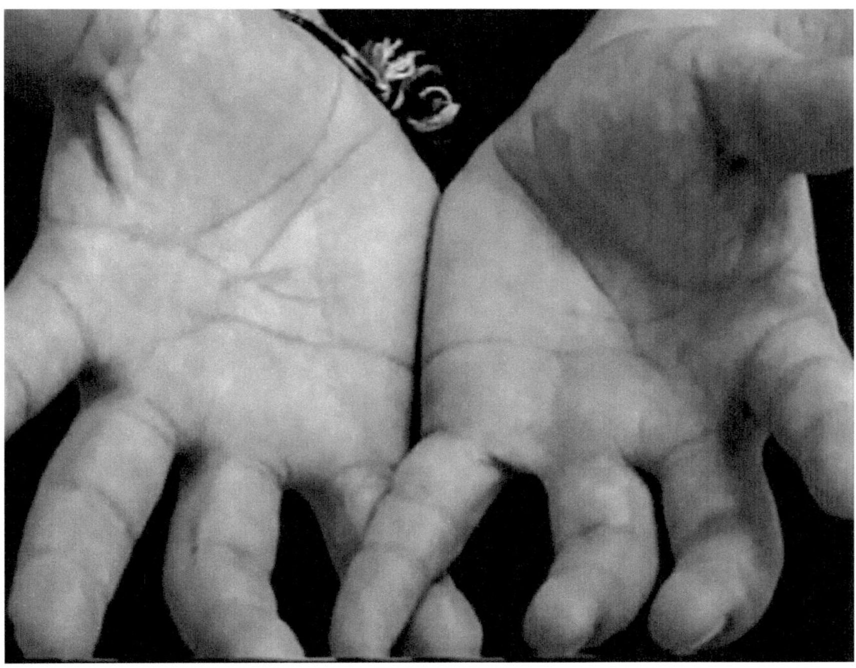

Video Machete, still from *Ju-Nam*, digital video, 2000.
Access at https://vimeo.com/158076201.

Story Four: Ongata Rongai, Reading from the Archive Differently[28]

Travelling to each other's worlds is to position ourselves in a complex web of interrelation, in which we understand and sense ourselves as we exist both inside and outside of each other's worlds of sense. Creative emanations from this perspective are multi-sited and pluriversal, to use Arturo Escobar's term[29], and open to the production of multiple tools and artifacts across communication media – sung, spoke, felt, danced, or written, etched, drawn – with their context constructed in perhaps temporary assemblages of people and meanings.

A group of people winds down a dirt road, then follows a path across fields and through bush to the river, Enkare Nairobi (place of cool waters). Some know these roads and paths and others do not. It is a place named Ongata Rongai (narrow plains). We are gently led, with no imposed tempo. But there is a direction towards which we are collectively moving, although each of us takes a somewhat different route. We all move towards the water. We listen along the route and upon our arrival. This is an exercise in considering the difference between listening and hearing. As we walk, then, with this shared intention, we think about what it is we are hearing and ask ourselves if this is, in fact, listening. We hear our own and each other's footsteps, and the rustling of the grass. Eventually, we hear the rushing water, and when we arrive at the river, we are silent. We each find a place, in near proximity or distance from one another. We work to listen. Some of us take notes, some close our eyes. We think about the sound of the river, the sound of the distant city of Nairobi, the sound of our recent conversations. To learn to listen to the complexity of a place, any place, is a first opening of the senses to a decolonial way of being.

The collective work of the Center for Arts, Design + Social Research (CAD+SR), which I founded in 2017, and where I am currently the Research and Program Director, is an ongoing experiment in decolonial arts and design education, research, and activism. The words that follow evoke, but do not fully capture, the complex alterities, visualities, auralities, and other communicative and sensorial experiences of the people and collectives that make up the Center. While we engage theoretical approaches to decolonial thinking and doing, our work is in relation to but not identical with existing explanatory frameworks. The role of institutions of education in repressing forms of knowledge while sustaining and reproducing the modern/colonial/capitalist world-system has been widely discussed and analyzed by diverse theorists, situated in very different contexts. With much nuance and methodological differences, decolonial thinkers understand education as a primary site of the reproduction of key characteristics of modernity/coloniality.[30] This includes the deliberate project of producing knowledge hierarchies that mirror and reproduce geo-political, racialized, and gendered social hierarchies, causing the division of the sciences from the arts and humanities that intensified in the post-World War II period and now structures institutions, geographies, and fundamentally forms the disciplines.[31] It is also reflected in the reproduction of domination that is the central goal of compulsory schooling, which emerged in the twentieth century and was 'universalized' alongside projects of colonial and imperial occupation.[32] On a continuum with plantations, workcamps, barracks, and prisons, schools are explicit in their exercise of the surveillance and domination of human bodies, undermining the agency of students and instead creating dependency on systems of control. To sum up these decolonial critiques, education is a set of social practices that marginalize the ways of knowing of the oppressed.[33]

An understanding of the geopolitics of knowledge – the positioning of knowledge production in a global hierarchy of political power that has divided the world according to North and South, East and West, as well as in a chrono-politics of the discourse of development – is crucial to elaborating a liberatory project. Contributing to theorizations of the coloniality of power and the modern/colonial/capitalist world-system, Dussel posits Eurocentric modernity as the episteme that maintains the stability of the world-system.[34] It centers itself and peripheralizes the rest of the world and its other ways of knowing. What is at stake in liberatory education, then, is challenging the social reproduction of this epistemic coloniality and its attempt to produce functional subjects within a dominating order, situated as they are in geographically, culturally, and economically diverse assemblages of contradictory elements.

The positing of our collective difference, or to use Escobar's phrase, 'difference-in-equality,'[35] as our knowledge archive, is a challenge to the dominant knowledge hierarchies that structure existing institutions of art and schooling. We understand the strategies we employ, our iterative, critical pedagogies as being situated in a set of liberatory pedagogics that are co-constructed with our research community. Dussel's distinction between pedagogy, understood as the science of teaching and learning, and pedagogics, the philosophies that frame the teaching and learning encounter, is useful here. All education expresses pedagogics, including contemporary schooling and its pedagogics of domination. Its practices are so deeply acculturated that they appear to be commonsensical, even natural. A critical de-naturalizing and recognition of historical and geo-political specificities produces other pedagogics.

The scene described above, in Ongata Rongai, Kenya, was imagined and led by Joseph Kamaru aka KMRU, a sound artist based in Nairobi and Berlin, during the De/Archive East Africa research residency held by CAD+SR in January 2020. The convening was focused on the politics of archives:

> The modern archive is both an instrument and artifact of power, no more dramatically apparent than in the recent history of East Africa, where Britain and Germany used archives as an essential foundation of colonial power. More than half a century after independence, the meaning of these colonial archives remains an area

of important social contestation, one which offers the possibility of radically new understandings of the past and even more radical imaginings of the future. How have artists, writers, thinkers, and activists addressed this tension to rethink the role of archives in the East African context? How might we rethink both knowledge and memory in relation to an official record based on exclusion and silence? What might a radical archive be? [36]

CAD+SR residencies are structured by this kind of knowledge sharing, with participants invited to respond to collective research questions and to create their own workshops or learning exercises. The Nairobi meeting was co-convened with Senior Research Fellow Syowia Kyambi, with the additional goal of creating a permanent artists residency in Ongata Rongai. In this altogether invented place, over 20 artists, designers, activists, and researchers from 12 countries gathered with Nairobi-based artists and collectives, all of whom, over the course of 10 days, led workshops along the themes of their research. KMRU's practice, predicated on radical listening, served as an exemplary framing of the convening. We listened for those things that are wrongly understood to be silent, absences that we came to know as being present.

These research residencies and workshops extend the Center's transnational fellowship program through which arts, design, and social researchers receive funding and other forms of support for their research projects. During residencies, held both in-person and virtually, fellows gather to share their work, lead workshops with each other and multiple publics, and engage in emergent conversations and collaborative projects towards building complex communities and relationships across multiple registers of difference. While not fully capturing the complexity of their identities, the fellows' national locations include Brazil, Cuba, China, Denmark, France, Italy, Kenya, Mexico, Pakistan, Palestine, Russia, South Africa, Taiwan, Turkey, Uganda, and the United States, constituting a radical geographic and cultural diversity of experiences and knowledges, that extend to embrace queer, non-binary, and trans-gender identities.

The residencies and workshops are migratory, and, besides Kenya, have been held in Brazil, Denmark, Finland, Ireland, Italy, Mexico, the United States, and online. The Center collaborates with artists, activists, and researchers in each locality of a residency or workshop to create the conditions for people to enter into each other's worlds of sense and place. This is both an epistemic and spatial practice of a radical intersectional traveling that María C. Lugones terms "'world'-travelling and loving perception.'[37] A critical engagement with our worlds of place and sense infuses our approach. We understand not only physical locality, but also digital technology, as an important location, both spatially and epistemically. Further, we recognize the role of technology in discourses of modernization and development that reinforce the epistemic hierarchies produced by the geopolitics of knowledge, making it a space of crucial decolonial intervention.[38]

                                    De-/Anti-/Post-colonial Feminisms

As a further turn in the planetary spatialization of modernity/coloniality, neo-liberalism emphasizes a flattening of the time-space of the planet, representing the world as wholly bounded, explained, and functioning according to its economic principles. The conceptualization of spaces of exteriority that precede, elude, and resist this universalism, not incorporated by modernity and coloniality, but on its underside, provides an entry point for imagining privileged sites of emancipatory thought at which a decolonial arts pedagogics can be sited. As Dussel writes, 'exteriority is a process that takes off, originates, and mobilizes itself from an 'other' place (one 'beyond' the 'world' and modernity's 'Being,' one that maintains a certain exteriority…) than European and North American modernity.'[39]

How we conceive of the location of exteriority as a collective imaginary has consequences for our pedagogics. We acknowledge, as discussed by Dussel, Escobar, and others, the singular importance of the planetary ways of knowing of Indigenous, 'Abya Yala/Afro/Latino América" communities and ancestral practices of 'Earth Thought'.[40] Our pedagogics also posit exteriorities as not a singular stable location or group of people. Exteriorities are multiply located, digitally, temporally, and spatially, crisscrossing existing planes of the arts, cultural practices, institutions, economies, geographies, nation-states, and digital media. Exteriorities are dispersed across spaces of institutionalized and informal learning and culture, including art worlds and global media flows.

Decolonial pedagogics define themselves in response to these heterogeneous spaces of domination and resistance, interiorities and exteriorities. Pluriversality includes the recognition of ways of being and doing that emphasize the interconnection, always in motion, of humans and the other living beings of the earth, as well as our multiple cosmologies and places. Escobar underlines the praxical invitation of the pluriverse: 'Living in accordance with the idea that there are multiple worlds, partially connected but radically different, entails an entirely different ethics of life, of being-doing-knowing.'[41]

We link these questions of the pluriverse to the potential of diverse forms of cultural practices and pedagogics to disturb and upend the ontological certainties of not just art worlds – the economic and social spheres constructed by the production and circulation of art – but also the flat, neo-liberalized, mediatized world that is of a piece with modernity/coloniality's 'global design'.[42] The invitation to engage in a pluriversal approach to culture, and a decolonial pedagogics, destabilizes disciplines and demands a reformulation of assumptions about what constitutes arts, craft, design, and visual culture education. This includes rethinking scope, method, genre, form, content, and purpose, and a recognition of the multiple genealogies and histories of making that inform planetary cultures.[43]

The recognition of the pluriversality of planetary cultures is at the core of our work. This recognition occurs in the contemporary context of the arts:

institutionalized arts education has been challenged by multiple pressures. Perhaps the most important among these is the increasing neo-liberalization and instrumentalization of all education, including the division of human knowledges into the hierarchical disciplines and the devaluing of the domains known as the arts and humanities.[44]

Culture is a site of struggle for marginalized and excluded communities, a place for emergent forms of social possibility from which to imagine the world otherwise. The projects of the Center's research community test such ideas in situated, praxical contexts. In the Center's practice, gatherings of researchers in residencies and workshops constitute a threshold to study through a matrix to connect distinct ways of understanding the world. Denaturalizing disciplines and their hierarchies, and making their terms cultural artifacts for critical reflection, requires cultivating a respect for the skills and knowledge of others in an open field of inquiry that can accommodate diverse modes. It is to imagine diversity without separation, in equality, an idea of community that encourages heterogeneity, including dissidence, conflict, and interrelation across difference.

  De-/Anti-/Post-colonial Feminisms

Notes

1. "World"-travelling is discussed in María C. Lugones' essay, 'Playfulness, "World"-Travelling, and Loving Perception,' *Hypatia*, vol. 2 no. 2 (Summer, 1987), pp. 3-19.

2. The *Pravda* article is quoted in Victor Volkov's article, 'When opera was a matter of life or death' for *The Telegraph* (London), 8 March 2004, https://www.telegraph.co.uk/culture/music/classicalmusic/3613515/When-opera-was-a-matter-of-life-or-death.html [Accessed 4 June 2023]

3. Ibid.

4. Gilles Deleuze and Felix Guattari, *A Thousand Plateaus: Capitalism and Schizophrenia*, trans. Brian Massumi, Minneapolis: University of Minnesota Press, 1987, p. 98.

5. Dalida María Benfield, *Canal Zone/La Zona del Canal*, 1994, Hi-8 video and Super-8 film, transferred to U-Matic SPA 60, 28 minutes. Stanford University Library, Women in the Director's Chair Archive.

6. Juan Downey, *Invisible Energy in Chile Plays a Concert in New York* (1969), acrylic, pencil and collage on cardboard mounted on panel, 49½ x 39¾ in. (125 x 100 cm). Private collection.

7. Richard explains the role of *testimonio* during the dictatorship as follows: 'the Chile of the dictatorship made the *testimonio* a privileged format that 'gave voice to the voiceless,' textualizing life stories and biographical narrations situated at the margins of those visions constituted and institutionalized through the master narratives of the social sciences and politics. *Testimonio* – as a subjectivized instance of knowledge that demythologizes the 'totality' – proposes a situated capturing of the real (relative, partial) that corrects the totalizing gaze of a macrosocial focus. But despite that partializing and relativizing quality of testimonial speech, which seeks to refute the universal fiction of an absolute subject, those exponents of testimonio that monopolized the attention of Chilean sociology during the period of reconstructing memory and national identity continued to portray characters (the political victim, the woman, the indigenous person, etc.) whose marginality and oppression symbolized a national consciousness sustained by the communal paradigm of denouncement, no matter how fractured its enunciative viewpoint.' Nelly Richard, *The Insubordination of Signs: Political Change, Cultural Transformation, and Poetics of Crisis*, trans. Alice A. Nelson and Silvia R. Tandeciarz, Durham, NC: Duke University Press, 2004, p. 15.

8. This echoes Deleuze and Guattari's explanation of the constancy of 'man': 'It is obvious that "man" holds the majority, even if he is less numerous than mosquitoes, children, women, blacks, peasants, homosexuals, etc. That is because he appears twice, once in the constant and again in the variable from which the constant is extracted.' Gilles Deleuze and Felix Guattari, *A Thousand Plateaus*, 1987, p.105.

9. See Gilles Deleuze and Felix Guattari, 'November 20, 1923: Postulates of Linguistics,' *A Thousand Plateaus*, 1987, pp. 75-110.

10. María C. Lugones, 'Heterosexualism and the Colonial/ Modern Gender System,'

Hypatia. vol. 22 no. 1 (Winter, 2007), *Writing Against Heterosexism*, pp. 186-209, p. 192.

11. See María C. Lugones, *Peregrinajes/Pilgrimages: Theorizing Coalition Against Multiple Oppression*, Rowman and Little, 2003, for an extensive discussion of these and other approaches to theorizing intersectionality.

12. Lugones, 'Heterosexualism and the Colonial / Modern Gender System' (2007), p. 202.

13. Ibid. p. 195.

14. Enrique Dussel, 'World System and 'Trans'-Modernity', *Nepantla: Views from the South* Durham, NC: Duke University Press, 2002, pp. 221-244.

15. Enrique Dussel, *1492: El Encubrimiento del otro: Hacía el origen del 'mito de modernidad'.* Santafé de Bogotá D.C., Colombia: Ediciones Antropos Ltda., 1992, p.13 [author's translation].

16. Lugones, *Peregrinajes/Pilgrimages,* 2003, p. 98.

17. Trinh T. Minh-ha, *When the Moon Waxes Red: Representation, Gender, and Cultural Politics,* London and New York: Routledge, 1991, p. 59.

18. Ibid. p. 60.

19. Ibid.

20. Lugones, *Peregrinajes/Pilgrimages,* 2003, p. 216.

21. Ibid. p. 217.

22. Gloria Anzaldúa, *Borderlands/La Frontera: The New Mestiza.* San Francisco: Aunt Lute Books, 1987, p. 90.

23. Anzaldúa, *Borderlands/La Frontera,* 1987, p. 91.

24.Ramiro Rodriguez, 'Nightmare,' poem read as soundtrack to Division 11 Diary, U-Matic SP 60 video, collectively produced by Video Machete, Chicago, Illinois, 1993. Access at https://vimeo.com/158076201.

25. Unpublished document, collection of the author.

26. Linda Tuhiwai Smith, *Decolonizing Methodologies,* London: Zed Books, 1999.

27. Ollie Mould, *Against Creativity,* London, UK: Verso Books, 2018.

28. This story is adapted from "Histories and Pedagogics from the Underside of Modernity," co-authored with Christopher A. Bratton, in Amanda Alexander and Manisha Sharma (eds.), *The Routledge Companion to Decolonizing Art, Craft, and Visual Culture Education,* New York and London: Routledge, 2023.

29. Arturo Escobar, *Pluriversal Politics: The Real and the Possible,* Durham, NC: Duke University Press, 2020.

30. See Frantz Fanon, *Black Skin, White Masks,* New York: Grove Press, 2008; Paolo Freire, *Pedagogy of the Oppressed,* trans. Myra Bergman Ramos, New York, NY: Continuum International Publishing Group, 1970/2000; Nelson Maldonado-Torres, *Against War: Views from the Underside of Modernity,* Durham, NC: Duke University Press, 2008; Walter Mignolo, *Local Histories/ Global Designs: Coloniality, Subaltern Knowledges, and Border Thinking,* Princeton, New Jersey: Princeton University Press, 2012; Wa Thiong'o, Ngugi, *Decolonising the Mind: The Politics of Language in African Literature,* Nairobi, Kenya: East

                                        De-/Anti-/Post-colonial Feminisms

African Publishers, 1992; Sylvia Wynter, '1492: A New World View' in Vera Lawrence Hyatt and Rex Nettleford (eds.), *Race, Discourse and the Origin of the Americas: A New World View.* Washington, DC: Smithsonian Institution Press, 1992, pp. 5-57.

31. Immanuel Wallerstein, *Open the Social Sciences: Report of the Gulbenkian Commission on the Restructuring of the Social Sciences*, Palo Alto, CA: Stanford University Press, 1996.

32. Ivan Illich, *Deschooling Society*, New York, NY: Harper and Row, 1971.

33. Paolo Freire, *Pedagogy of the Oppressed* [1970], 2000.

34. Enrique Dussel, *The Pedagogics of Liberation: A Latin American Philosophy of Education*, California, US: Punctum Books, 2019.

35. Arturo Escobar, *Pluriversal Politics*, 2020.

36. 'De-Archive East Africa', Center for Arts, Design, and Social Research, 2019, https://www.centerartsdesign.org.

37. As discussed, Lugones posits this notion in the context of women of color organizing. She asserts the essential necessity of traveling to each other's world in order to build coalition: 'Without knowing the other's 'world,' one does not know the other…By traveling to other people's worlds, we discover that here are 'worlds' in which those who are the victims of arrogant perception are really subjects, lively beings, resisters, constructors of visions…' Lugones, *Peregrinajes/Pilgrimages*, 2003, pp. 96-97.

38. The Center for Arts, Design, and Social Research hosts, amongst other research groups, the Affecting Technologies working group, focused on critical approaches to technology. This group has organized numerous transnational convenings, including hackathons and symposia, most recently resulting in a book, *Afetando Tecnologias, Maquinando Inteligências/ Affecting Technologies, Machining Intelligences,* Boston, MA and São Paulo, Brazil: Center for Arts, Design, and Social Research, 2021. The group's critical research informs the organization's overall approach to digital media.

39. Enrique Dussel, 'World System and 'Trans'-Modernity,' *Nepantla: Views from the South*, Durham, NC: Duke University Press, 2002. pp. 221-244. p. 234.

40. Escobar, *Pluriversal Politics,* 2020, p. 40.

41. Ibid. p. 27.

42. Walter Mignolo, *Local histories/global designs*, 2012.

43. The term 'planetary' echoes the call made by Paul Gilroy for a planetary horizon of imagined collective futures; see Paul Gilroy, *Postcolonial Melancholia,* New York, NY: Columbia University Press, 2005.

44. Wallerstein, *Open the Social Sciences,* 1996.

Art on our Mind: South African Women Creatives-of-Colour Talking Creatively

Sharlene Khan

In 2015, after completing my PhD in Art studies, I returned from London to South Africa (SA) where I took up a lecturing position at Rhodes University in 2016. There I wrote a proposal for a research project called 'Art on our Mind' to the South African National Research Foundation (NRF)[1] for a public dialogue series with South African women-of-colour[2] visual artists, receiving the requested funding in 2017. Since then, these dialogues have generated significant primary information on the invited artists, which are available on the Art on our Mind website[3], alongside the project team's collation of secondary research materials.[4] When we started, we aimed to generate some of these texts ourselves and to establish a 'speaking' archive of women-of-colour visual artists, some of whom had great websites and others none. As the project has grown and developed, we have built an historical record of contemporary artists' trajectories. This chapter reflects on this project between its initiation in 2017 up to 2021, and what I believe to be the value of 'women's talk' (and the way women talk) as scholarly, creative methodologies. As such, this text itself contains dialogue between my own reflections and responses gleaned from the various Art on our Mind dialogues (while there is some editing, the texture of the live dialogues is retained as much as possible).

There were multiple reasons for the ways in which the project was set up. The first is that South Africa has amazing women visual artists-of-colour of all ages and, in the last decade, their work has received much international attention but critical written discourse has lagged behind, with little in-depth analytic scholarship on their practice and historicisation of their work. As someone who grew up under apartheid in a segregated Indian township, but had still learned about many Black artists in high school through a radical visual arts teacher, and was surrounded by Black, Indian and Coloured classmates at my university which had an Africanised arts curriculum in the second half of the 1990s, I found myself at odds with the kind of textbooks on Western and South African history of art that were presented to me as 'canons'.[5] In the textbooks we were offered a canon that consisted of mostly White artists, one or two Black men artists and no Indian, Coloured or women-of-colour artists. I looked around me and I saw many artists-of-colour who were training, or who were my lecturers, but their names did not appear as actual accomplished artists that were validated and historicised in writing.[6] This developed in me a keen sense of distrust for the narratives crafted by history, discourse and writing and those invested with the power of representational life (and death), even as I started to understand through Edward Said's *Orientalism* (1976) how epistemic and representational power becomes cultural power that translates into civil and governmental power.[7]

The importance of representation and the central influence on the Art on our Mind project – and the person whom the project honours in name – is renowned feminist, cultural thinker and educationalist bell hooks. Her 1995 book *Art on my Mind* was an utter revelation when I encountered it.[8] bell hooks's *Art on my Mind* is a collection of different essays on cultural production, dissemination and creative theorisation. hooks talks through the refuge that art became in her life, how she came to her understandings of creativity and why perhaps African American communities do not 'see' themselves in fine arts as opposed to popular culture, which seems much more accessible. She takes apart the issue of the gaze and gazing in nuanced ways, focusing on the power of representation for individuals and communities and the struggles of being a black and/or woman creative. She combines these critical essays with conversations she has with African American artists about their work. hooks's oeuvre is marked by these kinds of dialogue – she has interviewed rappers, filmmakers, women in community groups and scholars as she sought to deconstruct the 'essentialised' and the 'normative' to reveal their social habitus and constructed behaviours and practices. She imagines new forms of being and doing, with an overarching belief that critical education could be liberatory, not just for society and collectives, but for individuals within their own lives.

Most importantly, hooks validated that it was possible for us, as people-of-colour and as women, to centre ourselves in our conversations, to have the nuanced and difficult conversations for ourselves, regardless of who is listening in on the conversation. For someone, like myself, who only encountered a White person when I was sixteen years old, this was confirmation of what seemed obvious to me: I, and people like me, were the centre of our knowledge universe. So it was strange when I started to encounter the wider South African and international world that so much emphasis has been placed on what White people and men think of us. I felt this all the more when I went to London to do a PhD as everything was constantly in relation to the white colonial Empire and presented in this way; as if we did not have our own theories, philosophies and methodologies before White Empires. Just as problematic was the myth that colonial systems were so all-encompassing as to have eliminated everything that came before. The idea of an African Feminisms conference began bubbling in my head, as did the Art on our Mind project, as I realised women-of-colour needed their own platforms to speak in a Self-referential manner and have nuanced discussions about their own range of perspectives, without having to speak to Whiteness. And that this was possible in a Black majority country like South Africa.

The Art on my Mind series has held public dialogues with South African women-of-colour visual artists in order to ask them about their biography and inspirations, their views of the art field and life challenges, as well as their creative content and methodologies. I wanted to create an easily accessible archive of these women that could be used by scholars, whether they were based at school, university or independent. As an artist myself, over the years I have often received requests from school children about my work from various geo-spaces across South Africa and beyond, and I understood why this form of documentation was important. Thus, the aim of building this archive of women-of-colour visual artists was that it should become a resource for artists who didn't have websites and, also, for researchers who wanted to find information on them in a curated and coherent manner linked to other online platforms and resources. The Art on our Mind research team – which consisted of Honours and Masters degree-level women visual art students (who had received bursaries from the NRF), as well as some who volunteered for the project – spent about three months researching each artist and tracking materials. We then collectively generated questions for the artist from our engagement with the material, and these questions were asked by myself as host, or one of the team members or an invited guest, in one-and-a-half hours to two-and-a-half hours dialogues in front of a live audience. At the end of the dialogue, a set of 'humorous' questions were also asked, followed by a question-and-answer session between the audience and the creative. The dialogues were video- and audio-recorded and placed online, along with a full transcript of the dialogue. The reason for documenting the discussion in these different formats was to take into account scholars who might not have enough bandwidth to watch the videos and those who might have sight-issues. The creatives we chose were a combination of emerging, established and historical South African women visual artists, curators and theorists who are actively involved in thinking through African women's visual culture and artistic methodologies, but occasionally a member of the team or friend approached us to feature a South African women creative that worked in interdisciplinary ways that intersected with visual arts, even if they were not solely visual artists (e.g. we interviewed a dancer/choreographer and filmmaker).[9]

The Art on our Mind dialogues has run in tandem with three other initiatives: a fortnightly Black Feminist Killjoy Reading Group (BFK)[10] and Decolonial AestheSis Creative Lab that I founded, as well as the African Feminisms (Afems) Conference that

De-/Anti-/Post-colonial Feminisms

I co-founded. These initiatives fed into ideas of black-African creative theorisation, building into African-centred women's scholarly platforms and informal pedagogical sites. Thus, the Art on our Mind series is not an isolated project, but part of a holistic thinking through black-African feminist creativities and learning that I and others have been involved in, established on the bedrock of black-African feminist thought. The inspiration for these initiatives comes from reading and engaging with the works of Ama Ata Aidoo, Pumla Gqola, Yvette Abrahams, Desiree Lewis, Gabeba Baderoon, Betty Govinden, Patricia Hill Collins, Toni Morrison, Sara Ahmed, Danai Mupotsa, etc.[11]

Thinking Through

On my return to South Africa in 2015, I started the BFK reading group at Rhodes University as a way of returning to Patricia Hill Collins's notion of 'dialogue' in which she frames dialogue as the humanising speech between Subjects.[12] I was also influenced by decolonial semiotician Walter Mignolo's (2014) refutation of the word 'representation' (and its hidden Western aesthetic biases) in favour of 'enunciation', which indexes historically "certain actors, languages, and categories of thoughts, beliefs, and sensing"[13], as well as Stuart Hall's (1989/1991) understanding of enunciation in relation to positionality: "What we've learned about the theory of enunciation is that there's no enunciation without positionality. You have to position yourself *somewhere* in order to say anything at all."[14]

I heeded postcolonial theorist Homi K. Bhabha's idea of the dialectic sometimes being a kind of negotiated settlement between two parties, indicative of the dominance of one over the other[15], and Gayatri Spivak's refrain of whether the subaltern can speak[16] (not as to whether there were such voices in the first place, because, as Collins reminds us, black women have always been speaking, but rather we have not always recognised the platforms within which they speak). Can the subaltern be heard – in their languages, in the forms of articulations they engage – in spaces that authorise discourses and speak about and 'for' them?

Post-apartheid scholarship is an interesting case of sub-altern enunciation. I asked myself how do I navigate my accountabilities and responsibilities as an 'insider researcher' (as articulated by Collins and Trinh T. Minh-ha)[17] when I have grown up in lower-class conditions, achieved social mobility and am now in a position of some authority (as an associate professor in fine art at a university)? Irrespective of the lower-class background that I came from, my advanced university education has resulted in me feeling like an interlocutor in the best case and a ventriloquist in the worst. Oftentimes, such personal history and life experience may result in a researcher believing that they can speak for lower- and working-class communities because they have come from them, not recognising how much these communities evolve and change and how stepping out of them results in losing touch with, fixing or relativising experiences within them. The other end of this spectrum is that such a researcher might feel they are not able to speak at all on their communities because they have 'attained' another economic level, and, yet, many of us may constantly straddle these two worlds when we visit our families and continue to be entangled within working-class lives. In fact, one of the hardest things to negotiate is the segregationist terms of 'under-class', 'lower-class', 'middle-class', 'upper-class' (and equally 'left', 'right', 'centre' politics) when one has not been raised with such terminologies in the getting on with life. Black feminist scholar Betty Govinden (2019) in an Art on our Mind panel on creative theorisation explains these tensions:

> Lived experiences, I think, tends to be boxed. So lived experience is experience on the ground but that doesn't mean it precludes people in the academic world. We all, whether we are academics or not, we have lived experience. And I think for me, the theory that I have access to in the academy, has in a paradoxical way, sent me back to my lived experience. And so in a way, I was isolating and abstracting myself from my scholarship, that's how I was brought up, not to think of myself as a site for any kind of reflection. But, over the years, that's also linked and influenced the kind of research I did. Being brought up in a colonial tradition and then gradually reading all the theorists across the board made me begin to have a new understanding of lived experience. And so in many ways, I traversed the spaces of the academy, which is my ground, and the other grounds on which I live and which I inhabit. And for me, it's just the most liberating, exciting experience.[18]

These are not just negotiations for discursive scholars of knowledge production centres like universities but for creative practitioners, too, who have to straddle the marked differences between lives in their communities and the fine art/ visual arts fields. In these contestations, however, as Govinden states, there is a rich sub-soil of discursive material that not only negotiates challenges, but also presents possibilities of expanded and decolonised notions, and ideas of creativities and creative lives and how, we, as human beings, come to 'art'. Curator Natasha Becker's (2019) statements about her creativity being informed by experiences from childhood are revealing in this respect:

> So reading, music, cooking and baking was also big and I have the advantage of time and perspective, so all of this is retroactive. I didn't have that level of analysis as to what was going on but when I think about my formative years and what has formed me, [it is] homecraft – my grandmother knitted all of our jerseys. We had a beautiful garden. One [tenant] worked for the national parks in Cape Town and he would smuggle plants from the mountain and grow them, so I viewed the garden as being an extremely aesthetic, sensual and sensory place for me...

The everyday – thinking, speaking, doing, making – is key and influences sites from which we draw knowledge. Part of the Art on our Mind research project is to ask questions in a manner that does not reproduce an alienating 'art- or academic-speak'[19], but rather uses everyday language to solicit a depth of knowledge that we see in our fellow artists' practices. We wanted speech acts that maintained the identity of the speaker and for the artists to be able to talk freely about their practice, even as they were directed by questions from the group. We wanted to know about their biography, but we didn't want the biographical to become all-encompassing, as so often happens when dealing with women or artists-of-colour.[20] Biography is crucial for Subjects, as hooks, herself, has demonstrated in her own memoirs:

> the longing to tell one's story and the process of telling is symbolically a gesture of longing to recover the past in such a way that one experiences both a sense of reunion and release. It was the longing for release that compelled the writing but concurrently it was the joy of reunion that enabled me to see that aspect of self and experience that may no longer be an actual part of one's life but is a living memory shaping and informing the present.[21]

This view of Self-narration enables ways to connect the personal to larger collective experiences, and hearing someone's story in the first person, as we aimed to do in Art on our Mind dialogues, results in realising hooks's idea of 'textured narrations', linking together the historical, socio-political, economic, personal, everyday and the imaginative in ways that are not concerned with establishing facts and coherent linear memorialisation but rather in excavating 're-collections'.

Critical race theorist Richard Delgado discusses narrativisation as follows:

> Stories build consensus, a common culture of shared understandings, and a deeper, more vital ethics. But stories and counterstories can serve an equally important destructive function. They can show that what we believe is ridiculous, self-serving, or cruel. They can show us the way out of the trap of unjustified exclusion. They can help us understand when it is time to reallocate power. They are the other half – the destructive half – of the creative dialectic.[22]

In the above, Delgado shares not just his understanding of colonial imperialist narratives and the kind of self-serving, at the exclusion of others, that characterises them, but invokes the idea of counter-storytelling as the means by which marginalised groups communicate their own experiences, worldviews, motifs and imaginaries, which consistently poses a threat to dominant narratives and their attendant power. Rather than an essential universalist colonial modernist paradigm, Delgado sees the potential of narratives to view others through their stories and reshape our viewpoints, and this is akin to African American poet Nikki Giovanni's invitation where "the universal comes from the particular".[23]

Just as the imaginary can be hijacked as a force through which to fear others and the unknown, the imaginary can also be a locale whereby we can imagine past, present and future Selves and others and various contexts for transgressiveness and personal and political affirmation, as hooks does when she draws on and extends Audre Lorde's idea of the potentials of biomythography in this regard.[24] In telling one's story with all of its gaps, contradictions and ambiguities, this Self-voicing shows the various ways women and people-of-colour come to be creatives amidst widely differing and, often, decolonial ideas of creativities, as well as what constitutes 'learning' and 'training'. The authority of this voicing and Subjecthood also validates lived experience as textured histories which do not seek to uncomplicate memories, exceptionalise a person or set up absolute truth, but rather to communicate intersectional narratives and narration determined by a range of persons, social and creative field mechanisms.

When asked, *"Tell us a bit about where you grew up, what creativities you were exposed to as a child and how you came to art"*, the range of responses implicate race, class and gender in schooling opportunities, family and community circles. Here are four of the creatives' stories:

Senzeni Marasela (visual artist): I went to school in Boksburg, I went to a girls' school – St. Dominic's High School for Girls. I went there [in] primary school, high school from the 1980s until 1994 when I finished Matric. We had Art as a subject ... we had a one-day trip that we took to art school in 1992 – we went to Wits [University] and I just fell in love with that place and I made a decision that when I finish high school, I'm going to Wits and I did that. So I had art. I had that privilege.

Reshma Chhiba (visual artist and Bharatanatyam dancer): I was specifically raised in Benoni, which is in the east of Johannesburg. I went to Benoni Primary School – which was predominantly Indian – and then went to Benoni High, which was then a Model C school, which had access to art as a subject, which I didn't have before – you wouldn't find it in Indian high schools, so that really helped in peaking my interest in pursuing a career in the arts.

Lebohang Kganye (visual artist-photographer): I don't think I take those years for granted at all. I think it formed a huge part of my personality, the different exposures, being able to access suburban areas through school, but then going back home to the township and sort of needing to merge those two worlds which are completely apart. Being the only kid that could read English for the kids in your street – you know, if

　　　　　　　　　　　　　　De-/Anti-/Post-colonial Feminisms

they'd get a story book or a fairy tale, they'd make me read it and I think that comes across in my interests around interrogating these stories that we grew up reading, such as fairy tales, so the later work or my earlier work speaks to that part of my childhood … And I guess the earlier work also speaks to that, it speaks to me having the realisation that I spent a large part of my childhood wanting to articulate myself or just have a similar identity to these White girls that I had access to and then bring that into a township and then have a conflict with being in that space.

Mamela Nyamza (dancer, choreographer): Because it's kasi-life [township-life], ja? That's the life. Like anyone who grew up in the community. I mean growing up during those times, it was in the 80s. But that's when we used to play like abo ndize ndize, nidize (hide-and-seek) and if you actually have seen my work, all my work comes from that 'kakyard'[25] situation.

Despite often recited narratives that schools in townships did not have 'art' as a school subject, Marasela indicates that she did (as did I), while other respondents were only able to access art through (semi-)private schools. These responses sometimes undo stereotypes about apartheid schooling, with many of the respondents discussing how creativities still featured in their wider school curriculum in the form of poetry, performance and diary writing. There are also influences that many of the creatives we have interviewed mention: storytelling, childhood games, cooking, gardening and mother's kists with blankets, doilies and other handwork. This goes back to Govinden's remark around how we need to think through and interrogate everyday aesthetics, including the kinds of intuitive ways in which these come to nurture artistic practices. In response to the general question: *"Can you tell us about what influences your creative practice and modes of working?"* it is also clear how everyday creativities evolve into artistic methodologies:

Lebohang Kganye: My introduction to the arts was very much through poetry and when I was in high school, I took part in plays and we got quite exposed to theatre productions, so we were performing quite a bit – I think since I was about 13 until I finished high school. I suppose that what I do at this point allows me to integrate those different worlds: that I was exposed to performance and then my exposure to photography, so I think what I do now, allows me to merge those different worlds or interests but *B(l)ack to Fairytales* became the start of that journey where my work will always have an element of performance … because the work for me is very much like diary writing. So there is a part of me that I feel I explore through this process and photography, again, just allows me that ... it is to a large degree me playing out a reality but also a fantasy, because I think that a lot of my work really explores those elements of play – like playing out a certain fantasy, playing out an idea that I have of myself.

Mamela Nyamza: I think as artists, we are healers because when you put work on stage, we are there to heal others and healing ourselves, so being on stage and actually having had the trauma of my mother – my mother was also raped and killed. So that became a thing of who am I to sit down and not talk about this in my art? ... I guess all of that has healed me, even her – my late mom – and also those who watch us because we become prophets without knowing that we are prophets, because when we are on stage, we are not alone. We are carrying people with us that are actually sending us to be onstage to heal others. I never go on stage without getting sick and, after performing, I never leave the stage without feeling empty because I have opened myself to a whole load of strangers. And to come back to reality, you don't even sleep, because you're still on another level.

Senzeni Marasela: I guess that ties me back to my own mother, because my mother has a kist[26] at home that she got when she moved to Joburg in the 60s, and in there were all these old tablecloths and doilies that she would put on the couch and I hated them, but she had a whole lot of lace. Then I realised, after the time, that she inherited these things when older relatives died, those would be 'hand-me-downs'. Then, when I was trying to develop my own work, and also trying to find a language, those things became very important: why my own mother would keep them and why many other Black women would have them, these objects that were quite Victorian and very steeped in that tradition of owning doilies and tablecloths full of lace.

Shelley Barry (filmmaker): I always paint a white square in any room that I am in. A white rectangle, it's a screen, and for me it is a reminder to make stuff. You can put stuff on that empty canvas. For me it's a reminder to create and to think about the frame and think about what you're going to put in that frame because what you're going to put in that frame is very powerful.

The excerpts above demonstrate the ways in which the easy dialogue elicits information, locating how one's positionality and context informs one's working

De-/Anti-/Post-colonial Feminisms

methodologies, and what Nigerian feminist Molara Ogundipe-Leslie calls the potential of theorising from the 'epicentres of agency, looking for what is meaningful, progressive and useful to us as Africans'.[27] It challenges scholars to do the work of theorising from the epicentre of the artist's responses.

Talking Through

As a host in this series, although I have a list of questions that are prepared in a particular order, I need to hear the artist as they are speaking, be responsive to what is being said, adapt the questions and follow the dialogue and just move forward with one question after the other. As a writer and visual scholar, I am aware of particular ways in which the artist's work is being viewed, but I also try to see other potentials for theorising (there are times I push the artist a bit on particular aspects, even as I need to journey with them on what they want to talk about and highlight). Natasha Becker, for example, speaks about how she sees curating as a creative process itself:

> I like to approach things intuitively, I like to feel it out: What could be relevant here, what could be interesting, what's been done before? What's coming next, what is the space like? How does it feel? What kind of experience do I want to create? Also, I'm producing something, too, I'm making something, I'm making an exhibition. And what do I want to make? What do I want, how do I want to use this material – art – to create the exhibition and the experience, and, potentially, what questions do I want to respond to or address?

Becker is pointing to extending the individual creative process of making an artwork to a creative process that is collective and that is further 'made' through this curatorial conversation. Thus, the artwork is not just an end-product but a conversation that can be creatively furthered through curation and continued contextually. This idea of conversations creating community is exemplified by South African black feminist theorist Pumla Gqola in an Art on our Mind dialogue (2019) in the following way:

> I cherished, and I still do, the enormous value that word [feminism] has in connecting me to millions of other people in the world, who speak millions of other languages, who want to create the kind of world that I want to live in. So that's why I call myself a feminist unapologetically since then. I suppose like every movement, I think that I don't need all of us to do our feminisms in exactly the same kinds of ways. I think that, of course, we are going to disagree and, sometimes, we are going to fight and I think that's the risk you take when you are in a movement and I think that we are able to do different kinds of work and need to do different kinds of work. So for me, feminism is about changing the world. Feminism

is, also, of course, about pleasure. And I am unapologetic about that, not just the sexual pleasure (that too!). I believe in erotic justice. I believe in an entitlement to pleasure, unapologetically, sexual pleasure included… For me, there is enormous pleasure in being part of a feminist community and in being part of different feminist communities.

What Gqola hearkens to here is that even before one finds terminology to define and discuss, one can already be enunciating one's Self within positionalities and politics, and when one encounters a particular language, one can find solace in it or feel alienated by it. hooks argues in *Art on my Mind* that there is an alienating space between fine arts and a wider audience. She asks her sister if she ever thinks about art and her sister says it is easier to identify with movies, whereas 'art is something – in order to enjoy and know it, it takes work'. hooks rationalises that this might be because most black people don't know that there are many black artists creating diverse art (and, therefore, don't see themselves in it), or that art is something that is not valued or seen as elitist (in this regard, 'art' here is meant to be 'fine arts'). These were considerations for the Art on our Mind project, not just in terms of the format of the dialogue with the artist, but the audience in front of whom we present these live dialogues (and also the potential range of audiences that might access the videos online). In most instances, the live audience has been composed of university staff and students, the Afems Conference presenters and attendees, as well as general audiences. We have found that even university students struggled to connect with 'artspeak'. One of our most popular conversations was with visual artist Senzeni Marasela, who is someone who refuses to speak in art discourse terms and presents herself and her work in a conceptually congruent manner of the 'everyday' (in 2018 I was lecturing in Art History and Visual Culture and many students' final year essays referred to the Marasela dialogue and how it connected with, and impacted on, them). Some artists like Kganye say they make art, but struggle with the term 'artist' and the kinds of individual, Western male genius stereotype that it conjures.

To further attempt to demystify 'art' and the idea of 'the artist', Art on our Mind employed a range of quirky questions borrowed from the television series 'Inside the Actor's Studio', which started in 1994 and was hosted by actor/singer and scholar James Lipton. As part of his interviews with well-known Hollywood actors, Lipton asks a series of funny questions. These questions are based on a questionnaire that is associated with Marcel Proust (and adapted by Bernard Pivot), which aims at 'humanising' those they are in dialogue with, and the questions while being fun also purposefully give a break from the serious discussion of creative work.[28] Our version of the 'Marcel Proust-Bernard Pivot-James Lipton-Art on our Mind' questionnaire is a rapid-fire series of questions: *What is your favourite colour, if you could wish any artwork into your life what would it be, what art movement do you*

   De-/Anti-/Post-colonial Feminisms

dislike the most, what sound do you most like, what delights you, what is your pet peeve, what is your favourite book, how would you like to die, if heaven exists what would you like to hear God say? The following brings together, from different artists, their responses to these rounds made at different times.

Sharlene Khan:	***Do you have a favourite book or writer or if you were a literary character, what/who would you be?***
Natasha Becker:	*All our radical ancestors, women intellectuals, like Toni Morrison who died recently. Desiree Lewis is somebody who, since I was at grad school, I've followed and admired, so women intellectuals.*
Reshma Chhiba:	*I'd be Kali. [laughing] No, but* The God of Small Things *by Arundhati Roy.*
Sharlene Khan:	***If you could wish any artwork into your life, which one would you want to have?***
Lebohang Kganye:	*Ooh, a lot of video work, so I would need a cinema room in my house, so I need a house.*
Natasha Becker:	*Right now, Titus Kaphar.*
Shelley Barry:	*I would like to have quite a bit of Bernie Searle's work.*
Sharlene Khan:	***What turns you on?***
Lebohang Kganye:	*Red wine.*
Mamela Nyamza:	*My woman.*
Natasha Becker:	*Dancing.*
Shelley Barry:	*The mind.*
Sharlene Khan:	***What profession would you not like to do?***
Mamela Nyamza:	*I think I hate blood so I wouldn't like to be a doctor.*
Reshma Chhiba:	*Gynecology.*
Senzeni Marasela:	*Oh, become a doctor. [laughter] I have suffering friends.*
Shelley Barry:	*I wouldn't be able to be a doctor. All that blood.*

Sharlene Khan:	***What is your best virtue?***
Lebohang Kganye:	*Laughter.*
Mamela Nyamza:	*My kids.*
Natasha Becker:	*Hard working.*
Shelley Barry:	*I think I am kind.*

Sharlene Khan:	***How would you like to die?***
Lebohang Kganye:	*I think after a really good night out.*
Mamela Nyamza:	*I would like to die on stage.*
Natasha Becker:	*Peacefully.*
Reshma Chhiba:	*In my sleep. Just go to sleep and not wake up.*
Senzeni Marasela:	*Probably in my sleep in my late nineties, like my grandmother. Because she just went to sleep and didn't get up.*
Shelley Barry:	*Good Egyptian cotton, lots of flowers and at least one week to say goodbye to everyone while eating delicious food every day.*

These quirky questions usually elicit a lot of laughter and changes the tone of dialogue, which sets up the last segment where the audience directly asks questions to the creative. The audience also gets a chance to express their appreciation for the works of the artists and how they connected with something shown or said – this sense of shared understanding is a powerful aspect of dialogue as the listener is weighing up and thinking through their own lived experiences. One audience member, for example, responded to Mamela Nyamza: 'I just wanted to say I appreciate how much you trust your gift. You trust what you are doing and it's so powerful. It's so inspiring to know somebody who knows they're accompanied, and they're safe and they can take any risk and they're fine. It is just a powerful thing.' Most often artists are asked about how they entered and manage to negotiate the art field and the challenges they face – as the Art on our Mind dialogues have been hosted in a university setting, it is unsurprising that university arts students are concerned and struggle to understand the modus operandi of the field or the ways in which one sustains themselves in such precarity (or the leap from art student to artist as an actual career).

> ***Audience member [to Lebohang Kganye]:*** I have a question that's more about adulting hacks in terms of preserving your mental health obviously, your okayness while being like this person that is making these great things for yourself and to communicate ideas to the world. What has helped you gauge where you are? How do you keep in touch with yourself and how do you look at yourself and stay close to what you need as a

person to wake up the next day or live your best life and, and that being separate to what the artist needs to create her work?

Lebohang Kganye: I can separate myself from my work. I would say in most cases I would emphasise that I make art, I don't want to say I am an artist, I make art. I can create that separation for myself and I actually practice a lot of self-care things.

Audience member [to Natasha Becker]: I wanted to ask what advice would you give an aspiring curator?

Natasha Becker: Practice, practice and practice. You know that's it. Practice, practice and practice. It's the advice that you would give to a classical pianist, the advice you would give to a writer – just practice.

I mean, like I said, after six years I have been doing this, I went from total beginner here (and you heard my disaster story about my first show) to the Ford Foundation show, which was spectacular and off the charts. I have had everything in-between and you just practice it, it's your craft, it's your profession.

Audience member [to Shelley Barry]: I am very interested in this question of eroticism, because I think you have been very important in reframing the black body, the wounded body, the lesbian body, the body on film and I'm wondering how you dealt with the challenge of filming sex, filming desire, filming eroticism when perhaps so many images that are so burdening of representing this and, yet, it is so important for all kinds of reasons and I am really intrigued as a poetic filmmaker, what does that mean to render for us who also desire to see it portrayed in some other way, sexuality and eroticism?

Shelley Barry: I think the celebration of bodies touching for me is very important because, also, when we see queer bodies on screen, it's often framed in an attempt at eroticism and that's all it's about – it's like, "uh, this is how lesbians do it". For me it's very important to frame that in a way that's authentic and in a way that celebrates love, touch and connection. When I direct scenes like that, often, I will ask, in this case it was with the women, to just explore each other in a way that felt real to them.

Thus, while the Art on our Mind dialogues start with us – the research group – the conversation continues between a number of different people (live and online). In speaking of what we do, how we do it and why we do it, the very act of enunciation is a collaborative co-creation between speaker and hearers, and it co-creates not just the readability and understanding of things we make, but it creates Selfhoods in relation to what we do. This series of dialogues understands pedagogy not as something made by an authority, but as knowledge which is a fundamentally collective co-creation in which everyone is constantly learning and using that knowledge to transform their lives (I'm always amazed and delighted at how the transcribers of the Art on our Mind dialogues say how much they have enjoyed and learnt in the process). Using our lived experiences as sub-soil for creativities and theorisations further informs our lived experiences and how we come to understand them.

Creatively Theorising from our Epicentres

Pumla Gqola (2006) has acknowledged repeatedly that our epicentres, as African women, are infused with creativity, not as a side activity, but as a central aspect of our lives. As scholars, our discourse and theorisations equally have to emanate from such spaces. Black-African feminist creative theorisation is a thinking through that takes for granted that black-African-postcolonial women have always being speaking, making and doing and that these are messy and entangled.[29] It generates knowledge from dialogue and community ways of being. It is responsible and accountable to history, the now, Self and fellow members, productively keeping the tension between the individual and the collective (the 'I-am-because-we-are' ubuntu philosophy[30]). It is decolonial because black-African feminist work is decolonial by its very nature: if you think of the ways in which colonialism disregarded black-African women's intellectual and diverse creative capacities, then incorporating their ways of being, speaking, thinking, communing and making disrupts hegemonic ways of rationalising, compartmentalising and dealing with their knowledges, but also recognises the primacy of black-African women's ways and creativities that not only are pre-colonial but also exceed the disruptiveness of the colonial moment. Collaborative learning and un-learning is a world-making exercise as Gqola (2019) explains:

> that's the project, that creative texts theorise and they create worlds and they do these things. The how and the what they are theorising and what they enable us to do matters. And we are invested in them doing a certain kind of work and creation because they are always creating and creating something that is the opposite of this mess. Or not the opposite, but something more interesting than the mess that we are in… And that, for me, is creative theorisation. Not so much, 'yeah theory is creative'. That's nice. Yeah, everything is creative. But for me, the more important thing is what happens? What am I able to do when reading Koleka Putuma or watching Gabrielle Goliath? What am I able to do that happens in my head that changes how I relate to my children, changes how I relate to where I work, that changes where I bank with, that changes what organisation I work with

De-/Anti-/Post-colonial Feminisms

differently, that changes how I walk in the street, that changes what kind of politically transformative project I invest in?

Establishing the value of creative dialogue is not a simple extractivist or elite tool but is a creative act itself because speaking as a woman, speaking creatively requires one to communicate one's Selfhood to another Selfhood. To be able to speak of our mothers, aunts, Dolly Parton, doilies and fairy tales requires that one believes that the listener is receptive to, and cares for, what is being said and who is saying it. This kind of dialogue is a creative and scholarly methodology that taps into African and women's oral histories, validating its form and content, it's epistemological sense-making, even as in the sense-making it continues to make. It presupposes an audience that will imaginatively follow it as it 'talks through' the imaginative and the forms it lends itself to, and, importantly, as it demonstrates how the sharing of imagination allows us to connect with other humans across vast social differences.

Notes

1. Art on our Mind was funded by the National Research Foundation (NRF) South Africa and Rhodes University between 2017-2018, and the NRF and the University of the Witwatersrand in 2019 and then funded by the latter University and Sharlene Khan.

2. This text uses official South African racial categories when referring to the local context: Black, White, Coloured, Indian, Asian, Chinese. It also uses 'black' and 'people-of-colour' as politically affirmative ideology. 'African' is used to designate someone who was born and lives on the continent.

3. https://artonourmind.org.za/

4. The following Art on our Mind creative dialogues have been held since 2017: Art on our Mind Creative Dialogue with Sophie Peters, Nono Motlhoki and Sharlene Khan, African Feminisms (Afems) 2021 Conference, Cape Town, South Africa, 5 November 2021; Art on our Mind Creative Dialogue with Sharlene Khan and Lallitha Jawahirilal, The Point of Order Project Space, Wits University, 10 October 2019; Art on our Mind Creative Dialogue with Beverley Barry and Mamela Nyamza, African Feminisms (Afems) 2019 Conference, Wits University, Johannesburg, South Africa, 6 September 2019; Art on our Mind Creative Dialogue with Sharlene Khan and Natasha Becker, African Feminisms (Afems) 2019 Conference, Wits University, Johannesburg, South Africa, 5 September 2019; Art on our Mind Creative Dialogue with Sharlene Khan and Lebohang Kganye, The Point of Order Project Space, Wits University,

9 May 2019; Art on our Mind Creative Dialogue with Beverley Barry and Shelley Barry, African Feminisms (Afems) 2018 Conference, Department of Fine Art, Rhodes University, 29 September 2018; Art on our Mind Creative Dialogue Curating as World-Making with Sharlene Khan, Zodwa Skeyi-Tutani, Nontobeko Ntombela, Same Mdluli, Nomusa Makhubu, Nkule Mabaso, African Feminisms (Afems) 2018 Conference, Department of Fine Art, Rhodes University, 28 September 2018; Art on our Mind Creative Dialogue with Sharlene Khan and Senzeni Marasela, Department of Fine Art, Rhodes University, Makhanda, South Africa, 8 April 2018; Art on our Mind Creative Dialogue with Nontobeko Ntombela and Reshma Chhiba, Department of Fine Art, Rhodes University, Makhanda, South Africa, 27 October 2017; Art on our Mind public dialogue with Sharlene Khan and Nontobeko Ntombela, Department of Fine Art, Rhodes University, Makhanda, South Africa, 8 September 2017; Art on our Mind Creative Dialogue Thinking Through, Talking Back: Creative Theorisation as Site of Praxis-Theory with Sharlene Khan, Pumla Gqola, Yvette Abrahams, Betty Govinden and Neelika Jayawardane, Six Mountains on her Back: (Re)thinking African Feminisms Colloquium 2017, Department of Fine Art, Rhodes University, 21 July 2017.

5. See Sharlene Khan, 'Curatorial Statement: Sharlene Khan' in S. Perryer (ed.), *10 Years, 100 Artists: Art in a Democratic South Africa,* Cape Town: Bell-Roberts Publishing, 2004, pp. 13-14.

6. Sharlene Khan, 'Imagining an African Feminist Press', in Y. Camps, M. Grünke, P.Obolo, M. Pichler, P. Tabapsi and N. Mabaso (eds.), *Decolonizing Art Book Fairs: Publishing Practices from the South(s),* Berlin: Miss Read, Afrikadaa, and Mosaïques, 2021, pp. 86-95.

7. Edward Said, *Orientalism,* London: Penguin Books, [1978] 2003.

8. bell hooks, *Art on My Mind: Visual Politics*, New York: The New Press, 1995.

9. In 2021, the Art on our Mind creative dialogue with visual artist Sophie Peters was video recorded in her and her friend's home spaces and was screened at the African Feminisms 2021 hybrid conference. The video was screened to a live online audience and Sophie Peters was available online to field questions.

10. The Black Feminist Killjoy Reading Group (BFK) is a fortnightly reading group at Rhodes University (2016-2019) and then the University of the Witwatersrand (from 2019) that uses black-African women's creative texts (visual arts, film, poetry, theory, fictional literary texts, dance and food to interact within a university space that centralises black-African women's lived experiences. There are a few men and persons of various ethnicities that have also attended these sessions. In March 2020, the BFK sessions were paused for Covid. The African Feminisms (Afems) Conference has been held yearly since 2017 and provides a platform for the presentation of conventional conference papers, performative presentations, creative productions and exhibitions. The Decolonial AestheSis Creative Lab was started in 2018 and hosts workshops around decolonising ideas of creativities and Western aesthetic sensibilities (based on Walter Mignolo's ideas of aestheTics vs aestheSis).

11. I need to mention here my working partners Lynda Gichanda Spencer and Fouad Asfour as central to the work I do (and the various initiatives mentioned here).

12. Patricia Hill Collins, *Black Feminist Thought: Knowledge, Consciousness, and the Politics of*

Empowerment, New York and London: Routledge, [2000] 2009, p.279.

13. Rubén Gaztambide-Fernandez, 'Decolonial Options and Artistic/AestheSic Entanglements: An Interview with Walter Mignolo', *Decolonisation: Indigeneity, Education and Society*, vol. 3 no. 1 (2014), pp. 196-211.

14. Stuart Hall 'Ethnicity: Identity and Difference', *Radical America*, vol. 23 no. 4, (1989/1991), pp. 9-20. p.18.

15. Homi K. Bhabha, *The Location of Culture*, London and New York: Routledge, 1994.

16. Gayatri Chakravorty Spivak, 'Can the Subaltern Speak?' [1989] in R. Morris, (ed.), *Can the Subaltern Speak?: Reflections on the History of an Idea*, New York: Columbia University Press, 2010, pp. 21-80.

17. Patricia Hill Collins, *Black Feminist Thought* [2000] 2009; Trinh T. Minh-ha, *When the Moon Waxes Red: Representation, Gender and Cultural Politics*, New York and London: Routledge, 1991.

18. Art on our Mind Panel Thinking Through, Talking Back: Creative Theorisation as Site of Praxis-Theory with Sharlene Khan, Pumla Gqola, Yvette Abrahams, Betty Govinden and Neelika Jayawardane, held at the Six Mountains on her Back: (Re)thinking African Feminisms Colloquium, School of Fine Art, Rhodes University, 21 July 2017.

19. See Sharlene Khan and F. Asfour, 'Whitespeak: How Race Works in South African Art Criticism Texts to Maintain the Arts as the Property of Whiteness', in A.M. Kraehe, R. Gaztambide-Fernandez, S.B. Carpenter II (eds.), *The Palgrave Handbook of Race and the Arts in Education*, Cham: Palgrave McMillan/Springer International Publishing, 2018, pp. 187-204.

20. Art theorist Olu Oguibe in *The Culture Game*, reads into a textual conversation between Ivorian painter Ouattara and American critic Thomas McEvilley and how the critic reduces the painter to the biographical whilst the frustrated painter wants to talk about his artwork (this recalls Frantz Fanon's notion of how the black body is objectified to body, race, ancestors). Without "author-ity", Oguibe (p.12) writes that Ouattara "struggles to speechify, to repossess his body and reinvest it with humanity, with language, with articulation. He struggles at the borders of subjecthood." O.Oguibe, *The Culture Game*, Minneapolis and London: University of Minnesota Press, 2004.

21. bell hooks, *Talking Back: Thinking Feminist, Thinking Black*, Boston: South End Press, 1989.

22. Richard Delgado, 'Storytelling for Oppositionists and Others: A Plea for Narrative', [1989] in R. Delgado and J. Stefancic (eds.), *Critical Race Theory: The Cutting Edge*, Philadelphia: Temple University Press, 2013, pp. 71-80.

23. Nikki Giovanni quoted in Collins, *Black Feminist Thought* [2000] 2009, p. 288.

24. bell hooks, *Talking Back*, 1989; bell hooks, *Wounds of Passion: A Writing Life*, New York: Holt Paperbacks, 1997.

25. 'Kak' is Afrikaans for 'shit'.

26. Refers to a furniture chest.

27.Desiree Lewis 'Desiree Lewis talks to Molara Ogundipe, leading feminist theorist, poet, literary critic, educator and activist, about the interface of politics, culture and education', *Feminist*

Africa, Issue 1 (2002), p.6.

28. In 1886 Proust answered a set of questions that was a popular Victorian parlour game. Although he did not develop the game, it has since come to be called the Proust Questionnaire and has been asked of many celebrities. In 1975, this was further popularised by French talk-show host Bernard Pivot. James Lipton then further developed the questionnaire as part of the Inside the Actor's Studio series. According to Evan Kindley, Lipton "declared Pivot's questionnaire a 'verbal Rorschach test that told the viewer more about the respondent than an hour of questioning'". See Evan Kindley 'How the Proust Questionnaire Went from Literary Curio to Prestige Personality Quiz', *New Yorker*, 17 July 2016, https://www.newyorker.com/books/page-turner/how-the-proust-questionnaire-went-from-literary-curio-to-prestige-personality-quiz [Accessed, 17 June 2023].

29. 'By "creative theorisation", I intend the series and forms of conjecture, speculative possibilities opened up in literary and other creative genres. Theoretical or epistemological projects do not only happen in those sites officially designated as such, but emerge from other creatively textured sites outside of these', Pumla Dineo Gqola '"Crafting Epicentres of Agency"; Sarah Bartmann and African Feminist Literary Imaginings' *QUEST*, vol. XXX no. 1-2 (2006), pp. 45-76, quote p.50.

30. See Sharlene Khan 'We-All-Fall-Down: Thinking Through Lines of Proximity and Ubuntu as Decolonizing Praxis in South African Museum Re-Presentations', in S. Jang (ed.), *What Do Museums Change? Art and Democracy,* Seoul: National Museum of Modern and Contemporary Art, 2020, pp. 222-243.

De-/Anti-/Post-colonial Feminisms

Mnemonic Aberrations:
An Essay on the CounterPoetics
of Black Feminist Experimental Film

Ayanna Dozier

Let me begin with a brief film example of embodied remembrance. The character Nana Peazant in Julie Dash's *Daughters of the Dust* (1991) serves as her family's historian and through ritual performances of cultural memory becomes a living memory to others. Nana "exists outside" of the linearity of time in relation to her offspring. A former enslaved woman, Nana is the grandmother to a new generation of Black life born after the abolition of slavery who convene on Saint Simmons Island in Georgia one last time before many of them depart for the North as part of the Great Migration at the turn of the twentieth century. Nana's efforts to make memory a living history are aberrant and often deemed troubling – antiquated, even – by others. When she engages with a root work ritual, Viola, a devout Christian, shouts with indignation at the "pointlessness" and "demonic" nature of her grandmother in-law's labor.

Viola's condemnation of Nana's root work lies in the disruptive power her labor of memory enacts, a mysterious and affective force that transmits time not as a linear concept, but as a multi-temporal life process. Dash underscores the significance of Nana's ritual through the film's aesthetics, which feature, among other things, fluctuating frame rates and the narration of an unborn child who tells the story of the past.[1] Nana's ritual is an act of communion with the dead, who deserve to be remembered and whose memories provide insight to and agency for the production of our lives. Nana poignantly states to her children, 'We carry these memories inside us. They didn't keep good records of slavery. . . We had to hold records in our head.' To be a living memory is to embody a place of alterity and heterogeneity, a literal passageway between life and death that aims to affectively restore, and recode, time for others. This aberrant memory work – be it physical or filmic – is what I call a mnemonic aberration.

Mnemonic aberration is a critique of how time is measured and recorded. The mnemonic device becomes a tactic for destabilizing linear or colonial temporalities, but it is not a claim for an "ethno-aesthetic." Ethno-aesthetics refer to the argument that our cultural production is autonomously produced and can produce an inherent, essentialist, meaning within the film's aesthetics around the fact of Blackness.[2] I examine how Black activities of cultural production are anti-colonial acts that have shaped a Black cultural production rooted in alterity and a strident refusal of anti-Blackness. This work forges instead an ethic-aesthetic principle of care found within many Black feminist experimental works. Such a practice is not autonomously produced but is forged within the structure which it actively seeks to resist. Although it may speak to many of the same ethno-organizing principles of nationality and race, these practices are not inherent to one's identity. To label such works as an ethno-aesthetic is reductive, for it ignores the layers of activity and cultural production that come with such works. The principle of care I am describing is in opposition to oppressive structures and simply cannot be uniformly called a "Black aesthetic". Rather it is an ethic-aesthetic of care that is uniquely featured in Black feminist work around the ways they re-articulate Black life.

Black feminist experimental film is a key aesthetic archive by which we can recognize Black feminism's ability to unmake what we normally consider the quotidian experiences of time's movement. Black feminist experimental film and video utilize Black women's capacity for memory to unsettle the present (or what we consider the present), to recode normative orders of time and rebel against it. Experimental films and video achieve this rebellion through an ethic-aesthetic principle of rhythm, one that draws out time as a life process, which recodes time from our normative colonial structure as a measurement of financial value and labor given in 'time is money'.[3] In so doing, this shift, or "aberration," reveals time as the culprit of bodily control. As Denise Ferreira da Silva explains, this is how Blackness can return the necessity of time to the subject and demonstrate 'that the world and its categories thrive in the contingency of existence shared by the subject of whiteness and its racial others'.[4]

I use the word aberration to signal difference from a normative temporal order, a disruption or jam in the machine of how things are and how they "should be." Understanding aberration as the return to time as a life process, rather than a power over life, requires freedom from colonial temporality. Colonial temporality is the source of the market value structure by which we come to recognize and live time. A colonial time is a static one. As philosopher Alia Al-Saji notes, it is a "fixed" construction of the past that sits firmly within the colonial fabrication of (white) History and bodies.[5] She argues that racialized subjects are framed as possessing "delayed" bodies, ones that are situated to view time and their histories as unchanging pasts where change is only made possible through "progress" or

De-/Anti-/Post-colonial Feminisms

a "building towards a future" for colonial subjects.[6] This conception of time, implemented through the horrors of colonization, commodified Black life as the "for-profit object" that could facilitate colonial temporality's movement in its linear progress into the future. Against these colonial structures of time, Black feminism has marshaled memory as a living force, as a circuit of time that restores time as something lived and embodied to individuals and refused time's petrification.

Mnemonic aberration is a method for exploring an expansive Black feminist critique of time in which a counter-poetics of rhythm becomes its ethic-aesthetic principle. In my PhD, 'Mnemonic Aberrations' (McGill University, 2020) and in further writing/ photography/ film-making, I employ this term amongst other Black feminist methods to study, gather, analyse and construct the history of Black feminist experimental film and video art in the United States and the United Kingdom between 1968 and 1998. In my PhD, I identified and studied the following filmmakers: Madeline Anderson, Camille Billops, Julie Dash, Barbara McCullough, Judah (Martina Attille), L. Franklin Gilliam and Jamika Ajalon, among numerous others.

Some film analyses from my PhD include Judah's *Dreaming Rivers* (1988), which is exemplary for its use of the third space—between life and death—as a suspension of time where the protagonist Miss T manifests her consciousness to the audience to give an image and name to her existence. The rhythm of Miss T's home in St. Lucia emerges to aide her on her journey to the other side, but far from being utilized as background 'noise', this rhythm in the film affectively grids the autobiography of Miss T's life through her embodiment, memories, trinkets and the distant voices of St. Lucia. Through Miss T's "dreams", director Judah manifests the geographical activities of Black culture on St. Lucia at the fore of the cinematic images in *Dreaming Rivers*. Film enables a temporal return home for Miss T rather than a physical or spatial return, in that her dreams evoke the memories and feeling of St. Lucia rather than represent the island. Judah fashions consciousness for Black womanhood enclosed by anti-Black patriarchal structures to demonstrate a life that has been lived in face of a structure that denied her right to a life.[7]

L. Franklin Gilliam's *Sapphire and the Slave Girl* (1995) uses citations and "doubles" of the Sapphire detectives as memory-images of Black womanhood. These citations repeatedly mutate themselves in time in the film, changing clothes, appearances and bodies to convey a shared transformation of queer Black womanhood that constructs itself in spite of the colonial closure of time in which we are 'known' by and through controlling images (stereotypes). Rhythm in the film is used as a pluri-construction of being and parallels the queer multitudes of Sapphires spreading in the film constructing a commons that is temporally structured rather than spatially. This is to say that *Sapphire and the Slave Girl*'s sequentiality is determined rhythmically. Each appearance of a Sapphire and citation brings a soundtrack with them that shifts our focus from a plot-driven structure to images constructed to 'initiate sound's ebb and flow and its indeterminate boundaries.'[8] Such images allow for a free-for-all engagement with the images on screen, insofar as there are no clear predetermined images to accompany the beats of a song, so any visual can be foregrounded at any time.

Another example is Jamika Ajalon's *Memory Tracks* (1997), which stands out for its use of the specter of the revolutionary past coming as a source of aid to the protagonist and the audience. The liminality of *Memory Tracks'* central character, a mad woman, produces an image of self-recovery in her pursuit of agency. The film frames the spectrality of the dead as a metaphor of tearing the veil between this world and the next to manifest the space of awareness beyond coloniality. Aesthetically, Ajalon uses the gaze to name the cinematic memory of Man and her opposition to that image and its production. The specter in *Memory Tracks* imparts a memory of freedom to our protagonist, giving her an oppositional gaze to look back at the viewer and construct herself (within a system that condemns her body through racism, sexism and homophobia structuring her personhood in the world) in her own terms, through a mnemonic aberration. The protagonist reinvents the flesh through rebellious affective means where jazz music wafts our protagonist through the film and lures us into the construction of what is happening onscreen.

My own investment in studying and writing about these films and videos was and is to examine what they aesthetically do and make possible, rather than what they representationally mean. By shifting away from certain approaches to representation as that of "picturing" Black women's lives, I analyze these experimental films' illocutionary force that is, the procedures by which they do what they do.

In my writing/photography/film-making, I am interested in extending Sylvia Wynter's scholarship to more fully realize her undertheorized term, the "counter-poetics of rhythm." Her conception of a counter-poetics of rhythm was first introduced in a passing sentence in her first of two articles from 1992 on film analysis, 'Re-thinking "Aesthetics": Notes Towards a Deciphering Practice.'[9] Here she describes how aesthetics can affectively imbue a refusal of anti-Blackness in their doing rather than their representational meaning. One of the effects of this practice is to free time from its colonial fixity to a more mobile, affective register, where it can be shifted from its commodity value to a life process.[10] Utilizing an affective framework, I read time as it is manifest in these experimental films by Black Women filmmakers in relation to the life process, removing it from its commodity framing attached to money and imbuing it with the fullness of life.

                    De-/Anti-/Post-colonial Feminisms

Towards a Counter-Poetics

Sylvia Wynter conceives of a counter-poetics of rhythm as the social imaginary of a global popular culture whose insistent challenge to the hegemonic social imaginary of Man lies within the "new video-like Black popular music forms".[11] While Wynter never returned to the term in her scholarship, she further elucidates in her unpublished manuscript "Black Metamorphosis" that rhythm, as carried out in Black music, constructs a rebellious thrust in the performer and audience.[12] This thrust can be described affectively as the motion flowing through rhythm that links bodies with the beat. Wynter's turn to music video-like productions to explain the counter-poetics of rhythm uses the metaphor of sound to examine how film aesthetics can draw that thrust out with images to its audience.[13] I build upon Wynter's term to flesh out further the way Black feminist experimental film and video works use rhythm as a similar affective movement that imbues their film and video aesthetics with the affirmation of Blackness – that is Black life, Black culture, and specifically here, Black womanhood. This aesthetic strategy exploits moving images' ability to generate affect and to usher forth a rhythm of suppressed Black culture. I foreground this strategy through looking again at Black folkloric Southern and Caribbean spirituality ("conjure culture") as an ethical orientation in which kin relations are named and altered in the aesthetic "doing" of the film, rather than its meaning. Like the brief example of Dash's film above, the commitment to alterity in cultural memory is for the well-being of the community. As Nana states, 'It's up to the living to keep the dead alive.' My work identifies this ethic-aesthetic practice of rhythm – as a counter-poetics of rhythm – wherein rhythm is affectively embedded into the work, transcending the soundtrack and background noise. Rhythm exists within the matrix of memory and can be understood as central to and/or as part of the associative practices of Black life that correspond to and are linked temporally in the aesthetics of Black women's experimental work in film and video.

Wynter centers rhythm in Black culture for its 'aesthetic/ethic principle of the gestalt':[14] its form itself is the production of aesthetic doing, and, through this form, it transmits an affective economy of senses and sense-making attributes in its production. Rhythm as the ethic-principle of gestalt shifts our attention to the overall code of the cultural practice as well as the individual agents of that coding that carry associative meanings in their placement. Thinking about this shift in attention allowed me to interrogate Black life, memory, and its history for its struggles and resistance to colonial temporality through living and cultural practices evident in Black women's films. This is how my PhD 'Mnemonic Aberrations' constructed and mobilized a counter-poetics of rhythm through Sylvia Wynter's available scholarship on aesthetics, poetics and Man.[15]

The counter-poetics of rhythm is a critique of Western aesthetic and mythological ordering of Man forged in and through the anti-colonial, liberatory practices of Black cultural production. I define the aesthetic reproduction of Man as expressed through linear filmic narratives; this is diametrically opposed to the fashioning of Black feminist imaginary in film and video art that is simultaneously social and non-normative. Man's kin relations are mobilized through the ethno-class relations of commodity culture, where aesthetically the 'quality of life' has been coded through material and commodity-based redemption. Anti-Blackness is embedded within our present normative cultural hegemony, in which individuals are socialized as active participants in perpetuating anti-Blackness within every fraction of their being – intellectually, biologically and socially. In McKittrick's astute synthesis of Wynter's unpublished manuscript 'Black Metamorphosis: New Natives in a New World', she argues that Black cultural production – specifically music – participates in the activity of rebellious reinvention of Black life.[16] In so doing, I name my approach to Blackness as an activity fashioned through cultural production that foregrounds Blackness through its rebellious activities. At its best, this conveys how global Black life emerges through various racial categorizations and differences following the Trans-Atlantic Slave Trade, in which the activities of cultural production – like ritual, spirituality, art-making and more – enabled generations of enslaved and/or colonized subjects to name themselves outside of the 'biocentric categories of being that cosmically anticipate Black dyselection'.[17] My use of Blackness as an activity of existence that names itself through the refusal of anti-Blackness has shifted my attention towards the specific cultural practices and customs, like ritual and spectral conjuring, that are practiced in the films and video texts I analyze.

Why Experimental Film/Form?

"Mnemonic Aberrations" as a term is a form of experimental Black cultural production, one that is entangled with the alterities realized in filmic rituals, specters, and conjure culture. My focus on alterity enabled me to attend to aberrant threads of Black feminist experimental film and video that, when marshalled, draw out the temporal dimensions of affect as it is produced and experienced in film.

Black feminist thought, historically, presents an ongoing critique of Eurocentrism that has produced the colonial thought, ownership and practice realized in the representational body of Man. Many of the filmmakers included in my PhD acknowledge the role that Black feminism (or womanism) has played in their lives and filmmaking practices, and how their films are often inspired by and are extensions of Black feminism as a practice. To further clarify my interest in Black feminist cinema as a genre, I find Gloria J. Gibson-Hudson's principles to be a useful tool. She writes that Black feminist cinema does the following:

De-/Anti-/Post-colonial Feminisms

1. Acknowledges that Black women worldwide share a history of patriarchal oppression;
2. Validates Black women's experiences as real and significant;
3. Investigates the cultural history of Black women, including the survival techniques Black women employ to resist oppression and (re) formulate concepts of womanself;
4. Acknowledges and respects alternative knowledge systems and the means by which Black women "recall and recollect."[18]

All of the films that I analyzed in my PhD adhered to one, if not several, of the principles listed by Gibson-Hudson, albeit in different ways due to their experimental nature. Selecting these films as representative of the genre of Black feminist experimental cinema advances the aforementioned claims and propositions by inviting audiences to reorient their relationship to Black womanhood by feeling time. This ethical principle of care helps audiences to aesthetically shift their relationship with movement in order to name the origins of their mythological structures and their kin relations and then free ourselves from that system. This was also a Black queer feminist project, not just for the queer lives that I selected to discuss in my PhD, but also for how queerness opens subjects to heterogenous ways of living, thinking and relating with others in the world, and ways of living that rebel against the stratification or singularity of Man. I folded queer kinship relations into my articulation of Black feminist thought to address how Black feminism is articulated, and expanded, by Black queer women.[19]

Black feminist experimental film also poses a critical pedagogical challenge to what we as scholars, viewers, filmmakers and critics – myself included – have inherited from Western Europe with regard to our aesthetic definitions of experimental film. Part of my practice is to make more visible how the Black cultural production of alterity, like Nana's performance of ritual, manifests very diverse and experimental forms, and yet is often denied the appropriate terminology and categorization in mainstream texts and film programs because of its distinctive expression of Black cultural production.[20] I am also interested in how the placement of nationality and/or national allegiance in films by Black women is often utilized to undermine and contain their work within particular historical narratives that contribute to the over-representation of Western-focused scholarship.

I find the definition of "eccentric" proposed by Black cultural studies scholar Carla Peterson to be pertinent to this practice. In *Recovering the Black Female Body: Self-Representation by African American Women* (2000), Peterson delivers a brief historical account in her introduction of how eccentricity both binds Black women to the visibility of their bodies – for the purpose of labor or for accusation of criminality – as well as describes their cultural practice of using the body as a manifestation of the spirit because of the ways in which culture articulates appearance.[21] The tension of the eccentricity that frames how Black women exist and produce art is precisely the structure of alterity and liminality that I use to navigate experimentation for this body of work. Experimentation marshals, what Peterson describes as an empowering oddness that might lend itself to a freedom of mobility in the world for Black women.[22]

Additionally, experimentation moves forward a creative practice that holds and centers the lives, labor and bodies of Black women in culture. The denial of a cultural, creative practice for Black women is rooted in enslavement, where its effect was to render Black women's bodies as reproductive (in children and pleasure) and regurgitative (in labor) machines that render profits. Experimentation is critically the term and practice that more scholars should be attentive to when analyzing the lives, labor, and cultural production of Black women. Mainstream approaches to film studies have not published rich scholarship on experimental films by Black women.[23] What does this absence of Black women in this field tell us about our social imagination of experimentation or difference in the world?

To use the term Black is to consider – as Wynter does – activities of cultural production that refute global anti-Blackness and white EuroAmerican categorizations of humanity and cultural production. "Black" describes the diasporic – and thus global – cultural relationships of bodies who descend from and around Africa that forged humanity and human relations within a global structure of racial violence. "Black" attends to the cultural practices of adaptation and code-switching that Black individuals have practiced to work within systems that oppress and suppress all aspects of our bodies, hair, language, vernacular and cooking, among so many other parts of our lives. It also embodies a radical critique of white EuroAmerican culture and government.

This is why for me analyzing Black feminist experimental film is a recuperative project, one that utilizes remembrance not to fully reconstruct what is missing but to speculatively point to what could be and what was. Black feminist experimentation opens tears in the filmic frame and allows those ruptures to be formalized for an audience to envision something beyond the histories presented within it; in other words, to create a new consciousness beyond Man.

Notes

1. Jacqueline Bobo writes in her book, *Black Women as Cultural Readers*, that the experimental or challenging filmic approach of *Daughters of the Dust* did not hinder nor interfere with Black women's responses to nor their interpretation of the film. Many felt that the aesthetic poetic license was necessary to convey temporality, bodies (reflected in both the unborn child and the ancestors), and change that cannot always be visualize before us. New York: Columbia University Press, 1995. p. 183. *Daughters of the Dust* was not only a milestone for Black women's cinema but also for the question of Black feminist experimental cinema that I take up here. Unfortunately, Julie Dash was locked out of Hollywood for many years before mainstream audiences turned their attention back to her work and the question of Black feminist experimental film again. See Michael T. Martin, "I Do Exist": From "Black Insurgent" to Negotiating the Hollywood Divide – A Conversation with Julie Dash' *Cinema Journal*, vol. 49 no. 2 (Winter 2010), pp. 1-16; Cara Buckley, 'Julie Dash Made a Movie. Then Hollywood Shut Her Out', *New York Times*, 18 November 2016.

2. Sylvia Wynter [1992] 'Re-thinking 'Aesthetics': Notes Towards a Deciphering Practice' in Mbye B. Cham (ed.)l *Ex-iles: Essays on Caribbean Cinema*, New Jersey: Africa World Press, Inc, 1995, p. 241.

3. Experimental cinema is usually defined as cinema that 'typically features nonlinear structures, nonnaturalistic performance styles, challenging subject matter, obtrusive camera work, and unconventional editing patterns': Jean Petrolle and Virginia Wright Wexman (eds.),*Women and Experimental Filmmaking*. Urbana and Chicago: University of Illinois Press, 2005. p. 3. They also state that Feminist experimental cinema describes films largely produced by women who critique and challenge the 'masculinist avant-garde aesthetic dogmas by juxtaposing narrativity and non-narrativity, deploying narrative pleasure alongside narrative disruption, providing viewers with identification as well as critical distance'. Numerous scholars and filmmakers are quick to assert that women inherently creating experimental film does not make their work a feminist experimental piece, especially when so many white women experimental filmmakers in the mid to late twentieth century were adverse to the term feminist. Robin Blaetz (ed.), *Women's Experimental Cinema: Critical Frameworks*, Durham: Duke University Press, 2007, p.10; Lauren Rabinovitz [1991] *Points of Resistance: Women, Power and Politics in the New York Avant-Garde Cinema 1943-71*, Urbana and Chicago: University of Illinois Press, Second Edition, 2003. However, as other scholars have argued, if a film has a strong political critique of an aesthetic order then filmmaker intent is not sufficient to a avow a film from the category of feminist experimental cinema (Ruby B. Rich Chicks, *Flicks: Theories and Memories of the Feminist Film Movement*, Durham: Duke University Press, 1988, pp. 70-71.

4. Denise Ferreira da Silva, 'Toward a Black Feminist Poethics', *The Black Scholar*, vol. 44 no. 2 (2014), pp. 81-97, p. 89.

5. Al-Saji 'Too Late: Racialized Time and the Closure of the Past', *Insights*, vol. 6 no. 5 (2013), pp. 1-13.

6. Ibid. Al-Saji re-examines Henri Bergson's cone of memory as an effective demonstration of how, ideally, the past is filtered out for present encounters. Bergson's 'useful aide' of taking just enough of the past to inform the present is not applicable when dealing with racialized subjects, specifically Black bodies. Racialized subjects' bodily schemas have been over-determined by colonization so that each encounter pulls from the visual and ideological colonial temporality of existence. This is to say that history and the present is in time with colonialism and its fabrications (see Fanon [1952] *Black Skin, White Masks*, trans. Richard Philcox, New York: Grove Press, 2008, p. 2). Al-Saji places one's

racialized and marginalized past as a present problem. Frantz Fanon's *Black Skin, White Masks* reminds us that the past and memory lives on through the bodies of racialized subjects and is in fact open for change. Frantz Fanon, *Black Skin, White Masks*, [1952] 2008, p. 201). Thus we should move out of step with this colonial tempo that views the future and progress as the site for change and find (with the case of Blackness utilize) our own tempo/rhythm where possibility and change can happen at any moment; a tempo where the past is always open for re-animation and discussion. Ibid. Al-Saji writes, 'The privilege of a racializing past owes, then, not only to dominance but to a form of temporal exclusion or 'othering': delays that are at work in both present and past. Other pasts, while not erased, are marginalized and reconfigured through this delay, unfolded and relocated as backdrops to a white world. Extrapolated from stereotyped identities, reactions taken out of context, protective rigidity, and temporality lived under oppression, this racialized past troublingly remains my own, while being at once that of imperial fragmentation and compartmentalization.'

7. Sylvia Wynter, 'Africa, the West and the Analogy of Culture: The Cinematic Text after Man' in June Givanni (ed.), *Symbolic Narratives/African Cinema: Audiences, Theory and the Moving Image*, British Film Institute, 2000/2001, pp. 25-76, p. 30.

8. Carol Vernallis, *Experiencing the Music Video: Aesthetics and Cultural Context*, New York: Columbia University Press, 2004, p. 44

9. Sylvia Wynter, 'Re-thinking 'Aesthetics': Notes Towards a Deciphering Practice', (1992), pp. 237-79.

10. Ibid.

11. Ibid. p. 260.

12. Katherine McKittrick 'Rebellion/Invention/Groove', *Small Axe*, vol. 49 (2016), pp. 81.

13. Sylvia Wynter, 'Re-thinking 'Aesthetics' (1992), p. 260 n.37.

14. Ibid. p. 245.

15. Assembling the bulk of Wynter's scholarship was itself a special archival challenge as the majority of her earlier (prior to 2000) journal and chapter articles have not been digitized. This separate, but related, endeavor to my archival research took me two years to acquire and scan the chapters out of print books, journals, and plays that I have used to build my scholarship upon in Mnemonic Aberrations. This research is reflected in my PhD.

16. Katherine McKittrick,'Rebellion/Invention/Groove' (2016), pp. 79-91.

17. Ibid. p. 89.

18. Gloria J. Gibson-Hudson, 'The Ties that Bind: Cinematic Representations by Black Women Filmmakers' in Jacqueline Bobo (ed.), *Black Women Film and Video Artists*, New York and London: Routledge, 1998, pp. 43-66, p. 46.

19. Here I am thinking of the insightful opening paragraph by Yvonne Welbon for the introduction to her edited anthology on Black out-lesbian women media makers where she notes that a significant portion of Black women's media making (30%) is produced by this minority population. Yvonne Welbon and Alexandra Juhasz, *Sisters in the Life: A History of Out: African American lesbian Media-Making*, Durham: Duke University Press, 2018, pp ix-xix, p.1.

20. In the research that I have conducted thus far, I have found that Black women filmmakers create more short experimental films rather than feature length experimental films. One reason may be that, as short films require fewer resources to produce and finance, Black women have had greater access to making them. They also do not have to recuperate as much in the way of production costs for short films and they enable directors to experiment more with the medium. As a result, there may be a lower stake in regards to

audience reception insofar as these filmmakers are not dependent on audience box office returns to be funded.

21. Carla Peterson, 'Forward: Eccentric Bodies', in Michael Bennett and Vanessa D. Dickerson (eds.), *Recovering the Black Female Body: Self-Representation by African-American Women*, New Brunswick: Rutgers University Press, 2000, pp.ix-xvi.

22. Peterson writes 'the first evokes a circle not concentric with another, an axis not centrally placed (according to the dominant system), whereas the second extends the notion of off-centeredness to suggest freedom of movement stemming from the lack of central control and hence new possibilities of difference conceived as empowering oddness', Ibid. p. xii.

23. Examples of analyses that do discuss Black femme filmmakers are: Gwendolyn Audrey Foster's book ,*Women Filmmakers of the African and Asian Diaspora: Decolonizing the Gaze and Finding Subjectivity,* Carbondale: Southern Illinois UP, 1997; Lorraine O'Grady's essay 'The Cave: Black Women Film Directors' *Artforum* (Jan. 1992) pp. 22-24; bell hooks, *Reel to Reel: Race, Class, and Sex at the Movies,* New York and London: Routledge, 1996; Jacqueline Bobo (ed.), B*lack Women Film and Video Artists,* Routledge, 1998; George Alexander, *Why We Make Movies: Black Filmmakers Talk About the Magic of Cinema,* New York: Harlem Moon, Broadway Books, 2003; Phyllis R. Klotman and Janet K. Cutler (eds.), *Struggles for Representation: African American Documentary Film and Video,* Bloomington: Indiana University Press, 2000; Robin Blaetz (ed.), *Women's Experimental Cinema: Critical Frameworks.* Durham: Duke University Press, 2007; Mbye Cham and Claire Andrade-Watkins (eds.), *Black Frames: Critical Perspectives on Independent Black Cinema,* Cambridge, Mass.: MIT Press, 1988; Mbye B. Cham (ed.), *Ex-iles: Essays on Caribbean Cinema,* New Jersey: Africa World Press, Inc., 1995; Allyson Nadia Field, *Uplift Cinema: The Emergence of African-American Film and the Possibility of Black Modernity,* Durham: Duke University Press, 2015; Alexandra Juhasz,*Women of Vision: Histories in Feminist Film and Video,* Minneapolis: University of Minnesota Press, 2001; Allyson Nadia Field, Jan-Christopher Horak and Jacqueline Najuma Stewart (eds.), *L.A. Rebellion: Creating a New Black Cinema,* Berkeley: University of California Press, 2015; Christopher Sieving, *Soul Searching: Black-Themed Cinema from the March on Washington to the Rise of Blaxploitation,* Middletown, CT: Wesleyan University Press, 2011.

Decolonial Theory: Spiderwoman Theater's Missing and Murdered Women

Shanna Ketchum-Heap of Birds

According to Maori scholar Linda Tuhiwai Smith, 'decolonization is a process that involves, at its core, the interrogation of colonizing knowledges that position the superiority of Western knowledge above all others.'[1] While Native American/ First Nation's artists/artists' groups[2] have been widely exhibited and analysed in relation to both postcolonial theory, postmodernism and North American multiculturalism, it is my contention in this chapter that a renegotiation towards decolonial theories can problematize the erasure of Indigenous concerns in the international art world in favor of Indigenous presence and futurity. Decolonial theories and processes are inherent to the struggles of Indigenous Peoples worldwide[3] as they intersect with one another on local, national and global levels because they still live under settler colonialism and land rights/dispossession are key issues.

By internationalizing the debate concerning Indigeneity and decolonial thought in art practices, as well as examining the reception of Native American/ First Nation's artists in the art world, I am arguing that a more complex decolonial understanding of gender, sexualities, and race can move us away from heteropatriarchal understandings imposed by colonialist and anthropological thinking. My PhD research focused on four artists/artists groups – Kent Monkman, Rebecca Belmore, Spiderwoman Theater Company and James Luna – and I sought to question how we understand the colonial past through images, artworks, and performances to demonstrate that their works constitute acts of decolonization.

Following the approach of performance scholar Diana Taylor in *The Archive and the Repertoire* (2003), I realized my PhD research needed to mediate a path between two fields – performance studies and Indigenous studies – by putting the two fields in conversation with one another and privileging the voices, and perspectives of the Indigenous artists through interviews with them. Initially, my topic was concerned with the Indigenous content evident in their works, and I framed their performance activity (live performances, installations, narratives/storytelling, video) within a wider Indigenous social and political context focused upon cultural survival and self-determining agency. I speculated that these artists intentionally used performance strategies to critically engage cultural, social, and political issues inherent to their own tribal backgrounds, experiences, and understanding of pan-Indian community activism. As I progressed in the research and interviewed the artists, I started to realize that their performance strategies were not adequately addressed, theorized or explained by mainstream art historical analyses, such as postmodernist and postcolonialist frameworks, which I found to be predominant in the literature about their work. Their repeated concern with the "disappearance" and genocide of Native people unsettled "normalized" colonial discourses in a variety of subject areas.

By examining how these artists/artists' groups works sit amongst other contemporary, Western 'academic'-based debates and concerns, I realized that the critique of Eurocentrism and coloniality offered new dimensions to my research. I was able to identify how their contemporary Indigenous performances functioned in relation to broader social movements and became performances about social practices, utilizing decolonizing principles by de-centering Western canonical texts and privileging Indigenous Peoples, their minds and bodies. Using postmodern or postcolonial gaze theory, it was relatively straightforward to identify that key works by these artists in different media such as video, photography, painting, and performance often challenge oppressive categorizations constructed primarily through the white, male, European gaze. However, using a decolonial perspective on the colonizer/colonized gaze, their Native American/First Nation's artistic and performative practices highlighted critical links between activism and art, or politics and aesthetics, as responses to oppressive, imperial regimes. Even though the works I selected for my research spanned a range of times and locations, their performances consistently articulated a "re-use" of notions of history, time/temporality, spatiality and identity, strategically re-engaging or critiquing it through performance. I wanted to understand the divergent (and collective) ways each of the four artists constructed culturally specific, contemporary subject positions in a manner that challenged the frames of the settler colonies from which they emerge as well as the borders of the larger fields of postcolonial studies and theatre and performance studies. I tried to confront the constant dilemma that feminist Gloria Anzaldúa has described as 'how to write (produce) without being inscribed (reproduced) in the dominant white structure and how to write without reinscribing and reproducing what we rebel against.'[4]

Other prominent scholars in the field of Native American, or Indigenous, art have also questioned the debates about forms of exchange between Indigenous cultures and the global cultural and political spheres and dominant paradigms.

For example, Jean Fisher offers this astute assessment in her essay entitled '"New Contact Zones": A Reflection' (2006):

As an outsider, I can say nothing of the dynamic of contemporary art practices internal to indigenous societies as they might articulate around differing historical trajectories, filiations to community and territory, degrees of urbanization, and acculturation to dominant national society. Regarding dynamics with external national cultures, it is a truism that indigenous art practices have long been circumscribed by what nowadays is termed "branded culture"—culture interpreted, packaged, and mobilized to serve the ideological or economic ends of the nation-state.[5]

Fisher's essay was included in *Vision, Space, Desire: Global Perspectives and Cultural Hybridity* (2006), a publication that documented the proceedings and personal reflections written by artists, curators, museum directors, academics and critics from various parts of the world who attended a symposium (by the same name) during the Venice Biennale's 51st International Art Exhibition (2005). The occasion was an important opportunity for the Smithsonian's National Museum of the American Indian to convene a meeting where the existing discursive fields of postcolonialism and postmodernism were interrogated by participants from multiple Indigenous, and non-Indigenous, contexts and global spheres. Fisher's assessment of the shortcomings of postcolonial theory in 2005 were as follows:

Postcolonial theory, evolved largely by diasporan intellectuals in the wake of the collapse of militant liberation movements, refuses confrontational divisions in favor of discursive practices that speak of pluralized identities, border-crossings, and cultural hybridity. It is nonetheless criticized for privileging cultural and textual analysis over social, political, and historical realities.[6]

As Iva Polak clarifies in her 2005 essay 'Postcolonial Imagination and Postcolonial Theory: Indigenous Canadian and Australian Literature Fighting for (Postcolonial) Space,' the term "postcolonial" has proven difficult for many Indigenous scholars because,

the shifting and problematic term of "postcolonial literature" when applied to indigenous writing in Canada and Australia, is loaded with ambiguities that are problematic especially when considering the simple question: When was the "postcolonial"? and whether the "postcolonial" is too universalist a category which tends to swallow starkly different histories and places of utterance.[7]

Polak went on to outline the problems for even an expanded use of the "post-colonial", exemplified by the significant writings of Edward Said, Gayatri Chakravorty Spivak and Homi K. Bhabha in the late 1970s-1990s[8] who each 'made invaluable analyses of the signifying practices and psychosocial dynamics of neo-colonial relations' because their 'theories lacked grounding in the specificity of contemporary economic, political, and social realities [for Indigenous peoples], or recognition of complex subject formations of class and gender as well as race and ethnicity.'[9] Within Native studies, Elizabeth Cook-Lynn (Crow Creek Sioux), in her essay 'Who Stole Native American Studies?' (1997), similarly critiques postcolonial theory's failure to address the real material concerns of Native

De-/Anti-/Post-colonial Feminisms

American communities and implores scholars in the field to 'seek autonomy from other opportunistic epistemologies in order to promote indigenousness and sovereignty.'[10]

Since the publication of Smith's book *Decolonizing Methodologies* (1999), a large number of Native American, or Indigenous, scholars have addressed or built on her arguments in the past twenty years.[11] Smith's study was one of the first concerned with the 'institution of research, its claims, its values and practices, and its relationship to power'[12] and how it intersected with the worlds of Indigenous Peoples 'to the extent that indigenous communities were most often the objects or subjects of study by non-indigenous researchers'[13] and not 'considered agents themselves, as capable or interested in research, or as having expert knowledge about themselves and their conditions.'[14] Since 1999, some of the most remarkable developments in the field of Indigenous studies have been the development of research that is meaningful to specific Indigenous communities due to 'an explosion of indigenous research [that] has brought together an emergent body of intellectual work being conducted across the world by indigenous and non-indigenous scholars.'[15] For example, the field of settler colonial[16] studies has been more comprehensively theorized given that colonialism never ended and settler contexts, such as the US, Australia, Canada, and New Zealand, to name a few places, persist. According to Indigenous scholars Eve Tuck and K. Wayne Lang, theories of decolonization 'bring together critiques of settler colonialism, borders, and conceptualizations of antiblackness'[17] especially in locations like the US where the 'destruction of Indigenous Peoples to acquire land, and the enslavement of people from the continent of Africa as units of capital for trade, labor, and disposal'[18] are prevalent.

Understanding and locating Indigenous people within an increasingly global society is one of Maori scholar Roger Maaka's goals. He states that 'Indigeneity is about decolonizing to create national societies in which Indigenous Peoples come from the periphery of national life to being fully functional citizens without having to assimilate.'[19] This is where postmodernism fails the Indigenous subject in its 'valorization of multicultural diversity and decentered subjectivity.'[20] Postmodernist theory has also promoted what artist, curator and art historian Jolene Rickard (Tuscarora) describes as an 'absence, or invisibility' of contemporary indigenous subjectivity on the international stage.[21] Rickard goes on to argue that Native artists like James Luna and his work have 'to be understood [within] the ongoing construction of the primitive, the exoticization of Native cultures, the impact of colonization, missionization, and the forms of performance and installation art.'[22]

As Linda T. Smith and Eve Tuck have explained, a decolonizing methodology has everything to do with Indigenous struggles and with challenging settler-colonial power. In their book *On Decoloniality: Concepts, Analytics, Praxis*, Walter Mignolo and Catherine Walsh define decoloniality as the 'undoing of Eurocentrism's totalizing claim and frame, including the Eurocentric legacies incarnate in U.S.-centrism and perpetuated in the Western geopolitics of knowledge.'[23] Mignolo and

Walsh make the distinction between the postcolonial (which took place during the Cold War) and decoloniality (which took place after the end of the Cold War) by discussing the aims of their project in terms of "re-existence," or de-linking from coloniality, instead of "resistance."[24] Although the authors recognize the political legacies of decolonization associated with the Bandung Conference[25] (1955) and the Conference of the Non-Aligned Countries[26] (1961), 'the horizon [for them] is not the political independence of nation-states (as it was for decolonization), nor is it primarily the confrontation with capitalism and the West.'[27]

Since the late 1990s, when Aníbal Quijano introduced the key concept of "coloniality",[28] Mignolo and Walsh have been concerned with 'how modernity/coloniality have worked and continues to work to negate, disavow, distort and deny knowledges, subjectivities, world senses, and life visions.'[29] Walsh and Mignolo's interests are not situated solely in the United States but worldwide, what they call "pluriversal decoloniality" and "decolonial pluriversality," in order to disturb the totality from which the universal and global are most often perceived.[30] Walsh's chapter distinguishes different patterns of power in the Americas, specifically the forms of colonialism that the Indigenous Peoples of North America experience, beginning in the nineteenth century, if not earlier, and known as settler colonialism:

> Decoloniality has a history, *herstory*, and praxis of more than 500 years. From its beginning in the Americas, decoloniality has been a component part of (trans) local struggles, movements, and actions to resist and refuse the legacies and ongoing relations and patterns of powers established by external and internal colonialism—and the global designs of the modern/colonial world.[31]

Walsh also states that 'while settler colonialism is distinct from the coloniality of power established in the Americas of the South [...] its patterns of extermination, pillage, enslavement, racialization, dehumanization, and power are, without a doubt, related.'[32] Conceived of in this manner, the authors claim to introduce decoloniality's praxis, concepts, and analytics from a local point of view because, they argue, 'it cannot be otherwise since all theories and conceptual frames, including those that originate in Western Europe and the Anglo United States, can aim at and describe the global but cannot be other than local.'[33] American historian Roxanne Dunbar-Ortiz defines settler colonialism as 'modern from the beginning precisely because it included the expansion of European corporations, backed by government armies into foreign areas, with subsequent expropriation of lands and resources [...] settler colonialism is a genocidal policy.'[34]

However, as Ramon Grosfoguel documents in his essay 'Epistemic Extractivism,' leading Indigenous scholars such as Leanne Betasamosake Simpson (Michi Saagiig Nishnaabeg) and Silvia Rivera Cusicanqui (Aymara) believe that some decolonial scholars, such as Mignolo and Walsh, are engaging in what is called epistemic extractivism. Simpson takes the example of:

> The United Nations project on the environment and development, in which the ideas of indigenous people throughout the world are appropriated in order to colonialize them by assimilating them into Western knowledge.

    De-/Anti-/Post-colonial Feminisms

Through this assimilation, or, in other words, by subsuming these forms of indigenous knowledge within Western knowledge, the radical politics and "alternative" critique of cosmogony are stripped away to make them more acceptable, or else simply extracted from a more radical epistemic matrix in order to depoliticize them.[35]

Rivera Cusicanqui's critique of well-known intellectuals within the Modernity/Coloniality Network, such as Mignolo and Walsh, identifies similarly with Simpson's because of the extractivist processes which they both define as 'represent[ing] a mentality that does not seek any dialogue that implies an equal, horizontal dialogue between peoples or any understanding of indigenous knowledge on its own terms.'[36] Rather, as Rivera Cusicanqui observes,

> Through the game of who cites whom, hierarchies are structured, and we end up having to consume, in a regurgitated form, the very ideas regarding decolonization that we indigenous people and intellectuals of Bolivia, Peru, and Ecuador have produced independently. And this process began in the 1970s — the rarely quoted work of Pablo González Casanovas on "internal colonialism" was published in 1969 — when Mignolo and Quijano were still advocating a positivist Marxism and a linear version of history [...] Mignolo and company have built a small empire within an empire, strategically appropriating the contributions of the school of subaltern studies in India and the many Latin American variants of critical reflection on colonization and decolonization.[37]

This section outlining decoloniality is invoked to establish both subalternity and Indigeneity as resistant subjectivities that are exposed to decontextualization and depoliticization when recycled by certain scholars that, perversely, speak in the name of epistemological decolonization. In their essay, 'Becoming Indigenous: the "Speculative Turn" in Anthropology and the (Re)colonisation of Indigeneity,' David Chandler and Julian Reid discuss Indigenous methods and practices that 'are increasingly constructed as offering futural possibilities for "becoming" rather than belonging to the archives of an underdeveloped past.'[38] Similar to epistemic extractivism, 'central to this transformation has been the speculative or ontological turn in anthropological discourse, which [they] argue has opened up new possibilities for a Western and colonial appropriation of Indigeneity. The authors argue against this reduction of Indigenous lives to the speculative "other" of Western modernity [because] it inherently tends to reify or "exoticise" Indigenous thought and practices or, as [they] state, to "ontologize indigeneity".'[39]

Importantly, Chandler and Reid argue that these discourses (modernity/ coloniality via Walsh and Mignolo) have little to do with Indigenous struggles or with challenging settler-colonial power. In fact, they maintain, as Simpson and Rivera do, that 'instrumentalising indigeneity in these ways merely reinforces neoliberal hegemony, marginalising critical alternatives for both Indigenous and non-Indigenous Peoples alike.'[40] Other scholars such as Simone Bagnall and Daryle Rigney (Ngarrindjeri), in 'Indigeneity, Posthumanism and Nomad Thought: Transforming Colonial Ecologies,' argue that Continental posthumanism ignores the prior existence of Indigenous knowledge which 'registers an intimate and ontological connection of humanity with the ecological health of the environment that sustains life-forms and diversifies creative potential through rich networks of interconnectivity.'[41]

In all cases, there seems to be a consensus that a "more-than-human" way of knowing, being and acting characterizes the Indigenous life world which is shared on a global scale, across time and space, amongst Indigenous Peoples. In contrast to privileging a postmodernist or postcolonialist conception of these relations, Rivera Cusicanqui explains:

> There is no *post* or *pre* in the indigenous version of history which is not linear or teleological but rather moves in cycles and spirals and sets out on a course without neglecting to return to the same point. The indigenous world does not conceive of history as linear; the past-future is contained in the present. The regression or progression, the repetition or overcoming of the past is at play in each conjuncture and is dependent more on our acts than our words. The project of indigenous modernity can emerge from the present in a spiral whose movement is a continuous feedback from the past to the future—a "principle of hope" or "anticipatory consciousness"—that both discerns and realizes decolonization at the same time.[42]

One of the subjects I explored was how two Indigenous women/groups created performances about the missing and murdered Indigenous women and girls[43] (MMIWG) of Canada and the United States: artist Rebecca Belmore's *Vigil* (2002) and *The Named and Unnamed* (2002), and Spiderwoman Theater's *Material Witness* (2016). In Canada and the US, the number of MMIWG keeps rising at rates disproportionately higher than missing or murdered non-Indigenous women and this disparity reflects the unequal power relations and structures of domination still in place. Both the violence and police apathy against MMIWG are the result of what activist Winona LaDuke (Ojibwe/Anishinaabe) describes as how Native women are seen as possessing 'less stature and value than others because of the process of colonization, sexual violence, dehumanization, and marginalization.'[44] The representations of MMIWG in media discourses are saturated with a colonial imaginary, and not the absent, or haunted, subjectivity of Aboriginal or First Nation's women who are victims/survivors of violence directed at them.

The staging of violence against Indigenous women has been explored by other artists such as Teresa Margolles in *Cuidad Juárez* (2005) and Coco Fusco in *The Incredible Disappearing Woman*[45] (2000), to name only two artists whose work deals with what Ratliff describes as "feminicide" that is a term that 'expands beyond murder to include a larger culture of violence, both physical and symbolic, against women that is constructed and maintained by social, political, and economic circumstances.'[46] Margolles and Fusco each provide their own perspectives on the feminicide at the US and Mexico border where brutal crimes against women of color have reached national headlines, gathered international support and, mostly, feminist and academic discussions, while the violence continues and justice for victims remain largely elusive. Performance-based artworks about Indigenous victims of violence along the borders of the US, in Mexico and Canada often

De-/Anti-/Post-colonial Feminisms

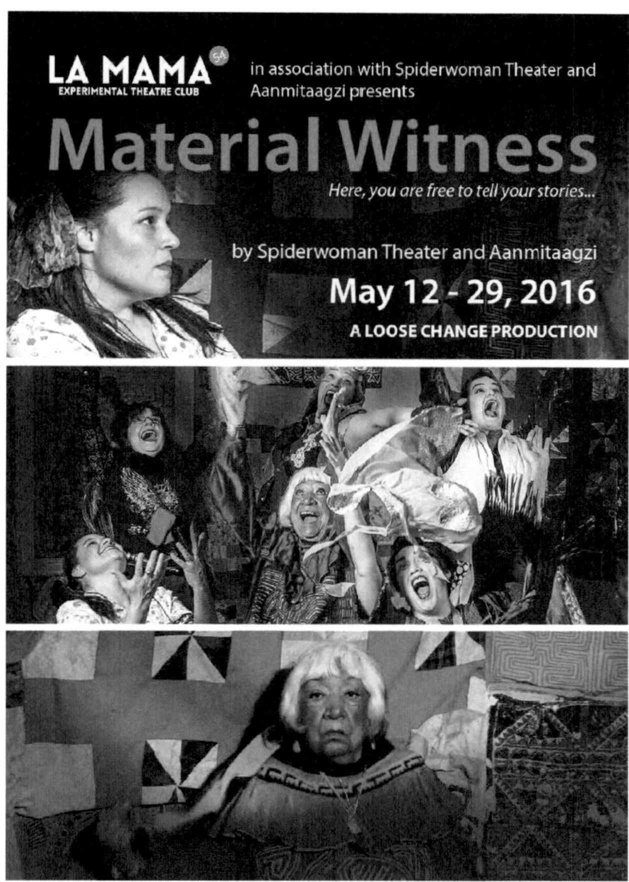

Material Witness poster, May 2016. Reproduced with permission of Spiderwoman Theater

employ practices, strategies and tactics to document, memorialize or represent the lives of missing and/or murdered women through live art, socially engaged theatre or gallery installations. Another approach to studying the impact of "feminicide", can be found in the book, *Remembering Women Murdered by Men: Memorials Across Canada*. Here, the Cultural Memory Group documents and analyzes 30 memorials placed across Canada, 'from Vancouver to Halifax as tributes to the lives of women murdered by men,' and their makers who tell about bringing public attention to feminicide in spite of running huge personal risks doing so.[47] While these works share some commonality as memorials, performance interventions, activist statements, and visions of social justice that respond to the actual murders of women, they differ in how their site-specific narratives encompass the everyday life and community struggles of the disappeared and those trying to find them.

I put forward the argument that the articulations of Indigenous female subjectivities in Spiderwoman Theater's *Material Witness* (2016) and Belmore's *Vigil* (2002) foreground decolonial strategies in their practice. Both articulate the formulation of an Indigenous feminist resistance grounded in critiques of settler colonial structures, the role of difference in the construction and representation of Indigenous women in the media, and the intersections of these frameworks in the voices and practices examined. For example, through her use of everyday materials and actions, Belmore carves out a space in *Vigil* (2002), cleans it, and marks it with her body to bring attention to the issue of MMIWG within the familiar event of candlelight vigils. For Belmore and Spiderwoman Theater, live art, or performance provides a decolonizing tactic for new meanings, and re-interpretations of media discourse, that have rendered MMIWG invisible due to the lack of attention paid to their concerns by the police or other state authorities.

Spiderwoman Theater's first production, *Women In Violence* (1976), an ensemble piece that explored violence against women, violence between women, and the violence women inflict on themselves, was the springboard for *Material Witness* (2016), which discusses violence against women in Indigenous communities specifically. My analysis of their work drew attention to how this early performance was grounded within the feminist movement of the 1960s and 1970s in an American theatre context. For the 2016 work, I considered how their practice was now informed by the strategic and political reframing of MMIWG as an international human rights problem by activists and scholars dedicated to promoting Indigenous self-determination and resisting forms of global capitalism and imperialism that have forced Indigenous Peoples to the peripheries of their nation-states, often through violence. Spiderwoman Theater offered a particular focus on Indigenous forms of activism and/or feminist knowledges and scholarship that are embedded within their theatre performances. There are other performances and plays by Aboriginal, First Nation's, and Native American people that also present Indigenous performance practices that infuse cultural traditions like storytelling, ceremony or ritual, and healing to honor the MMIWG, bring hope to families grieving and assign names to the faces they have lost and continue to commemorate.

The performance works by artist Rebecca Belmore in *Vigil* (2002) and *The Named and Unnamed* (2002), and Spiderwoman Theater's *Material Witness* (2016) ,directly address the MMIWG and offer shared critiques of the domination, colonial violence and gender violence that undergird the social existence of Indigenous women in the Americas. Even though these artists approach the subject of MMIWG in different performance modes, their memorializations and storytelling practices relate the narratability and political significance of the women who have disappeared and those trying to find them. Their works constitute acts of decolonization because of their repeated concerns with the continuing disappearance and genocide of Native peoples.

     De-/Anti-/Post-colonial Feminisms

Notes

1. Linda Tuhwai Smith, *Decolonising Methodologies: Research and Indigenous Peoples*, London: Zed Books, 1999, p. 20.

2. The term Indigenous refers to original societies even in trans-national contexts. The terms Aboriginal and First Nation's refer to the Canadian context, and the state-produced term Aboriginal is used contextually to refer to the designation of Indigenous people as colonial subjects via the *Indian Act* (1876). The terms Native American and American Indian refer to the US and are often used in that context. Where possible, I use the Indigenous nation's self-determined name.

3. According to Roger Maaka, 'today [the year 2012], Indigenous Peoples comprise an estimated 370 million people, which is 5 percent of the world's population, and they are spread over 90 countries. Indigenous Peoples speak 4000 of the world's 7000 languages, and nearly all of these 4000 languages are severely endangered. As they are excluded from political and economic power, indigenous populations are also disproportionally poor.' See Roger Maaka, 'Indigeneity and Locating Indigenous Peoples: To all our relations: Ki ō tātau karangataha maha' in Catherine de Zegher and Gerald McMaster (eds.), *18th Biennale of Sydney 2012: All Our Relations*, Woolloomooloo, N.S.W.: Biennale of Sydney, 2012, p. 366.

4. Gloria Anzaldúa cited by Catherine Walsh, *On Decoloniality: Concepts, Analytics, Praxis*, Durham and London: Duke University Press, 2018, loc. 529 of 7946. Kindle Edition. See Gloria Anzaldúa and Analouise Keating (ed.), *Light in the Dark/Luz en lo Oscuro: Rewriting Identity, Spirituality, Reality*, Durham and London: Duke University Press, 2015.

5. Jean Fisher, '"New Contact Zones": A Reflection,' in *Vision, Space, Desire: Global Perspectives and Cultural Hybridity* ,Washington DC and New York: National Museum of the American Indian Smithsonian Institution, 2006, p. 41.

6. Ibid. p. 43.

7. Iva Polak, 'Postcolonial Imagination and Postcolonial Theory: Indigenous Canadian and Australian Literature Fighting for (Postcolonial) Space,' *Theory and Practice in English Studies* vol. 4 (2005), p. 135.

8. Jean Fisher, 'Witness for the Prosecution: The Writings of Coco Fusco,' in Coco Fusco *The Bodies That Were Not Ours: And Other Writings*, London and New York: Routledge, 2001, p. 224. See Edward W. Said, *Orientalism*, with a new afterword, New York: Vintage Books, 1994; Gayatri Chakravorty Spivak, 'Can the Subaltern Speak?,' in Patrick Williams and Laura Chrisman (eds.), *Colonial Discourse and Postcolonial Reason: A Reader*, New York: Columbia University Press, 1994, pp. 66-111; Homi K. Bhabha, *The Location of Culture*, London and New York: Routledge, 1994.

9. Iva Polak, 'Postcolonial Imagination and Postcolonial Theory: Indigenous Canadian and Australian Literature Fighting for (Postcolonial) Space,' *Theory and Practice in English Studies* vol. 4 (2005), p. 135.

10. Elizabeth Cook-Lynn, 'Who Stole Native American Studies?,' *Wicazo Sa Review*, vol. 12 no. 1 (1997), pp. 9-28.

11. Within Indigenous studies in the US, seminal texts include Andrea Smith and Audra Simpson (eds.), *Theorizing Native Studies*, Durham: Duke University Press, 2014; Sandy Grande, *Red Pedagogy: Native American Social and Political Thought*, Rowman and Littlefield, 2004; Aileen Moreton-Robinson (ed.), *Critical Indigenous Studies: Engagements in First World*

Locations, Tucson: University of Arizona Press, 2016; and Glen Sean Coulthard *Red Skin White Masks: Rejecting the Colonial Politics of Recognition*, University of Minnesota Press, 2014, to only name a few. Publications by Grande and Coulthard represent a new strain of theory that explores the intersection between dominant modes of critical educational theory and the socio-political landscape of American Indian education.

12. Andrea Smith, 'Foreword' in Andrea Smith and Audra Simpson (eds.), *Theorizing Native Studies*, 2014, p. x.

13. Ibid.

14. Ibid.

15. Ibid. p. xii.

16. Settler colonialism is a form of colonization in which outsiders come to land inhabited by Indigenous Peoples and claim it as their own new home. Influential works for Indigenous activists include Lorenzo Veracini, 'Introducing: Settler colonial studies,' *Settler Colonial Studies*, vol 1. no. 1 (2011), pp. 1-12, and Patrick Wolfe, *Settler Colonialism and the Transformation of Anthropology: The Politics and Poetics of an Ethnographic Event* (Leicester, UK: Leicester University Press, 1999). See Eve Tuck and K. Wayne Lang, 'Series Editors' Introduction', in Eve Tuck, K. Wayne Lang and A. Smith (eds.), *Indigenous and Decolonizing Studies in Education: Mapping the Long View*, New York and London: Routledge, 2019, p. xii.

17. Ibid.

18. Ibid.

19. See Roger Maaka,'Indigeneity and Locating Indigenous Peoples: To all our relations: Ki ō tātau karangatahamaha', *18th Biennale of Sydney 2012: All Our Relations*, 2012, p. 367.

20. Fisher, '"New Contact Zones",' p. 44.

21. Jolene Rickard, 'The Local and the Global,' in *Vision, Space, Desire*, 2006, p. 60.

22. Ibid. p. 59.

23. Walter D. Mignolo and Catherine E. Walsh, *On Decoloniality: Concepts, Analytics, Praxis* (Durham and London: Duke University Press, 2018), loc. 145 of 7946. (Kindle Edition).

24. Ibid., loc. 469 of 7946. Re-existence is characterized by the cultivation of modes of life, existence, being, and thought *otherwise*—that is, modes that confront, transgress, and undo modernity/coloniality's hold.

25. The Bandung Conference, also known as the Asian-Africa Conference was a meeting of Third World countries which took place on 18-24 April 1955 in Bandung, Indonesia. Five countries – Pakistan, Indian, Burma, Sri Lanka, and Indonesia – were the co-sponsors of the Conference. They also brought together other twenty-four states from Asia, Africa, and Middle East. So, the representatives from 29 countries including Egypt, Indonesia, India, Iraq and China, met to consider the issues they deemed pressing. The main purpose was to discuss peace, the role of Third World countries in the Cold War, the promotion of Afro-Asian countries economic and cultural cooperation, and decolonization. See 'Bandung Conference (Asian-African Conference), 1955,' *Office of the Historian, US Department of State*, Retrieved from https://history.state.gov/milestones/1953-1960/bandung-conf, [Last Accessed, 17 August 2023].

26. The Non-Aligned Movement was formed during the Cold War, largely on the initiative of then-Yugoslav President Josip Broz Tito, as an organization of States that did not seek to formally align themselves with either the United States or the Soviet Union but sought to

　　　　　　　　　　　　　　　　　　　　De-/Anti-/Post-colonial Feminisms

remain independent or neutral. The basic concept for the group originated in 1955 during discussions that took place at the Asia-Africa Bandung Conference held in Indonesia. Subsequently, a preparatory meeting for the First NAM Summit Conference was held in Cairo, Egypt from 5-12 June 1961. See 'Non-Aligned Movement (NAM),' *NTI Building a Safer World,* 31 May 2018, Retrieved from https://www.nti.org/learn/treaties-and-regimes/non-aligned-movement-nam/, [Last Accessed, 17 August 2023].

27. Mignolo and Walsh, *On Decoloniality: Concepts, Analytics,* 2018, loc. 194 of 7946.

28. See Aníbal Quijano, 'Coloniality of Power, Eurocentrism, and Latin America,' *Nepantla: Views from South,* vol.1 no. 3 (2000), pp. 533-80.

29. Mignolo and Walsh, *On Decoloniality: Concepts, Analytics,* 2018, loc. 194 of 7946.

30. See Arturo Escobar, *Designs for the Pluriverse: Radical Interdependence, Autonomy, and the Making of Worlds,* Durham and London: Duke University Press, 2018. Escobar's study seeks answers to the question: Can design's modernist tradition be reoriented from its dependence on the life-stifling dualist ontology of patriarchal capitalist modernity toward relational modes of knowing, being, and doing?

31. Walsh, *On Decoloniality: Concepts, Analytics,* 2018, loc. 529 of 7946.

32. Ibid.

33. Ibid., loc. 145 of 7946.

34. Roxanne Dunbar-Ortiz, cited by Walsh, *On Decoloniality: Concepts, Analytics,* 2018, loc. 434 of 7946. See Roxanna Dunbar-Ortiz, *An Indigenous Peoples' History of the United States,* Boston, MA: Beacon Press, 2014.

35. Simpson quoted by Grosfoguel, 'Epistemic Extractivism: A Dialogue with Alberto Acosta, Leanne Betasamosake Simpson, and Silvia Rivera Cusicanqui', in Boanventura de Sousa Santos and María Paula Meneses (eds.), *Epistemologies of the South: Knowledges Born in the Struggle: Constructing the Epistemologies of the Global South,* New York and London: Routledge, 2020, p. 208.

36. Ibid.

37. Ibid. Rivera quoted by Grosfoguel, p. 210.

38. David Chandler and Julian Reid, 'Becoming Indigenous: the "Speculative Turn" in Anthropology and the (Re)colonisation of Indigeneity,' *Postcolonial Studies,* vol. 23 no. 4 (2020), p. 1.

39. Ibid.

40. Ibid.

41. Simone Bagnall and Daryle Rigney, 'Indigeneity, Posthumanism and Nomad Thought: Transforming Colonial Ecologies', in Rosi Braidotti and Simone Bignall (eds.), *Posthuman Ecologies: Complexity and Process After Deleuze,* New York and London: Rowman and Littlefield, 2019, p. 159.

42. Silvia Rivera Cusicanqui, 'Ch'ixinakax utiwa: A Reflection on the Practices and Discourses of Decolonization, *The South Atlantic Quarterly,* vol. 111 no. 1 (2012), p. 96.

43. The term missing and murdered Indigenous women and girls has been used since the early 2000s to denote the hundreds of mostly young women and girls that have been reported missing by their families in Canada since at least the 1980s. In some instances, this term has also included "two-spirit" people to refer to non-gender conforming individuals that have been murdered or missing as well.

44. Winona LaDuke, 'Foreword', in Andrea Smith, *Conquest: Sexual Violence and American Indian Genocide*, Cambridge, MA: South End Press, 2005, p. xvii.

45. Fusco dedicates the play to 'the memory of the 220 women, most of whom were *maquiladora* workers, who disappeared from the city of Juarez between 1993 and 1999.' See Coco Fusco, 'The Incredible Disappearing Woman,' in Coco Fusco, *The Bodies That Were Not Ours: And Other Writings*, New York and London: Routledge, 2001, pp. 202-220.

46. Jamie Ratliff, 'A War on Women: Teresa Margolles' *Cuidad Juárez'*, *n.paradoxa: international feminist art journal*, vol. 35 (2015), p. 57.

47. The Cultural Memory Group, Beth McAuley (ed.), *Remembering Women Murdered by Men: Memorials Across Canada*, Toronto, ON: Sumach Press, 2006.

De-/Anti-/Post-colonial Feminisms

The Question of Women and Craft, Pre- and Post-Independence India

Aarti Kawlra

The term craft, conventionally referring to practices associated with handmade objects in the West, carries the weight of an ideology in the Global South. As this chapter outlines, there is expanding literature on the Global South that demonstrates the place of craft at the nexus between anticolonial politics, post-independence nation building and Cold War diplomacy in the twentieth century. Viewed as a panacea to the ills of Western industrialism, with the potential to forge an alternative modernity, craft has offered cultural and political interlocutors in Asia and Africa the vocabulary and material evidence for reconstituting craft-based identities in narratives of rural rehabilitation, cultural self-determination, and national development. In this chapter, I interrogate elements within the trajectory of India's discourse on craft, that permeated policy and action in the pre- and post-independence period, from a feminist perspective. Asking the question 'Where are the women?' in the sphere of crafts, as does Cynthia Enloe (2014) in the sphere of international politics,[1] is to shed light on the ways in which women's activities are framed through the private and the domestic in the service of national and international goals. Seeking answers to this question also highlights the different spaces and roles women occupied in the renewed debates about crafts, as well as the intended and unintended consequences of foregrounding women's capacities in craft in relation to their home-based skills.

Communitarian Rural Rehabilitation Pre-Independence

By early twentieth century, knowledge production about the arts and industries in the colonies of the British empire had generated an influential global narrative legitimizing the notion of the "Indian craftsman". One of the showcases for this emergent male persona was The Delhi Durbar Exhibitions (1877, 1903 and 1911). These were the result of collaborations among (primarily male, white, colonial) museum professionals, art educators, and district collectors, who were responsible for the pre-selection of artisans and exhibits to represent specific regions across colonial India. George Birdwood's writing in the late nineteenth century had already promoted an arcadian view of craft in India, one that was 'rooted in religion and village community in which artisans had clear social obligations, patronage and hereditary traditions, passed from artisan-caste fathers to sons.'[2] That it was also a gendered view is unmistakable, not only in the discourse of the Indian craftsman but also in visual representations of living artisans on display at colonial exhibitions in the metropole who were, except for the women dancers, all male. Pamphlets accompanying these exhibitions described their physical attributes as part of the valorization of artisanal traditions which included, for example, 'his dress and adornment, racial markings, his movements and gestures.'[3]

In colonial discourse, the interchangeable terms - craftsman and artisan - not only articulated a distinctive taste for maintaining tradition but also encapsulated a singular gendered work imaginary in which male craft producers inhabited a space of time-honored skill and technique from an unchanged past. Craft producers were accordingly emblematized in colonial records and exhibitions as the native Indian craftsman represented visually in the image of an anonymous seated body at work.[4] Images of these male artisans, in postures specific to the tools of their craft, were shown widely in the colonial metropolis and in the colonies. These cottage-based producers were primarily male bodies engaged in the manipulation of handheld tools and making products from natural materials such as stone, wood, iron, gold, silver, cotton and silk, in keeping with the highest standards of skill and beauty. The question of women in craft appears eclipsed in this discourse even as the persona of the Indian craftsman, a male body at work, gained purchase in many of the visual records of the British administration.

Anti-colonial cultural and political interlocutors, Rabindranath Tagore (1861-1941) and Mohandas K. Gandhi (1869-1948) redeployed this colonial nostalgia for a pre-industrial past and the salience of Indian crafts in modernity, to critique the material and moral estrangement of factory production under capitalism. For them, crafts offered a civilizational alternative to the telos of progress underlying colonialism. Both carried out experiments in crafts-based education to counter the exclusion of India's masses from the formal system of colonial instruction that favored literary proficiency over physical labour.[5]

In the weekly boarding school set up at rural Sriniketan, Tagore and his collaborator Leonard Elmhirst (1893–1974), sought to use crafts apprenticeships as a means of catering to the needs of *any child* with a rural background. Yet Elmhirst's (1961) memoirs on the daily life at the school reveal that there were

                                                        De-/Anti-/Post-colonial Feminisms

clearly no girls at the school. He writes:

> The boys arrived on Monday morning, each with his little sack of rice, enough
> for five days, and went home on Saturday. At school they carried out a variety
> of duties, in dormitory, kitchen, garden, poultry-farm and dairy. They learned
> games, songs and plays, carpentry and some other craft, and their sums and
> writing were focused on their daily experience.[6]

Among the British educationalists who were part of Tagore's intellectual circle
was Sister Nivedita (Margaret Noble, 1867-1911), an Irish teacher who met Swami
Vivekanand in 1895 in London and joined the Indian nationalist cause to work in
Calcutta. She popularized manual training or craft work through a pamphlet titled
'Manual Training as a part of General Education in India' [1905]. Even though she
was concerned about the uplift of Indian women, the basic education agenda she
outlined referred to the training of boys and not girls:

> We have a right to plead for its inclusion in the school course.... other things being
> equal, a boy who has had manual training is in all ways the intellectual superior of
> him who has not. He has freshness and vigor of thought, due to the fact that he
> knows how to observe, and is accustomed to think for himself. He has daring and
> originality of purpose; And above all, his character is based on the fundamental
> habit of adding deed to dream, act to thought, proof to inference.[7]

Later, when she became embroiled in the nationalist movement led by Gandhi,
Sister Nivedita's perspective, even whilst making visible Indian women in the public
arena, reproduced what Janaki Nair (1990) calls a "housewifization" of women,
taking place both in India and back home in England.[8]

With the freedom struggle underway, women came to be viewed as sites
of resistance from the interior spaces of their homes. Gandhi is known to have
consciously included women in the anti-colonial struggle for independence, over
and above his plans for education, albeit in ways that reinforced their place in the
home. Madhu Kishwar, in her seminal piece on 'Gandhi and Women' (1986),
reveals that Gandhi's call for *swadeshi*, involving the boycott of foreign-made goods,
hand spinning on wooden *charkhas*, or wheels, and the wearing of *khadi* (handspun
and handwoven fabric), 'were eminently suited to the limitations imposed upon
the contribution of women by their roles in the household with which Gandhi
had no serious quarrel.'[9] She quotes his views on how the simple spinning wheel
could galvanize Indian women in performing their natural, and normalized, role of
promoting harmony through self-effacement and non-violence thus:

> The restoration of spinning to its central place in India's peaceful campaign for
> deliverance from the imperial yoke gives her women a special status. In spinning they
> have a natural advantage over men.... Spinning is essentially a slow and comparatively
> silent process. Woman is the embodiment of sacrifice and, therefore non-violence.
> Her occupations must therefore be, as they are, more conducive to peace than war.[10]

Gandhi's appeal to women to spin was aimed at every household in every corner of the country (contemporary India, Pakistan and Bangladesh, prior to partition), so that women from all income and class backgrounds could find reason and meaning in their domestic industry, not only as a livelihood option or a supplementary income, but also as a moral duty and code of conduct in the creation of a national sisterhood. In 1929, Gandhi instituted a charkha prize of a substantial amount to enlist people's participation within the khadi movement. It did indeed put a spotlight on what Shambhu Prasad (2001) calls the 'charkha atmosphere'[11] of scientific experimentation fostered by Gandhi at the Satyagraha Ashram in Ahmedabad, founded in 1915. Ironically, in this very public and nationally significant space, spinning was no longer a domestic industry, capable of psychological and moral upliftment for incumbent spinners. Shambhu points out that at this ashram or laboratory for Gandhian social engineering, 'more men spun than women ... despite spinning being traditionally a woman's occupation.'[12]

Gandhi's work on rural reconstruction was, in many ways, built upon the educational interventions of missionaries in post-famine rehabilitation in the previous century.[13] It reinforced missionary (Victorian) views on women's work, prioritizing the public/private separation of income for men and domesticity for women. Whereas orientalist knowledge on crafts was based on notions of craft as (ancient) Hindu tradition, for the missionaries, craft-based education was an occasion for imparting standards of physical, moral, mental and aesthetic discipline among pupils for gainful employment thereafter. The early deployment of craft in missionary agendas of self-help and economic and social uplift among the depressed classes is evident from the book *The Outcastes' Hope or Work among the Depressed Classes in India* (1912). It is here that Reverend G.E. Phillips demonstrates clearly how literacy and craft-based education was instrumental not only in instilling values of self-help and dignity, but also purging the caste-based bodily oppression of the "pariah". Craft products, processes and hand tools were deployed by missionaries to uplift the livelihood opportunities of the depressed classes in a gendered evangelist message of disciplined habits and industriousness. The industrial school which brought students away from their homes, and sometimes even villages, was meant for the training of boys:

> The object of an industrial school is not to develop an industry... but to train our Christian boys at crafts which they ply in their own villages to the improvement of the ways of living in those villages and to provide our Christian community, other sources of maintenance than the tilling of the soil.... It is our hope thus by precept and example to train the people of our communities to respect manual labour. To foster habits of industry and frugality.[14]

Missionary interventions in productive activity for livelihood creation paved the way for labelling certain types of crafts, together with their respective spaces of work

De-/Anti-/Post-colonial Feminisms

and labour, as being reserved exclusively for women. A major feature of missionary rural reconstruction was the creation of model spaces like special boarding schools, that facilitated the segregation of potential converts and trainees from everyday caste and gender prejudices in their home environments. In documents about planning women's education produced by missionaries during this period, we can find clear references to women as a separate group where craft production could be seen as an option to earn a future livelihood which could also insert low/lower caste converts into the local terrain of capital, production and consumption in colonial modernity. Interestingly, many of the crafts that were identified for training women were in the textile industries that had been the occupational preserve of men in both Hindu and Islamic traditions:

> Those reported are — rug weaving, silk embroideries, phulkari, drawn thread work, lace, handkerchief making, crocheting, knitting, plain sewing, weaving sarees, spinning cotton, durrie and tape weaving, embroidering shoes, making of chairs, baskets, and chics, rope making, gardening, and field work. Most of these employments are indigenous to the country, but hitherto, were the exclusive right of men, and are now transferred to the women.[15]

In her essay on 'Ironies of Emancipation' (2000), Jane Haggis cites the example of a missionary wife in early nineteenth-century Travancore (now Kerala state), Mrs Mault, who established a girls' boarding school where she trained convert girls in basic literacy and the art of lacemaking. Mrs Mault's idea was to market their handiwork in British military cantonments in South India and to enable her pupils to have an income from lace which also served as 'a reward' for continuing at school. Indeed, the boarding schools were often the only places in which instruction in the skill was available, and all hiring of lace workers was done through the missionary wife running the industry.'[16] Haggis reiterates the significance of the *place* where 'clean' laces were produced, emphasizing the emergence of a particular notion of women's work, one that was carried out in the order and privacy of the home, protected from the vagaries of hard manual labour in public spaces.

In her 2018 paper on women and weaving in Ladakh, Monisha Ahmed examines the role of Moravian missionaries in craft training and livelihood creation in one of the highest and coldest regions in the Himalayas.[17] Since many of the missionaries who came from Central Europe were themselves craftsmen, Ahmed observes, they concentrated their efforts on community self-sufficiency through productive work. However, it was the opening of an Industrial School in 1939 by Walter Asboe, a Moravian missionary posted in Ladakh from 1922 to 1947, that brought many women from Leh into weaving with the foot treadle loom for broad cloths, blankets and shawls. This foot treadle loom had been prohibited for women from nomadic pastoral groups in other parts of Ladakh. Ahmed tells us that with India's independence from the British in 1947, Asboe had to close the industrial school. In 1955, it was replaced by a handicrafts training center, mainly for weaving shawls and carpets, set up by the Indian government, and run by instructors who had first trained under Asboe. Ahmed observes that even though all the post-independence crafts skills training centers in Ladakh 'instruct and employ both men and women, … many more women than men train there.' She notes that women are now taking over from men in the village-based crafts like weaving, while men, in turn, are moving out to towns and cities pursuing newer professions in the army, tourism and government jobs. Ironically, it is the women who now see themselves as the practitioners and guardians of the textile crafts of Ladakh.

In colonial Madras, not just missionaries but even the colonial administration began to take interest in female education through promoting Home Science as 'an effective means of dampening political activism because it extended imperial modernity into the home.'[18] Mary Hancock's (2001) inquiry into the education of upper caste and upper-class females in formal schools, or through the *zenana* (women's quarters) or home-based tutoring, reveals that craft was part of the colonial Home Science curriculum which included needlework, domestic economy and moral education 'as a marker of the nationalist goals with which the field had been invested.'[19] Focusing their attentions on scientific applications to basic problems and concerns of daily life around home and community – food and nutrition, textiles and clothing, health and hygiene – would not only bring productive efficiencies into the life of Indian women from middle- and upper-class homes, but also help them better the lives of their 'poorer sisters'. Hancock argues that female education in colonial Madras sharpened the distinctions between private and public spaces, privatized domesticity, and framed elite homes 'as (feminine) "backstages" of new (masculine) public realms.'[20] This approach to middle and upper-class women's spaces of empowerment and action was crystallized at the national level with the opening of the Lady Irwin College of Home Science in New Delhi in 1932.

The entry of women onto the stage of anti-colonial politics was mediated by the Gandhian stance, which continued to prioritize upper-caste norms that placed women as the moral custodians of the home and, by extension, the nation. His choice of campaigns – liquor and foreign cloth – in which he summoned women to appeal to the public, 'was an excellent strategy. The effects of both – drunkenness and unemployment – affected the home directly. And that was the designated and chosen sphere of women. And the causes were popular enough to draw literate and illiterate women.'[21] In South India, and in Madras in particular, the anti-caste, self-respect movement led by non-Brahmin leader and political thinker, Periyar (E.V. Ramaswami), complicated matters, especially with respect to women and work. Though the movement did not acknowledge missionary experiments in crafts-based education for the uplift of the depressed classes, self-respecters did deploy a combination of literacy and industrial education as a means for gaining self-respect for social groups without privilege.

                    De-/Anti-/Post-colonial Feminisms

Muthulakshmi Reddy (1886-1968), who was among the women self-respecters, and the first Indian member of the Women's Indian Association (WIA), fought for legislative reforms to alleviate the caste-based dedication of minor girls to prominent temples run by influential Brahmin men. Having herself broken the shackles of patriarchy and caste to become a medical surgeon, Muthulakshmi nevertheless held the prevailing Gandhian conservative view that India's women should be chaste housewives in order to legitimise her opposition to the Devadasi system.[22] In 1931, the WIA opened the Avvai Home for girls and women under her guidance, which was later expanded to a much larger campus in Adyar, in present day Chennai. Her aim was to provide training in useful professions that would be suitable for uplifting the social and economic status of the many destitute and so-called 'fallen' women who came to the house. The 50th anniversary brochure of the home boasts many prominent, upper-caste donors and patrons, including a number of foreign visitors. Muthulakshmi Reddi's social reform interventions managed to bring national and international visibility to the cause of women from the depressed classes. Her goal of building self-respect through economic self-reliance translated into creating training programs for women that emphasized moral hygiene (housekeeping, midwifery, nursing, weaving, needlework, dressmaking, home science), which would ensure their acceptance and integration within India's caste system.[23]

The valorisation of the rural as a bedrock of civilization and authentic living in the early twentieth century, in crafts-based educational experiments of missionaries, Gandhi, Tagore, and women's rights activists of the WIA and AIWC had already linked rural India to wider transnational movements. They offered both the model and the roadmap for building new spaces for women and for the crafts, and helped establish the role of the developmental State through both protectionist and interventionist policies. By 1939, the sub-committee of the National Planning Committee on women's participation in the planned economy had been formed and it included Muthulakshmi Reddi, among other prominent women leaders.

The period of World War II was marked by visions of a transnational, non-Western modernity, one that would 'harness up-to-date "Western"-style scientific rationality, meritocracy, industrialization, and socioeconomic planning to the imagined, time-honored "Eastern" strengths of community, morality, and spirituality'.[24] For Kamaladevi Chattopadhyaya (1903-1988), who had stood as an independent candidate of the WIA in the General Elections of 1926, became the first secretary of the All-India Women's Conference (AIWC) in 1928, and was a volunteer in Gandhi's salt satyagraha in 1930, crafts revival and independence from colonial rule were interlinked agendas. During her world tour from June 1939-November 1941, Kamaladevi attended several international women's conferences in Europe, spent eighteen months in the US visiting social and political activists, lecturing on politics in India, and observing numerous social reform programs. The dialogues she had with counterparts in the different countries she visited in this period helped shape her political stance as a radical proponent of South-South exchanges and decolonization.[25]

Cultural Self Determination with a Transnational Socialist Inflection after Independence

In the post-War period, craft came to be accepted worldwide as a modernist project for decolonising Asian and African countries seeking to re-build their national self-hood. Pan-Africanist and pan-Asianist discourses recast craft as an aestheticized tradition predicated upon a disavowal of industrial mass production and its consequences of cultural alienation and individualism. Unhinged from its imperialist moorings in orientalist discourses and colonial spaces of representation, craft's clarion call from "Asia" in the first half of the 1900s was only the beginning of its subsequent momentum and consolidation as a node for Third World development later in the century. Lateral connections between the formerly colonized nations forged in the postcolonial context, first at the Asian Relations Conference in 1947 at Delhi and again in 1955 at Bandung, further crystallized this altered notion of craft in Asia and set the tone for its use in national and international development.

Kamaladevi's socialist views about the salience of crafts in the non-Western world underpinned her stance on Asian (and African) unity and emancipation from imperialist forces. In Kamaledevi's view, cultural decolonization in post-war reconstruction was as much the need of the hour as political independence, and could end the economic retardation experienced by continents like Asia and Africa under colonization. At the Inter-Asian Relations conference held in Delhi in 1947, the skill and self-conscious way of life of the artisan, and not the drudgery of the labouring factory hand, embodied, for Kamaladevi, the true purpose of craft in the awakening of Asia to its own living sources of knowledge and capacities for economic self-governance. Inspired by the Japanese state's patronage of craft and her friendship with the Kenzai family of potters, Kamaladevi acknowledged that her 'foundation for the development of crafts in India after independence was in truth laid in Japan' even though she was skeptical of Japan's emergence as an imperial power in Asia.[26]

Throughout her life Kamaladevi sought to infuse craft with an aesthetic sensibility whose cultivation, she believed, could be the well spring of a transnational, Asian cultural renaissance. An influential international voice on the subject in the post-war era, Kamaladevi's mission of decolonizing craft through an aesthetic self-assertion is latent in her reflection on the motivation behind her life's work in 1984: 'We had been made to feel primitive by the British—that we had nothing of modern aesthetic values ... we had to build our own sense of appreciation.'[27] Her writings reveal an embryonic perspective of the "South", including the South in the North, on the international stage of nations. Speaking on the role of crafts in the preservation of cultural values at the First World Congress of Craftsmen held in New York in 1964, Kamaladevi drew attention to the contemporary significance of crafts: 'Craftsmanship need not, however, be bound up wholly with tradition. While it continues to draw strength from the past, it has also to be tuned to the present, evolve a new relationship with the current flow of life.'[28] For her, crafts were not only a way of recognizing the significance of one's own culture, but also of developing a sense of appreciation of other world cultures as well. In a 1969 article titled 'The Crafts' in the May issue of the *Unesco Courier*, Kamaladevi proposes a universalistic view of craft:

> Craft has always been a basic activity in human society, in fact it is considered more cohesive and permeating in human relationships than even language, for it can penetrate many barriers to communication. Particularly has this been true of the older societies such as those in Asia, South and Central America, Africa and countries like Greece or Spain.[29]

Altering judgements of taste and consumption patterns, especially among the upper classes and castes and the emerging middle classes, was paramount in the recuperation of certain crafts in a new, culturally self-conscious India envisioned by Kamaladevi. Utensils, textiles, baskets, etc. as well as the local materials, tools, techniques, and cottage-based production processes involved in making these craft objects, became ideals of simplicity embodying the whole of Indian culture for her. Kamaladevi was instrumental in reminding urban consumers of the modest beauty of craft objects used in their daily life through establishing several travelling exhibitions, fairs, and interactive museums, and her work underpinned many new post-independence initiatives described in the next section.

Early on in her activism for the crafts, she had to contend with norms of patriarchy that governed women's entry into the labour market. In a pamphlet published in 1939, Kamaladevi was very aware of the pervasive gender-biased injustice in conceptions of work, labour, and wages that women were contending with:

> 'everywhere women are paid less – in some places about half of men's wages. This unjust system is part of the tradition handed down under masculine dominance. Masculine standard is the accepted one and according to that measure wages are fixed. That a woman worker spends proportionately as much energy and labour and is entitled to the same wage is lost sight of.'[30]

The model of co-operative organization for crafts introduced by Kamaladevi was to rectify this bias. Since the 1990s, however, neo-liberal policies have encouraged privatization in companies over collective organization, and protectionism of trades/types of workers as well as anti-unionization, over attempts to improve the general welfare for all artisans. Paradoxically, her interventions in the crafts did not encompass the sphere of women's work that was socially perceived to be non-domestic, non-familial or not rooted in Indian cultural traditions, nor did it cover women farm labourers, plantation wage earners, women in informal services or those working in the organized sector. It was the developmentalist state agenda that took over this task, as we will see in the next section.

Women and Crafts for Development

The recasting of artisanal work within a transnational critique of capitalist factory production in the first half of the twentieth century, spawned state-based valorization and protection of artisans and their products, within a wider Asianist imaginary.[31] The discourse drew attention to a common aesthetic ideal, one of self-conscious consumption of the labour and skill of the anonymous male artisan. It also helped establish craft as a de-politicized, yet gendered, way of building kinship with the socially marginalised and economically impoverished in the Global South from a developmentalist perspective.

Perceptions of local realities and gendered work from the lens of a shared craft aesthetic were now actively examined in order to be incorporated in state policy and soon came to be inserted into Third World development agendas of transnational bodies like the International Labour Organisation (ILO) and UNESCO. International development theorists, too, returned to the analysis of asymmetrically organized division of labour in productive households in Asia and Africa, to spotlight women's well-being and survival, and sought new ways to theorize the everyday conflicts of interest between men and women within family-based gendered work.[32]

In the years prior to independence Gandhi's economic advisor and secretary of the All-India Village Industries Association, J. C. Kumarappa, had already begun to situate craft as a cottage industry in the wider economic context of planned development and decentralization. Kamaladevi was instrumental in introducing cooperative organization as a key feature of developmental policies and institutions for artisans in independent India. Not only that, she also made it possible for other women from elite backgrounds to enter into the field of crafts resurgence, not only as the new urban consumers of handmade products but also, in forging a space for themselves in the advancement of India as a crafts nation.[33]

Many elite women of Delhi were enlisted to support Kamaladevi's cause of rehabilitating partition refugees at Faridabad town near Delhi. Faced with the dire situation of thousands of people camping in the outskirts of Delhi after partition in 1947, Kamaladevi and her advisor L.C. Jain decided to use the model of cooperative societies that was already functioning in some regions to create the Indian Cooperative Union (ICU), as the umbrella body that would form several producers' cooperatives under its fold. Among the early women activists responsible for institutionalising craft retail in India, Gulshan Nanda's (2013) study recounts how student volunteers were asked:

De-/Anti-/Post-colonial Feminisms

to identify women with the ability to sew and embroider using traditional stitches for which Punjab was well known…. Based on their assessment, the volunteers began organising the women's activity around handicrafts. Twenty machines were brought from the All India Congress Committee Office, arranged for by Sucheta Kriplani. Meanwhile, Sardar Patel had already been sending truckloads of fabric donated by mills in Ahmedabad. The volunteers were asked to segregate fabric suitable for garments, and for embroidered table and bed linen…. This sale of embroidered linen became so popular that one counter in Pandit Brothers became too small an area. Many of the customers were women who were well-off and eager to help the cause. More orders kept pouring in and Sheela Puri took charge of executing them. This, in my view, was the foundation of [handicrafts] retailing in India.[34]

The All India Handloom and Handicrafts Boards, implemented under Nehru's First Five Year Plan in 1952, formally initiated the newly emergent Indian government's agenda for protective policies on craft, and was instrumental in shifting the focus away from the patronage of princely states, who had lost their standing in the formation of the republic, to the burgeoning urban middle classes. The National Handicrafts and Handlooms Museum, set up in New Delhi in the late 1950s, was to support this new aesthetic for urban living with a mandate to 'source material for the revival, reproduction and development of crafts'.

Around the same time, with the appointment of Pupul Jayakar as the Chairperson of the All India Handloom Board in the 1950s, weaving clusters across the length and breadth of the country began to be supported by Weavers' Service Centers who would set up in their neighborhood and provide artistic, design, and technical assistance for creating new range of craft products. Pupul Jayakar herself encouraged rural women in Madhubani in Bihar to create their ritual wall drawings on paper and helped to bring visibility to their intricate artwork. In 1955 she initiated the idea of a 'national' design institute, which was set up in Ahmedabad with the help of American designers Charles and Ray Eames in 1955. Their proposal known as the 'Eames India Report' led to the founding of National Institute of Design (NID) in Ahmedabad, whose mandate was to address India's developmental needs through design whilst being mindful of its technical and aesthetic foundations exemplified by its craft traditions and exemplified by the handcrafted *lota*. NID became the training ground for many social designers working for India's underprivileged populations in collaboration with its artisans.[35]

In 1965, Kamaladevi set up the Crafts Council of India, a non-profit organization that works in tandem with governmental agencies for crafts advocacy and schemes for artisans, and is run almost exclusively by prominent women from each of the state-wise chapters. Among the 'formidable ladies' of the Delhi crafts council, Jasleen Dhamija became well known for her early writing on women's embroideries from

Punjab in the first Indian arts and culture quarterly magazine of independent India.[36] Dhamija was also among Kamaladevi's protégées enlisted to assist in international development projects focused on women. In her essay titled 'Handicrafts: A Source of Employment for Women in Developing Rural Economies' for the December 1975 issue of the *International Labour Review*, Dhamija was already established as a voice of women in crafts from the Global South, highlighting how 'in many countries women are already the custodians of crafts' and it is 'essential that the importance of handicrafts and the role of women in artisanal production should be recognised in development planning.'[37]

Training in co-operative organisation and product design development became the two pillars for inserting women in new India's developmentalist agenda. The familial aspect of craft work, the fact that it could be carried out from home, and that it involved patterns of interaction that women were already amenable to, made self-organising for home-based production a feasible goal: 'Indeed, the co-operative spirit already exists among the women, since they are used to working together on the occasion of festivities or during times of crisis. The strange thing is that in many areas co-operative education and assistance ... are given only to men, even where the women do most of the work.'[38]

From the 1970s, many non-governmental organizations led by women crafts revivalists and social design entrepreneurs reached out to artisan groups by providing them raw materials and other inputs for producing good quality products, in the comfort of their own homes. They took great efforts not only to promote the products in urban markets but also ensured the welfare of artisan families struggling to make ends meet and prevent them from migrating to cities under duress. Ritu Sethi, in her 2013 article 'Catalyzing craft: Women who shaped the way',[39] lists the pioneering efforts of many women's rights activists and social design entrepreneurs in reviving textile techniques among weavers, dyers and printers in different states, through innovations in the use of raw materials, rethinking design layouts, colour palettes and motifs, and setting up local museums, workshops and cooperative producer organizations for artisans, whilst providing them sustained employment opportunities in their own neighborhoods or nearby. Notable among them are Ela Bhatt, who founded SEWA in 1972, the 'Self-Employed Women's Association', and Renana Jhabvala and Mirai Chatterjee, who joined the organization to help informal women workers, both home or street-based, to organize themselves for their own welfare and self-respect in and around the city of Ahmedabad in Gujarat.

Others were involved in setting up educational programs *in situ*. Those that are relevant for building sustainable livelihoods among vulnerable communities include the Barefoot College in Tilonia, Rajasthan (Aruna and Bunker Roy); Kala Raksha Vidyalaya in Kutch, Gujarat (Judy Frater); and the Handloom Weaving School in Maheshwar, Madhya Pradesh (Sally Holkar). Platforms for direct marketing for

　　　　　　　　　　　　　　　De-/Anti-/Post-colonial Feminisms

artisans, like Dastakar and Nature Bazaar in Delhi (Laila Tyabji); Dastakar Andhra (Uzramma) in Hyderabad and Dilli Haat (Jaya Jaitly) in Delhi brought the urban consumer closer to artisans' doorstep. Disseminative platforms like the Crafts Revival Trust (Ritu Sethi) now serve as a growing digital archive for conversations and collaborations among artisans, designers and consumers. And even though some men have played a prominent role in the advancement of India as a crafts nation, at the core of India's craft leadership post-Independence, are these 'mothers and godmothers'.[40] World, national and state-level Crafts Councils continue the legacy of their mission to support the next generation of artisans and to inspire and educate young urban activists, a majority of whom are also women, in the ethics, aesthetics, skills and organization of the diverse and dispersed craft producers across the country.

By way of a Coda

This chapter sought to trace some spaces and actions of women in the deployment of craft in the context of rural rehabilitation, nation building, and national development in pre- and post-independence India, now visible in recent literature. My aim was to put a spotlight on the discourses about crafts and women in India, following the impetus of transnational movements advancing women's rights on the one hand, and craft skills training, on the other. It is interesting to see that both Muthulakshmi and Kamaladevi, despite being formidable among the first women leaders of India, preferred to move away from active party politics. Both chose to step-down from nationalist party politics and did not occupy any political office post-independence. C.S. Lakshmi notes that in the early days of their entry in the public sphere of nationalist politics, women were often confronted with conflicting loyalties on account of their framing within patriarchy. Many justified their stepping out of their homes by resorting to the metaphor of honorable service: 'Kodainayaki Ammal, for example, … explained her entry into the national movement in her journal…. "Some people wonder … how husbands allow their women to speak on the stage. There is nothing surprising in this. Those who look upon the home and the nation as one will not find anything unusual in this... Work at home is personal. But work for the nation is public service. It is something virtuous".'[41] Yet they were able to deploy the prevailing norms about women's domesticity, those that kept upper-caste women in their homes and lower-caste women out of respectable employment, into a global vision for women and crafts.

The commercialization of craft products in the colonial economy did 'systematically reinforce women's domestic, heterosexual, and familial identities', according to Michelle Maskeill's 1999 study of women's hand-embroidered shawls, or *phulkaris,* in Punjab. When these women started using imported mill cloths for embroidering these shawls, they were derogatorily dubbed as 'Manchester Baghs' in the colonial arts and crafts public sphere.[42] Post-independence as well, Maria Mies (1981) has argued that women's entry into the lace industry for the world market was predicated upon their societal definition as housewives and divisions between gender roles: 'whereas pauperised men try to do "business", they keep their wives at home to produce lace.'[43] There were other gendered as well as caste biases that crept into the nationalist aestheticization of crafts. This included the promotion of only those crafts that fulfilled the criteria of sanitary, moral and caste hygiene, over those that involved "smelly" processes, such as in leather tanning or indigo extraction.

Foregrounding women's home-based craft skills and capacities in the service of wider, national and international goals, as this paper has shown, has opened up some key spaces for understanding women's empowerment in particular textile crafts. Anonymizing occupational caste identities through craft skills training post-Independence did create possibilities for the remaking of women's subjectivities around dignified work, even if it was from home. More recently, a growing body of scholarship has focused on decolonizing women's work in the field of textiles. This literature takes into account how women negotiate control over their craft labour, in terms of resources and time within their domestic life, as well as in the material and narrative qualities of the very objects they produce. It was 'the promise of jacket' or respectability and freedom from the rules and restrictions of caste, that lured many lower-caste girls, who were otherwise forbidden to wear a breast cloth, to learn sewing in Sri Lanka, according to Mark Balmforth (2018).[44] He argues that the use of distinctive stitches, colours and motifs, including devotional verses in Tamil, found in the needlepoint samples of the Oodooville group, demonstrates that the trainees were forging a new subjecthood and identity for themselves. Pika Ghosh's (2020) study is another reminder to go beyond the nationalist valorization of craft skills and objects. She invites her readers instead to examine the *kantha,* running stitch quilt embroideries of Bengal, 'as traces of experiences and choices navigated by women in their everyday lives and selves.'[45] My own research in textile crafts and fashion, specifically on dyes and dyeing in the colonial archive and in postcolonial developments, has also veered towards a critical, narrative approach to the subject. Rather than focusing on a history of the extraction, production and circulation of indigo from a colonial, anti-colonial and postcolonial perspective (2016),[46] I am now interested in interrogating the subjectivities of the voices that narrate indigo in diverse contexts (2023).[47] Interestingly, it is the voices of women farmers of the indigo plant that appear to be silenced in all these registers.

Shifting attention to the question of where the women are in craft research is also a process of decolonizing one's own scholarship. Using textiles and women as an entry point of inquiry is a research methodology, as well as a kind of academic activism, needed for reframing our approaches beyond the colonial, anti-colonial and postcolonial.

    De-/Anti-/Post-colonial Feminisms

Notes

1. 'If we take seriously the politics of domestic servants, of women living on or near a military base, or of women who sew Gap and Zara apparel, we discover that international politics is more complicated' in Cynthia Enloe, *Bananas, Beaches and Bases: Making Feminist Sense of International Politics*, University of California Press, 2014, pp. 352-3, p. 358.

2. Quoted in J. F. Codell, 'Indian Crafts and Imperial Policy: Hybridity, Purification, and Imperial Subjectivities' in A. Myzelev and J. Potvin (eds.), *Material Cultures 1740- 1920: The Meanings and Pleasures of Collecting*, Aldershot: Ashgate, 2009, pp.149-70.

3. Saloni Mathur, 'Living Ethnological Exhibits: The Case of 1886', *Cultural Anthropology*, vol. 15 no. 4 (2000), pp. 492-524.

4. Deepali Dewan, 'The Body at Work: Colonial Art Education and the Figure of the 'Native Craftsman' in James H. Mills and Satadru Sen (eds.), *Confronting the Body: The Politics of Physicality in Colonial and Postcolonial India*, New York: Anthem Press, 2004, pp. 118-33; S. Mathur, *India by design: Colonial History and Cultural Display*, University of California Press, 2007.

5. Aarti Kawlra, 'Reconstituting Craft in the Idiom of Education for the Masses' in Milind Brahme, M. Suresh Babu and Thomas Muller (eds.), *Inclusive Education in India: Concepts, Methods and Practice*, New Delhi: Mosaic Books, 2018.

6. Leonard Elmhirst, *Rabindranath Tagore: Pioneer in Education. Essays and Exchanges between Rabindranath Tagore and L. K. Elmhirst*, London : John Murray, 1961.

7. Sister Nivedita, 'Manual Training as a part of General Education in India' [1905] in *The Complete Works of Sister Nivedita*, 5 vols., Calcutta: Ramkrishna Sarada Mission, 1996, vol. 4, p. 418.

8. Sister Nivedita's nationalist call was to emerge from the interior spaces of the *zenana*, to 'Let every Indian woman incarnate for us the whole spirit of the mother and the culture and protection of the homeland, Bhumia Devi'. Quoted in Janaki Nair 'Uncovering the *Zenana*: Visions of Indian womanhood in Englishwomen's writings, 1813-1940', *Journal of Women's History*, vol. 2 no. 1(1990), pp.8-34, p.23.

9. Madhu Kishwar, 'Gandhi on women', *Race and Class*, vol. 28 no. 1 (1986), pp.43-61.

10. Ibid, p. 45. (quote from Harijan – 2 December 1939).

11. Shambhu C. Prasad, *Exploring Gandhian Science: Case Study of the Khadi Movement*, Doctoral dissertation, IIT Delhi, 2001.

12. Ibid. p. 253.

13. Anandhi S. and Aarti Kawlra, 'Introduction to the special issue on 'Caste, Craft and Education', *Review of Development and Change*, MIDS, Chennai, vol.23 no. 2 (July-Dec 2018), pp. 5-18.

14. Ibid.

15. M. Abott, 'Progress of women's work' in *Report of the Fourth Decennial Indian Missionary Conference*, held in Madras, London and Madras: Christian Literature Society, 1902, pp. 258-263.

16. Jane Haggis, 'Ironies of Emancipation: Changing Configurations of "Women's Work" in the "Mission of Sisterhood" to Indian Women', *Feminist Review*, no. 65 (2000), pp.108-126, p.116

17. Monisha Ahmed, 'Women and Weaving in Ladakh: Missionary Interventions and the Making of a Craft Tradition', *Review of Development and Change*, vol. 23 no. 2 (July-December 2018), pp. 19-38.

18. Mary Hancock, 'Home Science and the Nationalization of Domesticity in Colonial India' , *Modern Asian Studies*, vol. 35 no. 4 (2001), pp. 871-903. https://www.jstor.org/stable/313194

19. Ibid.

20. Ibid.

21. C. S. Lakshmi, 'Bodies Called Women: Some Thoughts on Gender, Ethnicity and Nation' *Economic and Political Weekly*, vol. 32 no. 46 (15-21 November, 1997), pp. 2953-2962.

22. S. Anandhi, 'Women's Question in the Dravidian Movement c. 1925-1948', *Social Scientist*, vol. 19 no. 5/6 (May - June 1991), pp. 24-41.

23. *Avvai Home : 1931-1981*, 50th Anniversary Brochure, Adyar, 1982, no page numbers.

24. Ethan Mark, '"Asia's" Transwar Lineage: Nationalism, Marxism, and "Greater Asia" in an Indonesian Inflection', *The Journal of Asian Studies,* vol. 65 no. 3 (August 2006), pp. 461-493, p. 462.

25. J. L. Barbieri, *Kamaladevi Chattopadhyaya, Anti-Imperialist and Women's Rights Activist, 1939-1941,* [Master's thesis, Miami University, 2008]. OhioLINK Electronic Theses and Dissertations Center, https://rave.ohiolink.edu/etdc/view?acc_num=miami1218456911; Ellen Carol DuBois and Vinay Lal (eds.), *A Passionate Life: Writings by and on Kamaladevi Chattopadhyay*, New Delhi: Zubaan, 2017.

26. Aarti Kawlra, 'Sari-Kimono and the Making of a Transnational Craftscape' in Sushila Narasimhan (ed.), *India-Japan Narratives: Lesser Known Historical and Cultural Interactions,* New Delhi: Mombusho scholars association of India (Mosai), 2021. pp. 142-3.

27. Shakuntala Narasimhan, *Kamaladevi Chattopadhyay: The Romantic Rebel*, New Delhi: Sterling Publishers, 1999, pp. 77-9.

28. Kamaladevi Chattopadhyay, 'Preservation of the Cultural Values of a Society Through Craftsmanship', Speech made at the *First World Congress of Craftsmen*, American Craftsmen's Council, Columbia University, New York, 8-19 June 1964.

29. Kamaladevi Chattopadhyay, 'The Crafts', *The UNESCO Courier: A Window Open on the World*, vol. XXII no. 5 (1969), pp. 15-17, 32-36, p. 15.

30. Kamaladevi Chattopadhyay, *The Awakening of Indian Women,* Madras: Everyman's Press, 1939, pp 25, p. 32.

31. Aarti Kawlra, 'Sari-Kimono and the Making of a Transnational Craftscape' (2021)

32. Amartya Sen, 'Gender and Cooperative Conflicts' in A. Sen and I. Tinker (eds.), *Persistent Inequalities*, Oxford University Press, 1990, pp. 123-149.

33. Abigail McGowan, 'Mothers and Godmothers of Crafts: Female Leadership and the Imagination of India as a Crafts Nation, 1947–67', *South Asia: Journal of South Asian Studies,*

 De-/Anti-/Post-colonial Feminisms

vol. 44, No 2, (2021) pp. 282-297.

34. Gulshan Nanda, *Kamaladevi's Vision of Handicrafts Cooperatives: A Personal Narrative,* India: India International Centre, 2013, pp. 4-5.

35. In 2001, when the lives of many dyers and printers were affected by the Gujarat earthquake the 'Bandhani Development Project' at NID brought relief to these communities by raising funds, co-creating new designs and hosting exhibitions, sales and advocacy of their textiles.

36. Jasleen Dhamija, 'Bagh and Phulkari of Punjab', *Marg,* vol. 17 (March 1964), pp.15- 24.

37. Jasleen Dhamija, 'Handicrafts: A Source of Employment for Women in Developing Rural Economies' *International Labour Review,* vol. 112 no. 6 (December 1975), pp. 459-465.

38. Ibid. p. 464.

39. Ritu Sethi, 'Catalysing Craft: Women who Shaped the Way', *Indian International Centre Quarterly,* vol. 39 no. 3/4 (Winter-Spring 2012-2013), pp. 168-85

40. Abigail McGowan, 'Mothers and Godmothers of Crafts' (2021), p. 283. fn. 7.

41. C.S. Lakshmi, 'Bodies Called Women: Some Thoughts on Gender, Ethnicity and Nation', *Economic and political Weekly,* (1997), pp.2953-2962.

42. Michelle Maskiell, 'Embroidering the Past: Phulkari Textiles and Gendered Work as 'Tradition' and 'Heritage' in Colonial and Contemporary Punjab', *The Journal of Asian Studies,* vol. 58 no. 2 (May 1999), pp. 361-38.

43. Maria Mies, 'Dynamics of Sexual Division of Labour and Capital Accumulation: Women Lace Workers of Narsapur', *Economic and Political Weekly,* vol. 16 no. 10/12 (March 1981), pp. 496.

44. Mark E. Balmforth, 'Riotous Needlework: Gendered Pedagogy and a Negotiated Christian Aesthetic in the American Ceylon Mission' in *Review of Development and Change,* vol. 23 no. 2. (July - December 2018), pp. 63-92, Issue editors: S. Anandhi and Aarti Kawlra.

45. Pika Ghosh, *Making Kantha, Making Home: Women at Work in Colonial Bengal,* University of Washington Press, Global South Asia Series, 2020.

46. Aarti Kawlra, 'Recipes for Re-enchantment: Natural Dyes and Dyeing in India', *Marg* special issue. *Cloth and India: Towards Recent Histories 1947-2015.* (2016).

47. Aarti Kawlra, 'Narrating indigo: Telling and Re-telling Subjectivities of Craft in India' in Chandan Bose and Mira Mohsini (eds.), *Encountering Craft: Methodological Approaches from Anthropology, Art History, and Design,* London: Routledge, 2023, pp. 58-72.

Women's Tacit, Uncoded Knowledge: Ownership and Value in Conflict Zones

Neelam Raina

Since 2019, the work of the GCRF Gender, Justice and Security hub, has undertaken research in South Asia. Part of this research, led by the Culture and Conflict project, has taken a deep dive into analysing the practices of craftswomen who live and work in fragile and conflict affected states – specifically, Kashmir, Upper Chitral Valley (see Fatima Hussain's chapter), Jammu Region (India), Sri Lanka, Afghanistan – and what part craft plays as a solution to women's capacity to earn sustainable livelihoods as well as a methodological approach for understanding conflicts. My part as the lead investigator for the research in this project builds on two decades of work in crafts from South Asia. This chapter looks at different women's ability identified through this project to generate sustainable incomes from handicrafts in fragile economies where conflict is present, and considers the value placed upon women's tacit knowledge and skills in sustainable development policy about craft as income-generation.

What is it about "making" crafts that draws in women in conflict areas from across geopolitical divides? Why and how do crafts become the go-to activity with significant value, meanings and associations, when fragility becomes omnipresent in their lives? How has the knowledge of craft processes as a form of women's tacit knowledge become the fallback position for so many women? And how does their tacit knowledge provide the safety net for income generation, and for the ability to dream of a better future? The chapter offers some anonymised case studies[1] of individual women's situations to explain the dilemmas and contradictions women experience as makers in regions known for both their culture and political/military conflict and their subsequent identities as makers and practitioners.

Ameena from Srinagar in Indian Administered Kashmir, for example, has watched her mother and grandmothers work tirelessly as ancillary workers[2] within the supply chain for producing Kashmiri shawls. She has watched them, through days and months of their lives, spin, treat and wash the yarns needed to make each shawl into a piece of art. Women in Kashmir used to spin yarns for the shawls and men would weave this yarn. This role of women within textile crafts as spinners is something Kashmiri women have in common with counterparts across the world, for example, the women in the Otavalan community in Ecuador who also spin yarn for weaving and knitting as a means of income generation.[3]

Women, like Ameena and the other women in this chapter, however, exist between siloes in how the history of craft/culture, contemporary politics and economic development policy have been framed. In her home and region, the role of women in the craft sector is often excluded from how culture, as well as politics, are discussed. Here men are dominant in the narratives and documentation of the history of their community and region. This state of affairs is a problematic starting point for discussions about the women's needs and related policy making, because their practices are relegated to an informal part of the economy. I have heard their work being referred to as a hobby: as activities chosen by them for entertainment in their spare time. These women are invisible, even though they are essential workers in the process of shawl production, largely due to the way labour is organised in families, and by a patriarchy that silences and erases women, and political conflict that limits disagreement and exacerbates inequalities. While their work is sometimes included in reports on the labour market, it continues to be dismissed as the ancillary labour of tertiary workers, as support labour in the supply chain, not independent craftswomen. Most if not all of the women I have worked with have experienced how their creative work and time spent has been negated or stereotyped, pushing it behind the unpaid work of caring that most of them are responsible for in their households. The difficult politics of Indian Kashmir are well-documented.[4] In discussions about security and peace in the region where they live, these women are often excluded from consideration, despite global actions around CEDAW and UN Security Council Resolution 1325, which mandates that women be included and consulted, within spaces of security, about peace building and elimination of violence. These approaches explain why the women of Kashmir are constantly reminded of the many exclusions that they face politically, socially and economically.

In historical accounts of creative production of beautiful crafts from India that document the Kashmiri pashmina and its origins,[5] it is largely men who are depicted making this craft. It is emperors who wear them and bestow them on other men as gifts. Many books by travellers in the region during the last two centuries and more recent versions by South Asian authors often track and trace the craft and its making through a specific gendered lens, which prioritises men and overlooks the women involved (see Fatima Hussain's chapter). The limits of what has been recorded about women's production in handicrafts in culture opens the door to understanding further its juxtaposition with current development policy in conflict-torn states. The problems experienced by women in conflict states are presented as a 'problem of development' by the United Nations, led and guided by its Sustainable Development goals. The UN has tried to encourage narratives around development that place the needs of women in conflict zones alongside debates around human rights, rights of access to livelihoods, sustainable livelihoods, and the prioritising of women-focussed actions to promote a more sustainable, equitable world. Security Council resolutions like the UNSCR1325,[6] for example, now twenty-three years old, focusses on the role and significance of women in fragile, conflict-affected states. Analysing this approach is the focus of the UKRI GCRF funded Gender, Justice and Security Hub (2019-2024) of which the Culture and Conflict Project is part. The Culture and Conflict project set out to explore how economic development through culturally significant, locally valued craft practices could support and sustain women producers in fragile, conflict-affected states, and it began by recognising how women craft producers fall between the cracks of policies and decision-making agendas. It also explored the role of craft as an entry point into discussions about peace, violence and conflict – contentious issues in every intractable conflict.

Women often feature within politics and international relations debates in relation to words like empowerment and agency, but when security is discussed they are primarily instrumentalised as those who need protection or additional help, and their voices as political actors are not always heard in security forums. Women are often depicted and discussed as 'victims' of conflict and violence and are at best co-opted into peace negotiations or agreements. For example, in Afghanistan, the oppression of women by the Taliban in the 1990s was used as a rationale for starting the war against their regime in Afghanistan and this led to the presence of NATO forces for close to two decades in the country with the aim of changing women's position in public life, work and government.

Within policy-making for economic development, craftswomen do appear in specially targeted gendered inclusion policies and programmes but these initiatives often remove them from their everyday worlds of creativity and culture and rarely acknowledges their tacit knowledge and expertise or their lived experiences. Within discussions of craft production as a cottage or local industry, their labour is often dismissed as belonging either to a family business or to uneducated, inherited or traditional forms of learning and they slip between the cracks of literacy skills and formal contemporary qualifications through education or become invisible labour in a multimillion-pound handicrafts industry. Within discussions about culture, craftswomen are often depicted in romanticised notions as makers of beautiful objects in their 'spare time', linking them only to leisure and amateurism. These women are therefore located in the peripheries of each silo they are present in, which is why the research project I lead set out to challenge these views and present their experiences not as interlopers or other kinds of stakeholders, but as vital to the connections that need to be addressed to make change within a cross section of global challenges. Craftswomen and their practices, their relationship to their making, their landscapes, their personal identities, their ecologies and their communities are at the centre of our research.

We set out to understand how conflict re-organises gendered labour in a society, changes people's everyday lived realities and socio-economic backgrounds and affects the organisation of households. We have tried across the different regions we studied to correlate/co-relate specific conflicts and ongoing political struggles for their impact on women's decisions to earn incomes or support their families. We wanted to reconsider how the decolonised realities of knowledge production, tacit knowledge, and understandings about the value of livelihoods earnt when women have become more numerous as heads of households but still have to operate within the lens of what have been and are considered patriarchal and traditional societies affected by conflict. Postcolonial development theory suggests working and generating income does empower women and gives them a voice both within and beyond the family. We set out to explore if their ability to earn money reduces their marginalisation within society and how does it provide a new rationale for them to be viewed as active stakeholders by their families and community, in governmental and policy terms.

So how does this work for Ameena, a research participant in my work? In Indian Kashmir, women like those in Ameena's family, though of independent thinking, traditionally lead protected lives. These women seldom work as employees and though some have been educated to graduate degree or graduate diploma levels, they have rarely undertaken formal employment.[7] Once married, however, they are considered wholly responsible for decisions made within the household about domestic chores, caring for the very old and the very young in their extended families, planning the education of their children, arranging the marriages of their children, siblings and relatives, collecting and making their trousseau, planning savings and expenditures, etc. It is significant to note here that the logistics of planning and managing income and expenses, large-scale weddings, educating their children and securing savings require skills which Kashmiri women have a long history of doing. This ability to organise, manage and delegate, drawn from past experiences, are strengths amongst Kashmiri women today. In many of the conflict areas I studied, women have become *de facto* heads of households.[8]

In Kashmir an increasing number of women have been working within the crafts sector in the last decade and Ameena is one of them. These women are new entrants to the sector and they have chosen to work in crafts to generate incomes, often as heads of households. Men were traditionally considered as protectors who provided continuity of income and security: in their absence, women now fulfil these roles. This shift from traditional roles for women, where the (patriarchal) virtues of silence, obedience, chastity, domesticity and motherhood were promoted, is a pattern across many nations and traditional societies, especially in South Asia. Women are often seen as the moral compass and the benchmark against which virtue is measured and value judgements made of families and communities.

Our research project set out to explore some of the motivations through which women chose to use their tacit, uncoded, prior knowledge in craft-making as a route for generation of an independent livelihood. To earn a livelihood generated through craft-making enables their financial independence through dignified routes and increases their ability to support one's own family and self. For women, crafts are embodied practices that they have observed for many years, as they have been users and consumers. Prior knowledge of crafts as users and consumers is a huge benefit to the women of South Asia. They have in the past received craft-made textiles as wedding presents, as ancestral heirlooms passed from mother to daughter and from the matriarchs within their families who invested money in craft-made goods. They value the rich tradition of making and trading of handicrafts in all four areas of South Asia that we studied over many decades. This reliance on prior knowledge has been noticed in Saharawi refugee camps by Thomas (1996)[9] where women seek and maintain skill continuity by working within the handmade textiles area. It has also been seen in the conflict beset areas of North Caucasus where Chechen and Ingush women deal in textiles to generate incomes.[10] Thus exploring crafts as a source of income for women is not unique to South Asia alone.

The need for women to work to generate income for themselves and their families in fragile locations is not an exception but a norm in the case of South Asia, Iraq and Afghanistan. Like their counterparts in Saharawi, Bosnia, Lebanon, Sulawesi and other places of conflict, the women of South Asia, when faced by a pressure to earn, few marketable skills and very little work experience, have resorted to craft making to generate incomes. Although a key finding of the UNDP Gender Thematic assessment conducted in Central Sulawesi in 2004 was that in areas of conflict the social, political and economic role of the women shifts from domestic spaces to public spaces, where women now have the opportunity to generate income differently. This assessment[11] found women to have more freedom of movement than men; although they are sometimes harassed, most

　　　　　　　　　　　　　　　　　De-/Anti-/Post-colonial Feminisms

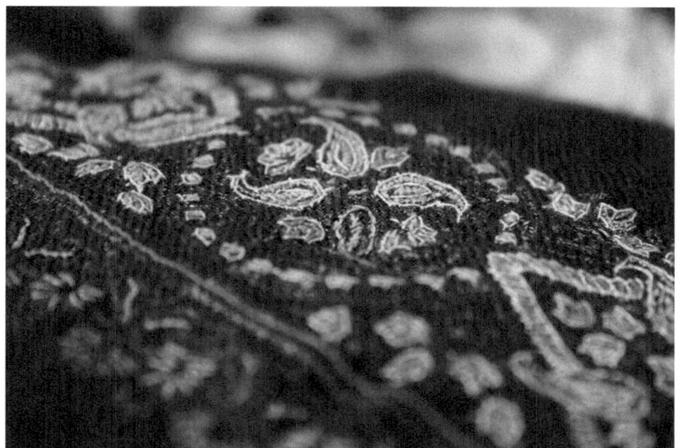
Detail of sozni embroidery, Srinagar, Kashmir, India. Photo: Neelam Raina

women are not subject to as much suspicion, questioning and searches by the security forces as men. This ability to move and generate income gave some women more decision-making power within the household and the community as a direct outcome of the conflict. However, this "freedom of movement" provides challenges that arise from their identity as women in conflict zones, including sexual violence directed against them.

Farheen from Charsadda in Pakistan creates beautiful hand embroideries which are often used in making traditional Salwaar Kameez for women in her region of Swat. She told us about her ambitions and desires stitched into the clothes by her own hands. She spoke about the economic status of her family, the lack of employment opportunities for women who have had little access to formal education, are often married at a young age, and the responsibilities she now carries looking after her extended family. Her lack of formal education holds her back from accessing formal higher paid employment. Her gender limits her mobility to other parts of the country and her love for her region, her family and her loved ones makes her hesitate from thinking about a career and employment outside of Swat. Her landscape and her craft are a space of silence and meditation for her, she calls it her hobby and thus any income she makes from this practice is a bonus for her. In a fragile place – both politically and environmentally she is aware of the lack of employment options for people like her.

Kamala from Basohli, in the Jammu region of India, which shares a long, contested border with Pakistan, spoke to us about her work as an artist who paints traditional miniature paintings in the Pahari school style, often depicting women in love in outdoor floral garden spaces. She learned about drawing on paper these famous female characters, with a side profile, from her community.

This art form, famous for its fine lines and detailing, depicts romantic narratives around the woman who feature in most of these paintings, has now seen an increase in women artists when it was previously dominated by men. Some women are trained formally through certificate and diploma level qualifications, while others have acquired knowledge of this art form through their own learning or informal means in the community which surrounds them. Basohli miniature painting is widely recognised as part of the Indian art map and was recently given a Geographic Indicator label by the Government of India.[12] These paintings, made with patience, painted in traditional colours, depicting stories of love, yearning, separation and joy, are now made by women in the district. It takes Kamala, days to complete a painting, and she sells them intermittently, when her personal family life allows her to step out to sell them. Painting gives her time away from other domestic chores, a chance to explore her own creativity and to generate an income. By generating income for herself through painting, Kamala hopes to pay for her own further education, with the ambition of joining the Indian civil service.

Savitha from Batticaloa, Sri Lanka, spoke about her experience as a weaver of sarees in a community which has experienced varying levels of exclusion in the immediate aftermath of the Easter Sunday bombings in Sri Lanka. Weaving is a skill she developed through peer learning from women's groups in her region. The ability to access a loom, within her home, with support of local groups (who are research partners on the project that I lead) allowed her to set up her own workshop. From within the confines of her home, she now weaves beautiful cotton sarees on a simple two pedal loom. The creativity is enhanced and complimented by her own awareness of the sarees worn in the community and region around her, and she is a keen observer of the market and what sells in which season. She is aware of the role of this piece of cloth within her community and culture. She explained to us that new clothes are purchased for key cultural and religious celebrations in Sri Lanka and this is why she observes the role colour plays within her country and location. Her ability to understand the texture, weight, length, and pattern/design of her weave allows her to generate her own income, which she sees as central to supporting the future educational ambitions of her children. With the current economic crisis in the country, her income is crucial for the survival and well-being of her family.

In Afghanistan, the crisis that unravelled in August 2021 followed close behind our research which had begun in Feb 2019 in Mazar-e-Sharif, Kabul and Kandahar. As an activist and a feminist, watching the accelerated impact of this political crisis, followed closely by religious edicts that removed women from the public space within months of the NATO forces leaving the nation, is a rather long, horrific, ongoing narrative. What became clear quite quickly was

De-/Anti-/Post-colonial Feminisms

that working on crafts, from the confines of the home, through a practice which is considered feminine and traditional, was perhaps one of the very few options left for women to pursue to generate incomes. Afghan women, makers of the exquisite *charmadozi* and *khammakdozi*, were now, once again, placed within their homes, unable to pursue jobs, careers or education in the face of the new regime in place since August 2021. The embroidery skills that many Afghan women know and are taught since a young age, are widely understood as both tacit and uncoded. They have come back once again into these women's lives, showing a glimmer of hope in the face of one of the largest human disasters of this century. Afghan women have learned embroidery from their female family members as young girls, yet this knowledge is taken for granted and not acknowledged or recognised or spoken about by the Afghans. Farida and Homeerah spoke to us about needing to focus on embroidery to keep them sane and occupied whilst they are surrounded by a bleak political situation, which many see as a gender apartheid. Professor Karina Bennoune developed the concept of gender apartheid[13] and it is broadly defined as practices which condemn girls and women to a separate and subordinate existence, and which turn boys and men into the permanent guardians of their female relatives' chastity. Instances of gender apartheid lead not only to the social and economic disempowerment of individuals but can also result in severe physical harm for any breaches of its strict code. We wanted to explore whether working from home represents a more secure choice in these circumstances, in contrast to other workplaces where women face an increased risk of violence in conflicts and wars.[14]

Working from Home

What is appealing about home-based working, and why and how does craft become a default setting to revert to when times are tough and the landscape where one lives is both fragile and constricted? During the pandemic, many of us pivoted to use digital technology platforms to work from home. Emerging data now indicates clearly that returning to working full time from offices has proved to be slow as the Covid 19 pandemic recedes, as most people prefer to retain a degree of flexibility that working from home provides. This flexibility of work – which allows us to save commuting time, money spent travelling, multi-tasking domestic chores, having more time with family and, most importantly, being safe from the threat of illness and death that the virus brought with it, finds resonance with reasons women choose to work in craft making from home to generate incomes in conflict-affected regions.

Working at home on craft production may reduce the need to travel, independently or in company of known men/women. It certainly reduces the effort for women to be productive in remote locations with little access to transport. The Culture and Conflict project also considered the situation of women craft producers in remote locations, like the Jagti refugee camp in Jammu, located on the outskirts of a city, where public transport is unreliable and intermittent, and expensive to use on a regular basis. As extreme weather, usually intense summer heat starts appearing with regularity on most parts of South Asia with global climate shifts now visible, this has become yet another factor for choosing to work from home.

For women across the world, working on craft from home whilst simultaneously looking after the household and the family remains appealing. In some close-knit communities and cultures, the duty of care and the definition of family is not limited to immediate family and children under eighteen years of age alone. In South Asia, family includes older in-laws, unmarried siblings, children who are over eighteen and living at home, even if they are not financially dependent, siblings of parents, and other relatives who live in the same household even if they are distantly related. Such families, often called 'joint families', make up a larger household who live together and depend on each other economically. Working from home allows women to be home within this understanding of family and to look after the needs of other family members. In some of the remote regions we studied, women who live in single unit families and were also head of household had little access to childcare, and this also prevented them from leaving the confines of their homes. In most conflict areas, the number of women headed households rises for a range of reasons, primary amongst these is the fact that the combatants are primarily men.

Women craft producers interviewed in South Asia spoke about a lack of confidence about going to work in formal employment settings such as businesses, organisations or factories. Many had low literacy skills. They spoke of anxiety at the idea of travelling alone to work or to look for work, and although having no income caused them great stress, the search for jobs caused even more stress according to them, lowering their confidence further. Their dependence on public transport for travel, combined with restrictions on how far they could travel to work, affected the way these women could find employment. The lack of economic development on account of the conflict in their region, meant that there were even fewer jobs to go around. They were unable to find jobs in the formal sector because they were in competition for these jobs with potentially more qualified men. In hiring women to replace roles vacated by men because of the conflict, many employers showed little interest in supporting women working in male or mixed sex environments, or felt it would not be in their business interests given a fragile economy. Crafts therefore appeared to many of these women to be a possible safe option, a middle ground for self-employment, piecemeal work, or work in the home. These skills and practices, therefore, became default positions

　　　　　　　　　　　　　　　　De-/Anti-/Post-colonial Feminisms

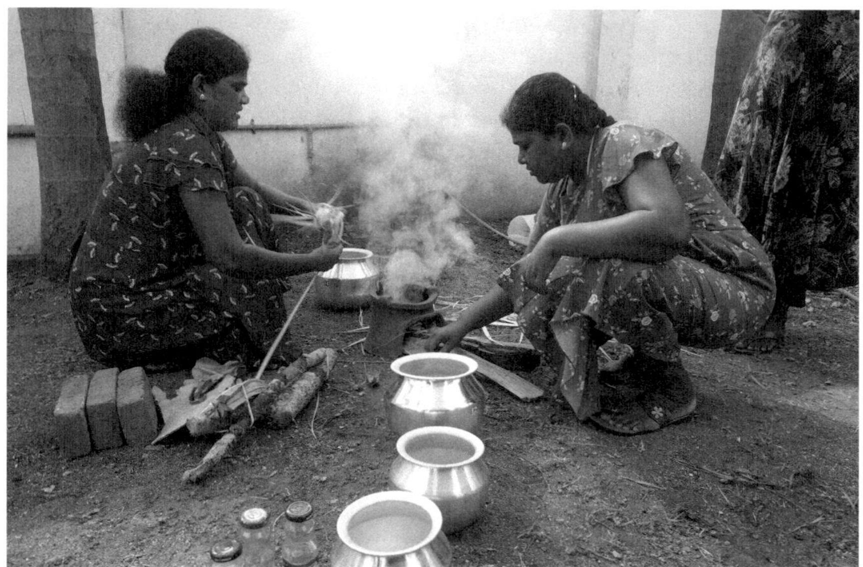

Fieldwork and training for Palmyrah craft, Vavuniya, Sri Lanka. Photo: Neelam Raina

that women return to in challenging times, as they attempt to remain resilient and survive in the face of violence and conflict.

The fluidity of employment in this sector is another reason why women chose to work in crafts. As freelance makers, they can earn a wage without being formally employed by a particular business. The crafts sector in the areas we researched showed not only the presence of the women's expertise, but also systems of trading and marketing, supply chains for raw material, presence of local businesses which continue to trade. For women, this pre-existing structure allows them to enter the sector without significant financial investments in equipment or materials of any kind.

The Landscape and Sustainability

The reason why crafts are a popular area for women seeking employment should also be seen within the context of the ready availability of raw material provided by the geography where they live, the local beauty that inspires the crafts people to create, the extreme weather which prohibits working outdoors during the harsh winters, the traditional use of craft-made goods in the everyday, the long-standing tradition and history of craft-making and related pride in these industries. This research indicates that cultural industries that include working in sectors which are linked to specific cultural identities are those valued by most communities. Textiles here play a key role, as a range of textiles – from clothing and dress, to floor coverings and tapestries – are often visible in the everyday lives of communities. Very often these practices continue to be present and part of the everyday as they are made using locally available raw materials and skills. People are often proud to wear their traditional clothing or share their heritage in forms of practices that have historical roots and a long, often undocumented, knowledge of being made and used.

Practices also follow a seasonal pattern due to the same reasons, vegetables and dyes, animals and their fleeces, harsh winters and low agricultural production/labour through changing seasons, often determine when textiles are made and out of which raw material. Communities in Pakistan for example, have indicated through our research that their relationship with the animals they rear is part of their practice; their food and their care leads to a pattern of making, a practice, that is embedded deeply within the landscapes in which they live and work.

Sustainability of the environment through raw materials, blends seamlessly into the sustainability of communities and their relationships through these practices of craft making. Very few craft practices are ever undertaken by one person alone, there is interdependency between practices for support from others in their reach. The person who spins yarns, provides materials to the weavers, who in turn depend on others to build their looms, warp their yarns, and then also dye them, embroider them and trade in them. These processes are interlinked, interdependent and connected, and this interlinking contributes to making them resilient even in times of conflict. This also leads to community ownership of the practices and a collective pride in their skills and materials.

Conclusion

There is a range of reasons for the survival of these practices within communities of South Asia. These practices have survived across generations because the transmission of these skills – orally and through an old apprenticeship system that rests within families and community groups. The transmission of these skills take place in real time, and demonstrates considerable resilience, which is not built or instigated by external actors or international development policies. In decolonial terms, we can characterise this as an indigenous resilience, a complex system of thinking, making, learning, teaching, holding, storing, memorising, and valuing cultural knowledge which is embedded within communities. Resilience is a word which is commonly heard within development narratives, as something to inspire in others, something to be built, a solution to global challenges, a key component of the sustainable development goals. Yet our research explored the existence of resilience in its locally held and often overlooked forms, surviving in communities torn apart by conflict. This

                                    De-/Anti-/Post-colonial Feminisms

resilience is locally owned and valued, even when it is neither documented or showcased by those communities. This knowledge, which appears uncoded or tacit, provides practical and viable prior solutions to many women who face multiple inequalities and inequities. In times of crisis, this knowledge, becomes a default position based in observation and consumption that they can call upon. Such practices become solutions for conflict areas like Afghanistan, they become anchors for development in post-conflict regions like Kashmir, they become a source of income, joy, learning and community healing in areas emerging from decades of war like Sri Lanka, and they become beacons of hope for communities excluded from economic development pathways for women in Pakistan.

Our ongoing research in South Asia has indicated, as one of its key findings, that women who access these practices to generate incomes and reach markets ,both in their home country and overseas, are able to change their own personal life trajectories and those of their families. Income generated through commercialisation of this work in this project allowed women to pay for tuition fees for their children, including girls. Some built permanent solid roofs for their homes. Other decided to explore self-help groups where makers come together to build small home-based businesses that trade in crafts. Incomes provide opportunities of choice to women. In conflict zones within patriarchal societies, they allow women to have a voice in their futures and provide them dignity in making an income that can shift them away from poverty and its related traps. We set out to demonstrate how we need to value these practices and see them, and their makers, as partners in development and peacebuilding. The women craft producers should be seen not as passive recipients of policy initiatives that aim to shape their futures, but as key stakeholders in policy making, in a collaborative manner. They should also be viewed as experts on resilience and community based and owned development initiatives, which can transform livelihoods and build sustainable incomes.

Notes

1. All the case studies are anonymised with name changes for safeguarding and ethical reasons.

2. Ancillary here refers to tertiary support work within the long production chain for craft making characterised by piecework with temporary pay. This is work in pre phases of production for example spinning yarn, washing and ironing finished goods.

3. D. Kyle, 'Otavala Trade Diaspora: Social capital and transnational entrepreneurship', *Ethnic and Racial Studies*, vol. 22 no. 2 (1999), pp. 421-446.

4. See P.N. Bazaz, *The History of Struggle for Freedom of Kashmir*, New Delhi: Kashmir Publishing, 1954; S. Bose, *Kashmir at the Crossroads: Inside a 21st-century Conflict*, New

Haven: Yale University Press, 2021; P.S. Jha, *The Origins of a Dispute: Kashmir, 1947*, London: Pluto, 2003; A.J. Kabir, *Territory of Desire Representing the Valley of Kashmir*, Minneapolis: University of Minnesota Press, 2009; J. Korbel, *Danger in Kashmir.* Princeton, New Jersey University Press, 1966; A. Lamb, *Kashmir: A disputed Legacy, 1846-1990*, Karachi: Oxford University Press, 2003; R. Pandita, *Our Moon has Blood Clots: A Memoir of a Lost Home in Kashmir*, Gurgaon, Haryana, India: Penguin Books, an imprint of Penguin Random House, 2022; V. Schofield, *Kashmir in Conflict: India, Pakistan and the Unending War*, London ; New York ; Oxford ; New Delhi ; Sydney: I.B. Tauris, 2021.

5. F. Ames, *The Kashmir Shawl and its Indo-French influence*, Woodbridge:Antique collectors club, 1997; P.L. Barker, *Islamic Textiles*, London: British Museum Press, 1995; J. Gillow and N. Barnard, *Traditional Indian Textiles*, London: Thames and Hudson, 1993; S. Gordon, 'Robes of honour: a "transactional" kingly ceremony,' *Indian Economic and Social History Review*, vol. 33 no. 3 (1996), pp. 225-42. M. Levi-Strauss, *The Cashmere Shawl*, London: Dryad Press, 1986; A. Mathur, *Indian shawls: Mantles of Splendour*, New Delhi: Rupa and Co, 2004; S. Rehman, and N. Jafri, *The Kashmiri Shawl, from Jamaavar to Paisley*, Ahmedabad: Mapin Publishing 2006.

6. 'Landmark resolution on women, peace and security (security council resolution 1325)' (no date) United Nations. Available at: https://www.un.org/womenwatch/osagi/wps/ [Accessed: 11 July 2023].

7. *Annual Digest of Statistics*, Department of Education, Government of Jammu and Kashmir, 2000-2001

8. E. Date-Bah, 'Women and Other Gender Concerns in Post-Conflict Reconstruction and Job Promotion Efforts' in E. Date-Bah (ed.), *Jobs After War: A Critical Challenge in the Peace and Reconstruction Puzzle*, Geneva: ILO, 2003, pp. 111–48.

9. A. Thomas and G. Wilson, 'Technological Capabilities in Textile Production in Sahrawi Refugee Camps,' *Journal of Refugee Studies*, vol. 9 no. 2 (1996), pp. 183-198.

10. K.S. Layton, 'Post Conflict Pro-Poor Private Sector Development: the Case of Timor-Leste', *The Online Journal for Peace and Conflict Resolution*, vol. 66 no. 1 (2004), pp. 241-271.

11. G. Brown, Y. Tajima and S. Hadi, *Overcoming Violent Conflict – Peace and Development Analysis in Central Sulawesi*, London, Department for International Development (DfID) Bureau for Crisis Prevention, 2005.

12. Sanjay Khajuria / TNN, 'Kathua's 'basohli painting' gets gi tag', *Jammu News - Times of India, The Times of India.* Updated: Apr 3, 2023 (no date). Available at: https://timesofindia.indiatimes.com/city/jammu/kathuas-basohli-painting-gets-gi-tag/articleshow/99219407.cms [Accessed: 11 July 2023].

13. 'Gender apartheid', (2016), United Nations Economic and Social Commission for Western Asia. Available at: https://archive.unescwa.org/gender-apartheid [Accessed: 11 July 2023].

14. E. Date-Bah, 'Women and Other Gender Concerns in Post-Conflict Reconstruction and Job Promotion Efforts', 2003. pp. 111–48.

De-/Anti-/Post-colonial Feminisms

Recognising Choice in the Practices of Making

Fatima Hussain

Empowerment is a long-established approach in postcolonial development interventions targeting women. Empowerment refers to 'the processes by which, [those] who have been denied the ability to make choices, acquire such an ability'.[1] As such, this approach is understood to help improve the ability of women to have greater agency and autonomy in their lives, expanding their freedom and capabilities,[2] participation in decision-making, and through economic gains enabling them to challenge oppressive structures[3] and achieve sustainable development outcomes.[4] Within empowerment initiatives in craft-making the focus of postcolonial development has been on a production-orientated programme, typically making an increased quantity of objects directed at local or transnational markets. The making of craft objects is often reduced and simplified within a quality-controlled production cycle, where the maker's dependence on specific markets limits their autonomy and self-determination and the craft itself is severed from the previously inseparable material entities and relationships that emerge through the interactions between people, animals and materials in their environment. The subtlety of practices embedded in complex relations between people and their livestock, land and traditions is often lost, and this is where a decolonial approach can be beneficial. My argument here illustrates how empowerment in postcolonial development, with its focus on the commercial success of women, risks imposing a single, narrow definition of choice – that of producing and selling commercially successful commodities – rather than giving priority to the actual experiences and perspectives of women while making craft, which a decolonial approach to research can reveal.

This chapter arose in relation to a gender empowerment intervention by the Culture and Conflict project, funded by the UKRI Gender Justice and Security (GJS) hub, to support female craftspeople in Upper Chitral Valley,[5] Pakistan (2019-2024), that I led as a researcher. This research project had four case sites across South Asia (see chapter by Neelam Raina): Afghanistan, Pakistan, India and Sri Lanka. The project as a whole looked at communities of women in conflict and post-conflict settings in mountainous regions to map how their practices of craft-making are embedded in their everyday lives. The project sought to explore how they use their skills, tacit knowledge, creative and culturally relevant practices as craftswomen to rebuild their lives. The project's examination of an ecology of cultural practices that might be able to enhance and uplift the value of products, contributed to these women's economic empowerment as well as their justice and security, but it also provided other insights about the question of empowerment and this has become the basis for a decolonial approach for research. While many empowerment initiatives map the production process of the practice of craft from its raw materials to the finished object, our creative participatory action research took a slightly different route in the Upper Chitral Valley. The project did offer direct technical assistance to the women involved to help make their craftworks ready for market, and linked these women into national and global markets. However, as this chapter will show, the focus on transforming craft into a commercially successful commodity proved inconsistent with the capacity of these women to make other choices about their craft production in terms of maintaining their traditions, communities and customs.

Craft-making is influenced by a variety of factors, including cultural traditions, economic opportunities and personal aspirations. The women in the Upper Chitral Valley have to negotiate complexity in balancing these factors, and the choices they make, in turn, impact their own definitions of what social and economic empowerment mean for them. The Culture and Conflict project attempted to explore how empowerment initiatives should address broader changes that go beyond individual economic gain, such as promoting 'greater economic social security or justice' for women. Most of the indigenous communities that the project worked with reside in mountainous regions. Living in harsh terrains with a difficult climate is a key part of these women's daily life experience. The project, designed to work over the course of four years, supported women in these indigenous communities by providing them with the capacities and resources required to turn around the craft they were creating for their personal use into craft

                                   De-/Anti-/Post-colonial Feminisms

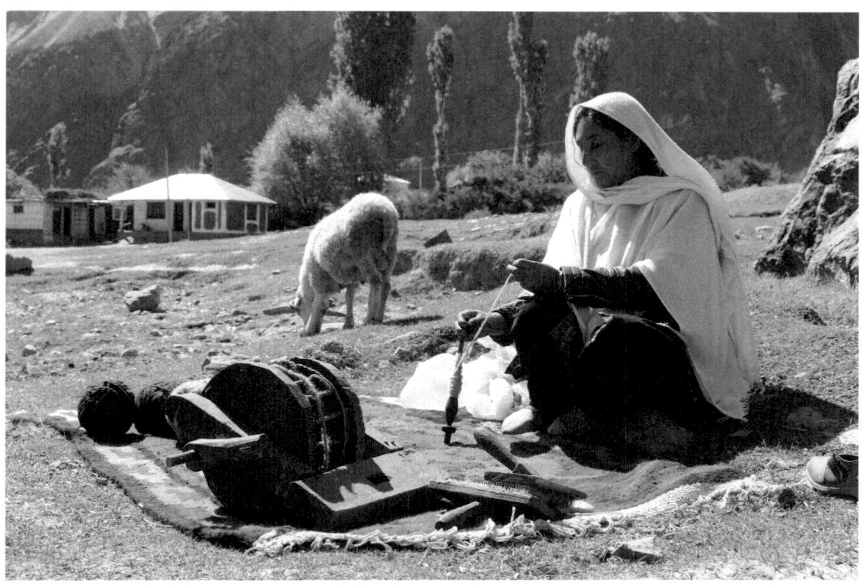

Shared Practice of Making, Laajverd, 2020. Photo: Laajverd archive, Culture and Conflict project

that could be produced and sold for economic benefit. The researchers sought to identify and use the skills, tacit knowledge, and creative and culturally relevant practices of these women and, through workshops and activities, find ways to assist them in developing economic opportunities that would enable them to rebuild their lives. The expected outcome of giving the women access to the economic opportunities offered through the project was that they would have greater agency and autonomy in their economic as well as social lives.

During the formative phase of this intervention, the project conducted field research in these communities and gathered data around the production chain of the crafts practiced in each area, the experiences of craftswomen and their lives, livelihoods and their interest in uplifting the practice for a wider market.[6] The project documented over 20 practices ranging from weaving, to needlework, spinning and woodwork from the four locations by using observational research and focus group discussions. The observational research – which consisted of live observations and photography – revealed the prevalence of the women's shared and collaborative methods of making crafts in group situations and within communities. The fieldwork, however, revealed limited descriptive information, shedding very sparse insight into why the women were

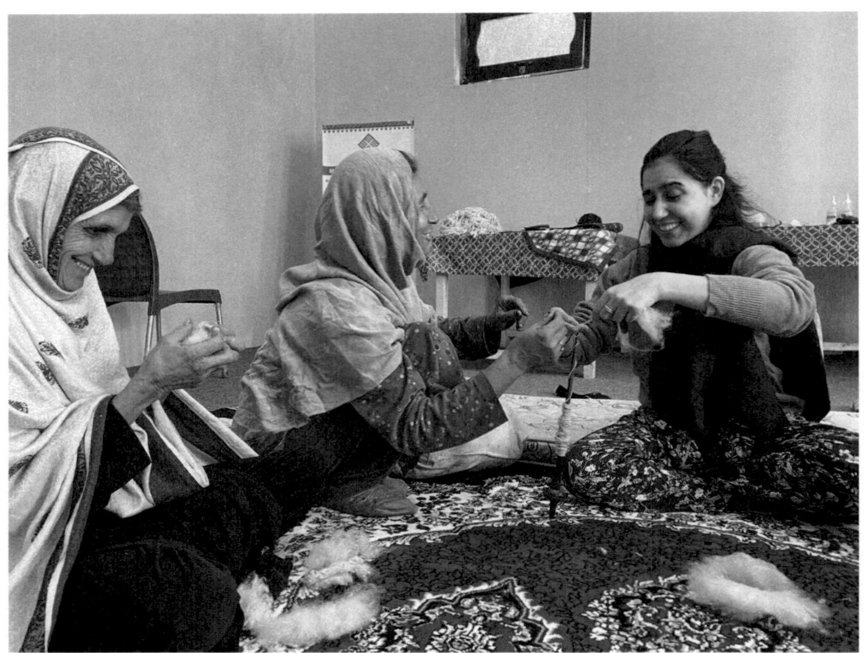

Shared Practice of Making, Laajverd, 2020. Photo: Culture and Conflict project

pursuing their specific practices of making. There was little insight as to what generated these practices in the first place. For example, during focus group discussions most of the women articulated these practices as driven by economic motivation while also claiming that there isn't a market for their products locally, and the objects made are mostly used by them in their communities.

In response to the limited information gathered from the focus groups and the insights of observational research, the project then pursued a second phase of creative participatory action research that directly emerged from the crafts that were produced through women's shared methods of making. To understand and coherently map the practice, the research tapped into the most prevalent shared method of spinning yarn and weaving carpets and paired local makers with researchers to jointly make finished craft pieces. Textile designers who were primarily based in Islamabad, and undergraduate design students from National College of Arts, Lahore and Rawalpindi, travelled to the communities as researchers and were 'paired' with a craftsperson in the field. Although the researchers were trained textile designers and were able to engage in the making of

                                        De-/Anti-/Post-colonial Feminisms

the object, they were unfamiliar with many of the methods of this region's communal practice. The materials and processes that are taken for granted in the studio spaces became alive; for example, how to care for an animal in order to get clean wool to make yarn. The communities' shared language of making also became the method for the exchange of knowledge between the researcher from the urban setting and the maker from the community. In pairs, the two would work together, actively sharing their knowledge while making the crafts. This collaborative method helped bypass some language barriers between Khowar (the local language) and Urdu and allowed for knowledge and skills to be exchanged through collaboration and participation rather than extracted by observers.

This form of indirectly peeking into the practice unearthed a plethora of nuanced knowledge that was not evident in the responses to either the focus group discussions or the observational research. Instead, it revealed a lot of key insights about the motivations behind these women's choices in making what they make, how they identify themselves during the process of making and what their understanding was of who the artist/ producer is. In the case of yarn-making, for example, the women who spin the yarn often identified themselves as "grandmothers" because there is no particular name for a person who spins the thread in the Khowar language and the woman who spins, as a participant in the craft-making process, is rarely, if ever, acknowledged for her work. Through this collaboration, the project succeeded in recognizing the importance of this activity of spinning yarn in the making of craft. This led to a shift in the researchers and maker's own perception of the yarn-maker's hand as an equal actor in the craft-making process rather than an unnoticed tool. The method of action research collaboration also allowed researchers to consider more closely the motivation to make as centred around the material of the practice, to identify the location of craft practices within daily life both in a particular place and at different times in the year, and how the craft object acquired a living essence/or values and meanings as a result of the process of making.

These collaborations changed how craft and its makers were perceived at various stages and processes, by recognising and valuing the role of each actor (the individual, their material, a process) involved in the craft-making process. We started to see craft as a living thing that has several makers within its creative process – such as the relationship between the tools, material, the land, and the hand that makes it – while also arguing for each being an actor with agency and the need to understand how all of these parts were woven together in their context.[7] The philosophy of the researchers shifted from a postcolonial to a decolonial approach where the craft object was transformed into a living entity seen within the process of its making, and this shift started to support a more holistic and nuanced understanding of the craft. Central to this shift was the recognition of the importance of spinning the yarn in making local crafts, and this hand was identified as an equal actor amongst other contributors to the craft. It is important to note that this represented a revised approach to thinking about making that was not limited to the craft object itself but extended to the perception of the craft-making process and the actors involved. The collaboration allowed for a deeper understanding of the affective aspects of craft-making which were often lost in traditional ethnographic research and could contribute to a decolonial approach.

What this approach to shared relationships in making craft did was remove the focus on the individual who is the craftsperson and place a stronger emphasis on the relationship between the actors. It brought our attention to the fact that if the craft is seen as only an economic object destined for a market, it is severed from the flows that brought it to life.

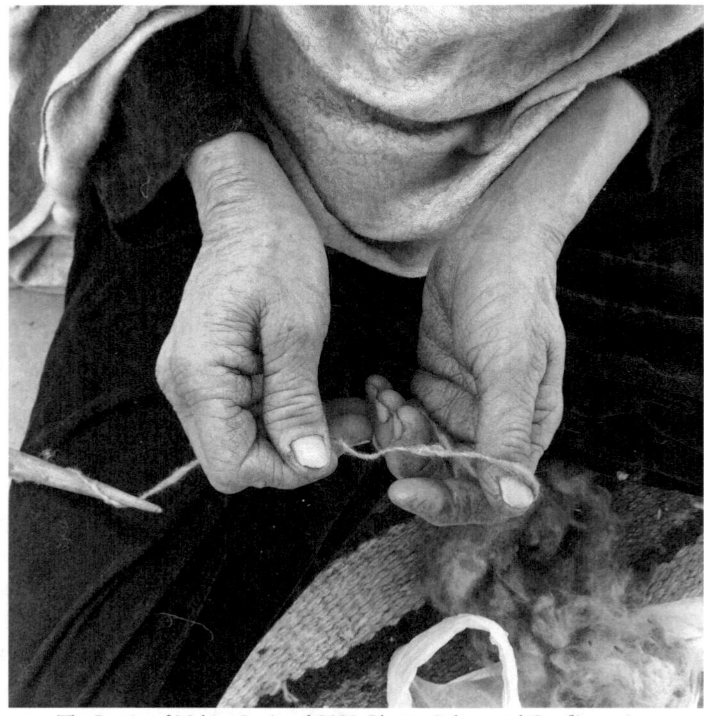

The Practice of Making, Laajverd 2020. Photo: Culture and Conflict project

                                        De-/Anti-/Post-colonial Feminisms

This mapping allowed us to see the generative capacity of the practice in which forms arise through an entanglement[8] of relationships where the emphasis is not as such on the material properties of the final product but the social, economic and life processes which determine the fluxes and flows of material.[9] This inseparability of entities suggests that these materials and relationships do not pre-exist in their interactions but rather emerge through and as a result of the 'intra-actions'[10] which involve both material and discursive dimensions. It is through these intra-actions that these entities emerge. The capacity within the practice does not lie in how well or swiftly the hand moves, but rather in the entangled intra-action between the hand and the material it interacts with. According to Karen Barad, the material not only passively receives the hand's actions but also possesses its own agency to act back, allowing it to make what it otherwise could not. In this understanding, the practice is not a one-way interaction where the hand imposes its will upon the material, but rather a dynamic and reciprocal process of entangled agency and responsiveness, where the material's properties and potentials actively participate in the generative possibilities of the practice. The hand that moves along the wooden spindle while women talk and laugh in a communal setting also has a memory of its own, learnt over generations. It is the spindle, the conversations, the temperature, etc. surrounding the hand within which it has learnt to spin and motivated it to make that becomes important in why and how these craft objects are made. The conversations, myths, and beliefs, and the unsaid demand of the yarn needed to make carpets is what surrounds the hand and wool that interact to produce the craft object.

The notion of entanglement was also significant in understanding the motivation behind making the work. Motivations were highly variable and they did include functional and economic rationales. Sometimes women stressed how making craft was useful as an activity undertaken to pass time or a tool to socialise through in communal making, but just as often they made statements about the importance of their management of natural resources. One example of this was the practice of yarn making that is used for the purposes of weaving carpets, weaving cloth for shoka (waistcoats) and making ropes. To understand how this yarn is spun, a standard approach to researching it as a production process in business or anthropology would be to map the tools and the steps that are undertaken to make the yarn which include shearing and cleaning the wool, combing the wool then spinning the thread, and then making it two-ply. In this approach, the tools and the materials become silent as the hand of the craftsperson becomes the driving agent, making the yarn and rendering it malleable and compliant. The observational notes and photos that we collected, however, can be used to tell another slightly different story about yarn production. In the photo of the hands spinning the yarn, the hands struggle to clean and soften the wool. The wool is abrasive and rebellious. It rubs against the skin of the hands and makes many shallow wounds. The hands look deft and unwavering when handling these difficulties in making the yarn. Nevertheless, it was a village elder who articulated this important nuance in our research when she said that 'the quality of the yarn depends upon how closely the animal is cared for.' This comment returns us to the importance of local farming/agriculture and the importance of animal care in the community for the craft-making process.

How Social Research Can Read Practices of Making

Craft-making exemplifies the diverse expressions and practices safeguarded under UNESCO's Convention for the Safeguarding of the Intangible Cultural Heritage, which encompasses traditional techniques, skills and knowledge passed down through generations. In this context, the process of making can be seen as more than just a physical act; it is a transformative endeavour that generates its own knowledge, shapes environments, gives form to thoughts, motivation, time, perception, and weaves together the various textures of material that are both tangible and intangible. Within the context of the craftsperson in these mountainous communities, it became imperative to look at their lives in this particular landscape, and what it meant to be within and with it in order to understand where making 'begins' and how practices unfold. When one charts the process of making, the journey from raw material to the object is not straightforward and neither can one craftsperson claim to be the single author of the work. There are many actors and materials that have an equal (if not more) stake in the process of making. This requires an investigation into the process of caring for, feeding and taking care of the livestock during the harsh seasons, and how their time in the pastures gives particular qualities to the wool. Therefore, the process of making precedes the shearing of the wool and now includes the relationship of the livestock with the people, the pastoral landscape, the seasonal lives of the people, how the animal is cared for, as well as the myths and beliefs surrounding these practices of rearing and shearing and finally spinning the yarn.

Rather than reading backwards from a finished object to the process, where one is essentially looking at the object as an outcome of raw material coming together or as an economic project which might counter the destitution left by the violence and conflict in the region, what is significant is that practice continues as an ongoing generative movement in which multiple agents are continually coming together with a variety of motivations. As part of the universe in which the practice is made, the object becomes not a final outcome but one of the many possibilities and perhaps a culmination of various forces. This coming together of various forces can be understood through the way the material contributes its properties, constraints and affordances that in turn influence the direction and possibilities of practice. Embodied knowledge plays a crucial role in handling, shaping and transforming the materials often to preserve identities, generate income, preserve heritage or natural resources. Such collective roles and interactions within the community contribute to the ongoing generative movement of practice.

For the researcher, it is important to unpack what can be understood by 'making' and 'practice' and what it means to create things in such an environment. How can the researcher unpack the way material is understood, seen and used? Who holds the agency within this process of making where forms arise? As our experiences with the focus group discussions showed, conventional methods could not capture what was happening in the practices of making. This methodological limitation made it 'important to reflect on the possibility that "unspeakable" elements may be the most significant aspects of the research subjects or the researchers' accounts of themselves.'[11] We determined that one way for ourselves and future social researchers to reflect these elements would be to consider further non-representational approaches to body-landscape relations. These approaches challenge traditional representational ways of understanding the relationship between the body and the landscape. These emphasise the sensory and affective experiences of the body in relation to the environment, rather than focusing on representational meanings and symbols in craft objects. These approaches consider bodies and landscapes as co-constitutive and interconnected, rather than as separate entities. Examples of non-representational approaches include embodied geography, affect theory and ecological psychology. These may help recognise that people – in this case craftswomen – 'are not simply rational actors in an inert landscape, but rather we are always in the process of formation with the landscape.'[12]

Let us imagine removing the environment and making a straight line between the wool and the yarn and by extending this line to introduce this object (yarn) to the market. Within this, many factors determine the material and none of these are immediately visible within the object/craft in the foreign/global market. What is most frequently discussed instead is

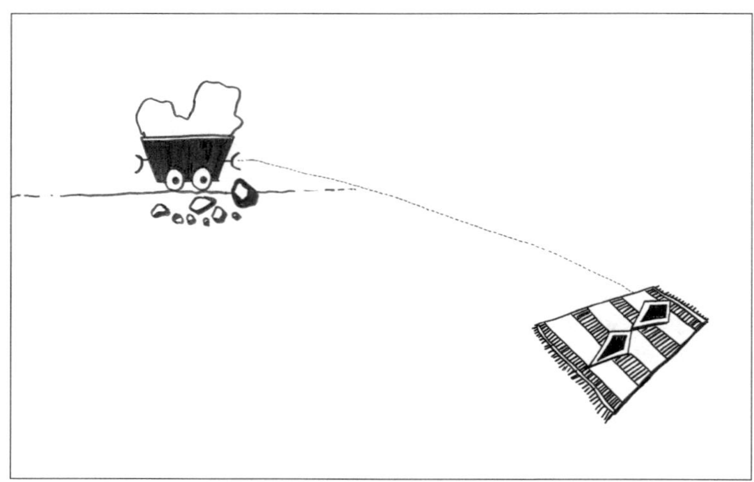

Fatima Hussain *Straight Line* (2022) drawing, marker on paper

how the hand produces in terms of tangible contributors and the time taken to make the object. Scaling up of these crafts to participate in the capitalist market often requires standardising processes (following factory models) with attention given to limited materials, palette, designs and the time taken to make it. This is because mass production requires standardisation and consistency in order to efficiently produce large quantities of goods. Such a method eliminates the many choices that the women may have in the making of the craft and poses the risk that the unique qualities and variations inherent in traditional practices of arriving at the craft may be lost. Mass production methods are in direct contrast to approaches used in traditional practices, where multiple factors and tacit motivations drive the making of the craft and may include variations in design, materials and techniques, even across the same type of object or craft process used in an object. These include factors such as temperature, motivation, time, folklore and the conversations that compelled the hand to make the object in the way that it was made.

Many empowerment initiatives do not consider the cultural significance of the craft practices and often encourage women to make changes to their crafts in order to appeal to foreign markets or tourism. This leads to the loss of traditional knowledge and practices, and the erosion of cultural heritage. In many cases, such projects create dependency on aid and discourage the development of self-sustaining business models and community-based enterprise. For example, in Pakistan, traditional

De-/Anti-/Post-colonial Feminisms

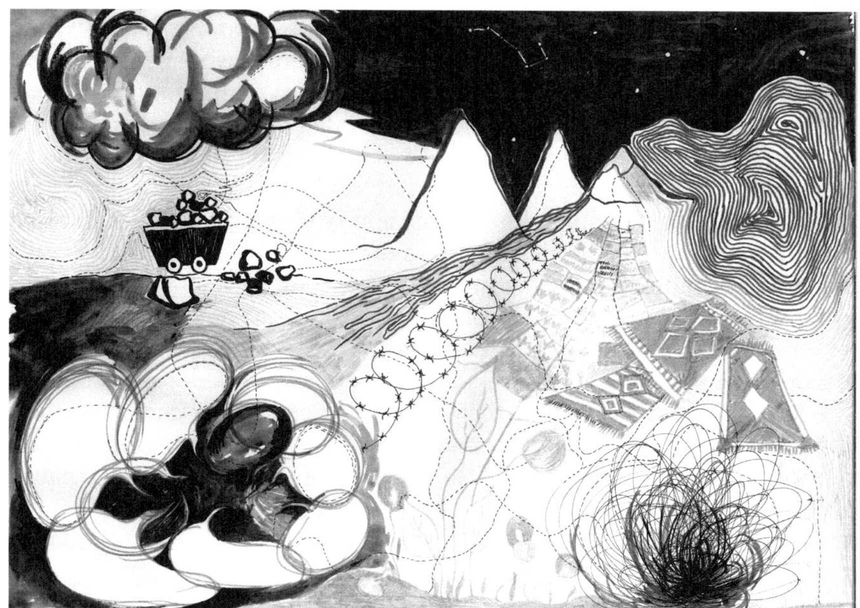

Fatima Hussain *The Web* (2022) drawing, marker and ink on paper

embroidery practices among women in rural areas have been declining due to the increased availability of mass-produced machine-made textiles. Many projects are initiated with the aim of offering short-term solutions to generate larger markets or more craft objects, and this is how they misunderstand empowerment as the capability of women to earn only for themselves by entering foreign markets. In many cases, one sees the craft being uplifted for immediate economic gain in sales of products, resulting in a completely altered craft that is being produced *en masse* for the consumption of a market that is completely alien to the maker.

The numerous conversations during the creative participatory action research revealed that women possessed their own ideas and definitions of 'empowerment' that were extremely different – almost unexpected – to that of empowerment as economic gain. The conventional understanding of empowerment initiatives in fragile and conflict-prone geographies, much like in the case of the project's work in Upper Chitral Valley, was that "gender equality" and "financial security" were important outcomes that could be achieved by helping women sustainably achieve an "economic gain" of some sort. Most of the craftswomen, however, articulated that being empowered meant someone who could "multitask". Consistent with what was highlighted above, this capacity to multi-task was situated within relationships. The women described an "empowered" woman as someone who had everything under control and was able to manage multiple roles with ease, such as being a mother, a wife, a daughter and a daughter-in-law, while also indulging in the practice of making a craft. For them, being empowered meant being rooted in one's community, able to speak the local language, use the tacit knowledge and work with local symbols and meanings with ease, and provide items for local consumption. The crafts made by the women were mostly seen as important if they were being used in their homes, and when they were made as gifts to be given away or to be kept as dowry for their children. This is what "wealth" meant and it was loaded with symbolic meaning and the importance of local exchanges. The profound connection between empowerment, community, and local exchanges highlights a richness that extends far beyond material wealth, challenging popular preconceived notions and revealing alternative dimensions of empowerment in this context.

Conclusion

One way to look at women's craft practices is to see it from a gendered perspective in which women's lack of access to power and the fact that they are discriminated against in terms of opportunities to work in the waged labour market are regarded as key. Commonly, empowerment initiatives focus on linking crafts to the market by creating inclusive and enabling environments where craftswomen access resources, gain decision-making power and challenge traditional gender roles. Engaging in economic empowerment initiatives are therefore seen as a successful outcome to change power relations, and it is believed that by uplifting the craft for economic purposes, the maker can transcend their geographical boundaries and participate in internationally-exchanged capitalist marketplaces. However, what this process most often does is introduce the craftsperson to a market, which can perpetuate discriminatory practices that were unfamiliar to them before, such as labour and skill not being adequately compensated, economic downturns and reinforcing existing power imbalances. This form of empowerment economically can generate an unexpected cost: the divorce of the product from its place in the midst of multiple factors and relations which had initially determined why the craft object was made in the first place. By overlooking these values, the local community and the ecosystem of the practice is disempowered. The commodification of the craft object alters the practice in a way that results in the loss of cultural significance and meaning of the craft as it reduces

                          De-/Anti-/Post-colonial Feminisms

craft objects to a product for sale and consumption in the global market. So, the single efficient line in this view of postcolonial approaches to empowerment emphasizes the link between raw material and production of marketable objects reducing and controlling the choices that these makers can exercise in the making of the craft. It leads to the erosion of the community's ability to preserve and pass down these practices by disrupting traditional systems of knowledge production and preservation.

On the other hand, if these practices are seen as ones based on full epistemologies that both shape and determine the maker, then this in many ways decolonises the way research – like the Culture and Conflict project itself - is done and understood. This opens up multiple ways in which empowerment can be seen and understood in terms of local perceptions and value systems. By situating craft within its landscape, both natural and social, one can start to study the traditional epistemologies such as tacit knowledge, transference of this knowledge between generations, different approaches to natural resource management, etc.. What then becomes evident is that ability of the hand to shape and reshape their environment is enhanced at the behest of a plethora of materials and processes involving time/commitment on the maker's part as opposed to a few tangible economic gains. This holistic perspective can address the ways in which most of the crafts are produced.

Let us again imagine the environment in which the making of these crafts is practised. We see that the practice occurs over seasons, where the livestock is reared, taken to the pastures in the summer, tended for in the warmth of the homes during winter and sheared in the spring. During this time, a special bond is developed with the animal. The wool that is sheared is used up by the older women of the household in cleaning and then spinning the yarn. Spinning is a communal activity, women sit together and talk, laugh, share stories while the hand moves deftly and spins. Children watch their grandmothers spin, often sitting and helping them as they tell stories. The children grow up having learnt how yarn is spun. In this environment, the entangled web of material comes together to make the thread. This web of material (See Fatima Hussain, *The web*, drawing, 2022) offers choice to women that they exercise while making the yarn. It is within this universe of the practice that the hand is in sync with the various actors around them. The web of entanglements, however, retains and expresses the choices women exercise in the practice of making craft. This heightened ability to make choices exists because of the plethora of material, and attention to the inter-actions of actors that shape and define the object being made; it also provides a respectful and decolonial approach to research.

Notes

1. N. Kabeer, 'Gender Equality and Women's Empowerment: A Critical Analysis of the Third Millennium Development Goal', *Gender and Development*, vol. 13 no. 1 (March 2005), 'Millennium Development Goals', pp. 13-24.

2. A. Sen, *Development as Freedom*, Oxford University Press, 1999.

3. J.H. Momsen 'Women and Development: A Dualistic Standpoint' *Economic Geography*, vol. 67 no 1, (1991) pp. 1-18. J. Gaventa, *Power and Powerlessness: Quiescence and Rebellion in an Appalachian Valley*, University of Illinois Press, 1980.

4. N. Kabeer, 'Resources, Agency, Achievements: Reflections on the Measurement of Women's Empowerment', *Development and Change*, vol. 30 no. 3 (1999), pp. 435-464. M. Friedman, *Free to Choose: A Personal Statement*, New York: Harcourt Brace Jovanovich, 1973.

5. Laspur is an administrative unit, known as Union Council, of Chitral District in the Khyber Pakhtunkhwa province of Pakistan, it includes 8 villages (Gasht, Shahi-Dass, Raman, Herchin, Brok, Phort, Balim and Sore-Laspur). The remoteness of the Laspur is due to a historical political conflict where the people of the Kingdom of Chitral revolted against the 'Mehtar' and took shelter in Laspur. For decades following this revolt, the valley was cut off from basic facilities, where ideas and cultures were formed in isolation with impressions from travellers of Central Asia.

6. The research was also able to see how the COVID-19 lockdowns impacted the women's craft-making both in terms of practice and market.

7. T. Ingold, 'Bringing Things to Life: Creative Entanglements in a World of Materials', ESRC National Centre for Research Methods' *NCRM Working Paper Series*, University of Manchester (5 October 2010).

8. Ibid: 'Thus, when we speak of the entanglement of things, it means this literally and precisely: not a network of connections but a meshwork of interwoven lines of growth and movement'.

9. G. Deleuze and F. Guattari, *A Thousand Plateaus*, London: Athlone Press, 1988.

10. K. Barad, *Meeting the Universe Halfway: Quantum Physics and the Entanglement of Matter*, Durham: Duke University Press, 2007.

11. D. Haraway, 'Situated Knowledges: The Science Question in Feminism and the Privilege of Partial Perspective', *Feminist Studies*, vol. 14 no. 3 (Autumn 1988), pp. 575-599.

12. H. MacPherson, 'Non-representational Approaches To Body-landscape Relations', *Geography Compass*, vol 4 no. 1 (2010), pp.1-13.

     De-/Anti-/Post-colonial Feminisms

A Particular Reality (APR):
Developing a Nuanced Pedagogical Methodology within Practice-Based Higher Education Courses

Michelle Williams Gamaker

This chapter, co-written with colleagues, aims to show the breadth of A Particular Reality's (APR) activities (2018-2023) and different facets of APR's decolonial and anti-hierarchical pedagogical developments in Art, Learning and Anti-Racism within the context of Fine Art, creative, practice-based Higher Education (HE) courses. Joanne Addison (Kingston University) and I (Goldsmiths University) co-founded APR[1] to support Black, Indigenous, People of Color (BIPoC) students to develop peer networks and diminish social isolation during their Fine Art degrees. APR has become a cross-institutional, educational collective where co-learning is paramount. It has been likened to an 'after-school club'; a reaction to the institution, but also one that exists in relation to it addressing both art and anti-racism, within and beyond fine art's models of practice-based learning. Here, I have brought together reflections on the multiple pedagogical approaches of the many contributors who are making this work possible, while drawing attention to the collective, intergenerational, layered and horizontal approach to learning that APR embodies.[2] Interspersed throughout this document are quotes from the film, *A Particular Reality: Art, Learning, Anti-racism.*[3]

In the past two years of work, APR has carried out 71 (and counting) events with over 750 students engaging in our extra-curricular programming, including artists talks, student-led workshops, gallery visits, in-conversation events, symposia and a Summer School: *Art School Backwards*, centred around practical exploration of anti-racism. APR is a resident at Goldsmiths CCA since 2021, offering an invaluable "Third Space" to carry out our work. We have

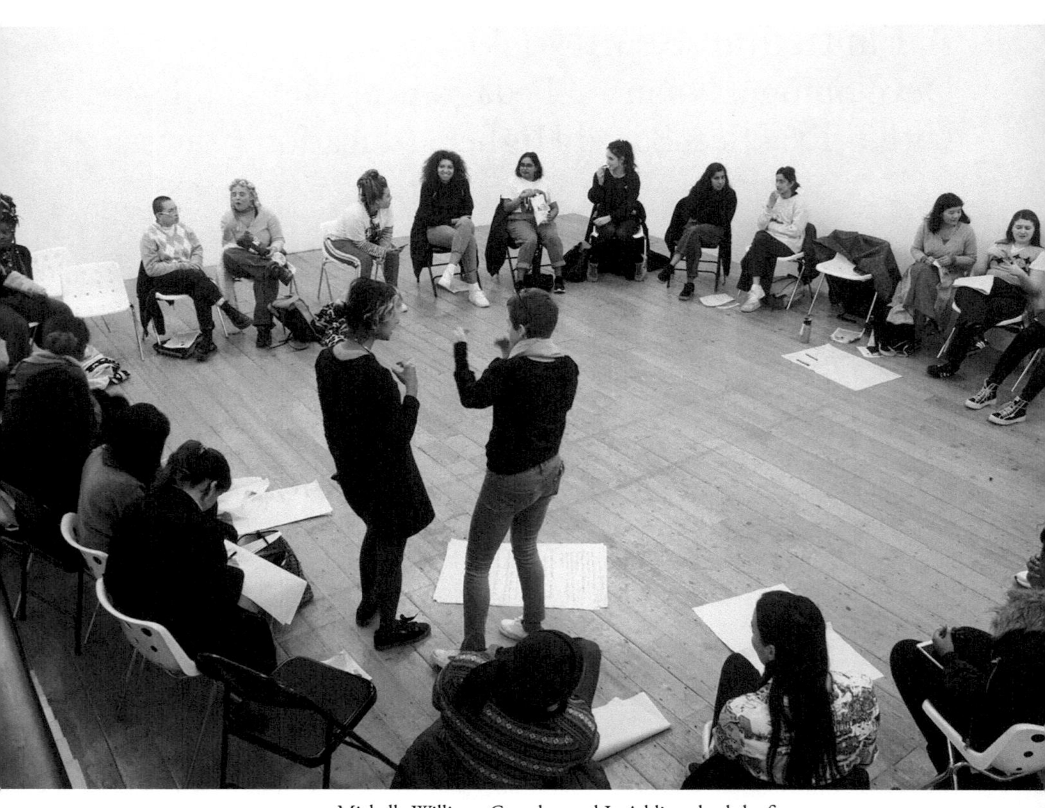

Michelle Williams Gamaker and Jo Addison lead the first
A Particular Reality: session 1: *Pairing*, Raven Row, February 2019

De-/Anti-/Post-colonial Feminisms

worked with organisations including South London Gallery, Autograph Gallery, UAL: Camberwell, Carlos Ishikawa, Gasworks, Bloc Projects, Thomas Tallis School and Kettle's Yard. APR has also collaborated with many artists including Kobby Adi, Simeon Barclay, Clémentine Bedos, Sutapa Biswas, Harold Offeh, Hetain Patel, Raju Rage and Olivia Sterling in addition to APR's facilitators who share their practice and experience of being artists with students.

As with many organisations, the Covid-19 pandemic impacted our capacity to meet, but with thanks to the dedicated support of a small number of APR alumni, a zine (distributed online) was produced that enabled us to share our project with students and colleagues.[4] Since 2021, the project has also been established at Manchester Metropolitan University, building on *The Intersectional Hydra*[5] project. In November 2022, Middlesex University's Fine Art department joined the APR network, reconnecting the history and intergenerational experience of past and present staff – including Jean Fisher, Lola Young, Sonia Boyce and Keith Piper – with the present ways these histories are felt in the needs of students, staff and recent alumni (including myself), whose call for an anti-racist and anti-colonial approach to art education remains critical.

APR continues to evolve with new voices that contribute and shape our programme; an important aspect of this project is its capacity to co-exist through artists, thinkers and pedagogues, who can share the scale of the collective work. This capacity to respond flexibly to the needs of our students, to effectively pass the baton on, between staff and graduates, through an intergenerational approach is an invaluable process in our work. Two APR Programme Leads, Ali Eisa (Goldsmiths) and Abhaya Rajani (Kingston) are now responsible for key programming, with additional curriculum development support from Francesca Telling, Laiba Raja and Clémentine Bedos (Goldsmiths), Alice Gale-Feeny and JJ Chan (Kingston), Sarah Howe (Manchester Metropolitan) and Alberto Duman (Middlesex).[6] APR is also supported by its alumni: Amrit Sanghera, Tara White, Elly Lukoszevieze and Shivani Patel have all initiated, led and facilitated projects. Having co-founded APR in 2018, Jo Addison[7] and I have recently moved to a more advisory role aiming to develop strategies for APR's continuation into the future.

Since 2018, the project has encouraged a reflexive stance, in which we question what our collectivity means for those who participate and for the structures we work within. In essence, APR invites its participants to come together to talk, think and make. Through this simultaneously enquiring, reflective and active approach, we discuss shared problems faced and we attempt to identify and articulate (through verbal and non-verbal modes of expression) what matters most to the group in terms of learning. Here, speculative and concrete content is proposed for a more inclusive curriculum, to match not only our participants, but more broadly for the culturally diverse students who are studying within Arts HE today, taking forward the shapeshifting qualities of APR's pedagogic methodology.

> We acknowledge that we exist alongside a history of decolonising movements in art practice and education, that we are constantly responding to and working in coalition with. We consider how futures are envisioned in ways that are inclusive, and through which students from many backgrounds can find inspiring role-models for their work.[3]

We continuously return to the concern of what questions we should and need to ask (and of whom) of the models of education we find ourselves working and studying within. We also think through what needs to happen to make our questions be answered. These structurally complex questions are too great in scope to be answered by any individual alone, but we propose that through encouraging collective frameworks, students might develop a more transparent understanding of their learning. From a distance, one might argue that HE courses in their very rationale already offer many multiple group and communal learning moments, but increasingly students who attend APR events tell us that they feel isolated in their learning.

Beginning Again: A Cyclical Landscape

In 2018, when Jo and I began APR, we were inspired by words spoken in 1986 by artist Gavin Jantjes:

A Black visual art is an innovative expression of a particular reality— a reality set in the framework of specific cultural and historic forces. These are: cultural domination by Western Eurocentrism and marginality to it; the experience of exploitation, appropriation, slavery, inequality, and racism; and the long and abominable history of colonialism. A Black art emerges from this framework and is vitalised by these forces.[8]

The question of intersectional identities and their expression will always be a particular reality,[9] and one that presents daily personal challenges to those who are also processing what it means to be marginalised within the white majority of a Fine Art course and beyond. My own marginality as one of the few tutors of colour in the institutions where I have worked has amplified the burden of trying to hold the concerns of my students of colour, who expressed a real desire to speak to their lived-experiences and to address the gaps in the curriculum that failed to respond to the questions of identity that had been arguably bypassed and overlooked in favour of a dated curriculum.[10]

   De-/Anti-/Post-colonial Feminisms

From our working knowledge of the Goldsmiths and Kingston departments of Fine Art, we mutually recognised that within our respective institutions, core teaching delivery failed to genuinely support or engage with our students of colour. These two HE institutions are not unique in this respect. We felt that, if left unchecked, the isolation that many of our students were speaking about was likely to increase, if the potential communities that could strengthen their practice remain atomised. As tutors we felt that more conversations were needed about experiences that often get overlooked because it takes hard work to find the words to talk about race, which intersects with sexism, class, ableism, gender and sexuality. What seemed worse was not talking at all.

As a contributor to our 2020 Zine wrote:-

APR broadcast our reality of being a POC in a white institute, a white building with white walls and majority white staff and students. Culture, Race, Heritage, Nationality. These are words that are overlooked. After two and a half years of plodding along, making art just for the sake of making, just to get a degree, along came A Particular Reality. A collaboration run by two very brave staff members of Kingston and Goldsmiths that allowed us to network with many POCs and for the first time we were not alone. We were many students going through the same struggle, the struggle of not being completely understood, not fitting in and of being tokenised.[11]

And another summed up what this meant for them:-

A Particular Reality provided us with the platform and support to investigate our own realities and identity and have the courage to make artwork that we are proud of, to make work for ourselves, without worry about how it might be perceived by our white community. It made us see our voices are important. Now that these conversations have begun to be discussed we can only hope that this is a start. A discourse that occurred 2 and a half years too late for us must ripple through all institutions and take place instantly for new students everywhere.[12]

These individuals, comprising UK and international students, formed an integral part of the student cohort, and yet described their experiences of encountering the course from the periphery. Their feedback reiterated that they could not find ways to meaningfully connect their nuanced, cultural perspectives in various teaching contexts: personal tutorials, group tutorials and more informally amongst their peer network. Where students and staff were able to talk at length about the work of white students in group crits, they often they came unstuck when approaching work based on different cultural perspectives, or rooted in the lived experiences of the maker through aesthetic and conceptual means. This sensation of being 'tokenised' within the course exacerbated disengagement and often left students feeling conflicted, ultimately impacting their confidence levels. Our students expressed a need for genuine recognition and parity. BIPoC students often felt instrumentalised in learning exchanges, and international students on higher fees acquired the uneasy realisation that they embodied "cash cows" to bolster university finances.

APR also sought to implement alternatives to the colonial narratives that underpin our curriculum. Within the arts and cultural sector, it is widely acknowledged that colonial narratives have skewed our understanding of the history of Art, which cannot be separated from the hierarchised value we place on certain forms of practice (and by inference certain practitioners) and how it is taught. Since 2020, sparked by the renewed focus on Black Lives Matter, multiple institutions have scrambled to be on the right side of history, with arguably performative, but well-meaning gestures to address the manifold issues of inequality within the cultural sector. Lack of diversity present within staffing, curation of artists of colour, dated programming and glaring omissions within national collections are just some of the areas in need of significant reappraisal.[14] As artist Harold Offeh suggests, 'The university is sorely intellectually impoverished without diversity'.[15]

While development of a sustainable framework within cultural institutions for this work is ongoing, with positive developments for more meaningful and robust strategies to address the representation of artists of colour, the fact remains that there is a very real possibility of invisibility and erasure of the labour of these artists; a depressing reality of the UK arts landscape.[16] Art departments are still populated by a majority of white academics (Goldsmiths, Kingston, Manchester Metropolitan and Middlesex Fine Art Programmes are no exception) and students of colour continue to struggle to find their lived experiences and creative aspirations reflected in the individuals who teach them.

The broader implications for creating alternative learning spaces are becoming clearer as Ali Eisa, explains: Specific concerns with how race and different cultural perspectives are represented in white-centered curriculums,

De-/Anti-/Post-colonial Feminisms

have opened out to broader questions of accessibility and rights to art education for neurodiverse, disabled and working-class people who identify as white, but are similarly marginalised and minoritised within current modes of art education. This extends to include APR facilitators who identify as white, developing a crucial role APR plays in building forms of allyship and coalition in the wider collective approach to anti-racism and decolonial work within the arts and HE sectors.

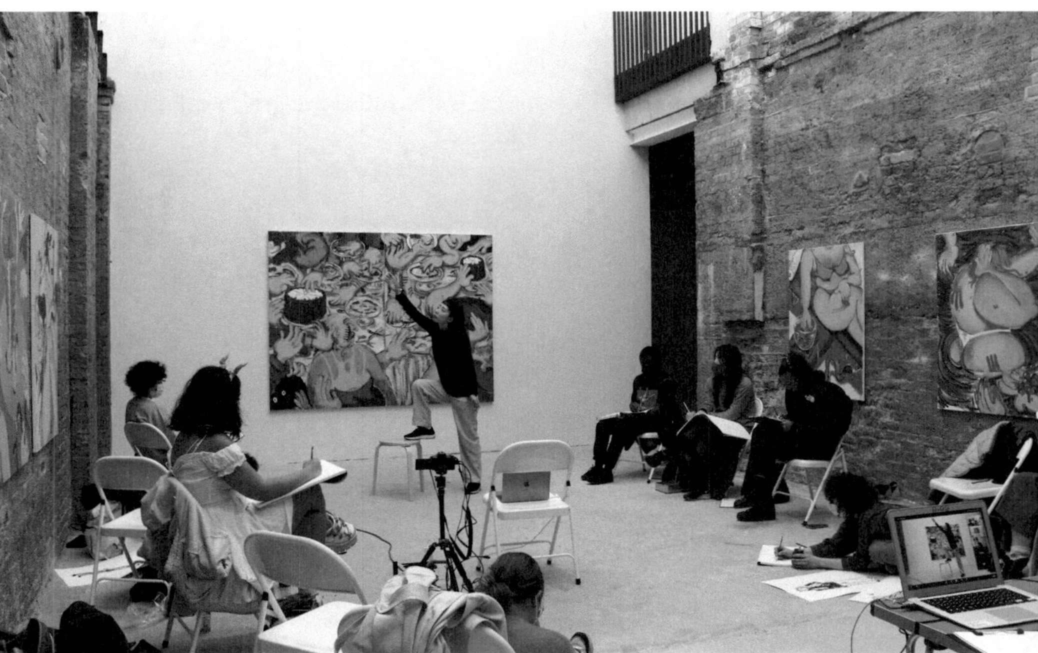

A life model poses for Olivia Sterling's Life Drawing Workshop within her solo exhibition
Really Rough Scrubbing Brush (Goldsmiths CCA, November 2021)[17]

Examining the Legacies of Colonialism – co-written with Abhaya Rajani
On 7 September 2022, APR collaborated with Bloc Projects, Sheffield as part of the *Harsh Light* series to establish an intergenerational enquiry on caste discrimination as a means to articulate the lived-realities of colonialism. APR members, Abhaya Rajani, Aaliah Qureshi and Shivani Patel, connected by their early-career pursuits in contemporary art as well as their South Asian heritage, participated in this collective discussion and communicated their experiences of casteism and how their art practice was formed in relation to this. This session opened with a collective reading of 'Annihilation of Caste' by Dr B. R. Ambedkar (1936), the historical anti-caste, undelivered speech investigating caste as 'a

graded hierarchy'. The key question APR raised was: What responsibilities do we have as young, diaspora artists to establish anti-caste discourse along with anti-racist values within and beyond contemporary art?

As Abhaya Rajani elaborates: This question has led to the continued collaboration between APR artists and Bloc Projects as they develop a research project called *Touching on Caste: South Asian diaspora and Caste (In)Tangibility* which will take place in January 2024. The artists started a dialogue about the caste system in an APR session, where for the first time ever, they felt safe to share their experiences of casteism with fellow South Asian practitioners. Discovering intersectional, marginalised realities within A Particular Reality and creating space for nuanced conversations is APR's strength to collectively navigate resistance for all oppressive injustices.

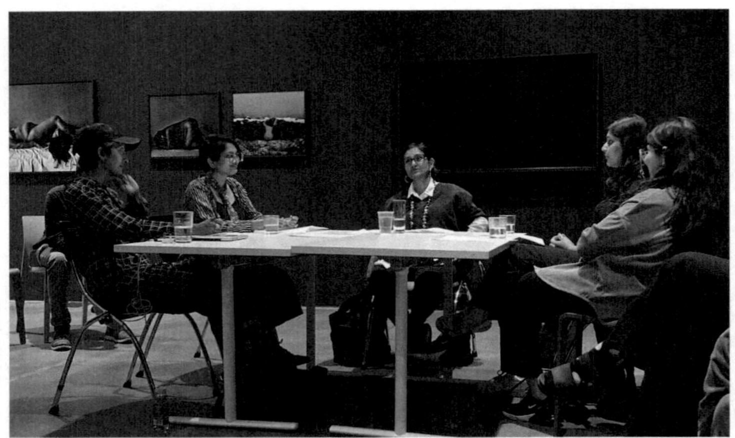

Michelle Williams Gamaker, Abhaya Rajani, Sutapa Biswas, Simran Kaur Bahara and Laiba Raja,
roundtable at Autograph, May 2022

The project continued in other visits and discussions. In January 2022, Francesca Telling took APR Goldsmiths and Kingston students to visit Kettle's Yard, Cambridge, to see Sutapa Biswas's exhibition *Lumen*. This visit was followed up in May 2022 with a visit to Autograph Gallery, London for the touring leg of her exhibition. APR Students watched one of Sutapa Biswas' films, followed by a fascinating intergenerational round table with the artist joined by APR facilitator Abhaya Rajani and APR students Simran Kaur Bahara and Laiba Raja (both of whom were researching her for their dissertations) and chaired by Michelle Williams Gamaker. The topics of discussion included the concept of making, Sutapa's practice around feminism and questioning the Eurocentric attitude towards Art and artists through her legendary work *Housewives With Steak-Knives* (1985), *Synapse II* (1987-92) and *Lumen* (2021). The conversation was shaped further by

                                           De-/Anti-/Post-colonial Feminisms

dialogue about breaking the stigma around the female body in patriarchal societies, the horrors of colonialism, practicing anti-racism in education institutions and complex ideas of racism penetrating through casteism. As a vital contributor to the Black Arts Movement in Britain and through her active engagement with art history, our students were able to see how visual disruption in Sutapa's work continues to challenge and reimagine our present time.[18]

The success of this roundtable encouraged us to continue to invite our students to present their artistic research, which developed into *Out of View*, our second APR Symposium in November 2022. This event provided a platform for Warsha Ahmed, Lucy Carter and Judith Gao (3rd Year Kingston Fine Art students and alumni, respectively) to present their current research at Kingston to students across APR's network. The conversation started with a grounding exercise led by APR facilitator Sarah Howe, and developed alongside Abhaya Rajani and Alice Gale-Feeny, each speaker then presented on the peripheral and its interpretation through their practice and research. Lucy explored the notion of redefining the definitions of known words to make them accessible, arguing that Google definitions can take away subjective meanings.[19] Judith analysed their relationship with beauty standards, unrealistic expectations to inhabit the body in certain ways in order to feel accepted by others and how they bring this personal experience into art practice which they initiate through painting personal objects. Warsha deconstructed the pressure which BIPoC feel to talk about their experience of discrimination through compassionately crafted poetry. The students observed how institutions can create a toxic environment where white people heavily rely on the trauma of BIPoC to enlighten themselves.[20] This can normalise the assumption that BIPoC have a greater responsibility to dismantle discrimination through an urgency to create a genuine dialogue. All three students discussed the necessity to create dialogues with others which encourage more active listening and non-judgemental sharing.

Cross-Cultural Making and Learning – co-written with Francesca Telling
Central to APR's pedagogy is its commitment to supporting the practices of students from the East and Southeast Asian diaspora, through fostering creative and collaborative expressions and building new bonds and allyship across peer networks. In 2021, APR collaborated with East Asian Women Artist Community (EAWAC)[21] inviting the group to facilitate a series of sessions in our Goldsmiths CCA residency space, open to anyone who identifies as from East and Southeast Asian diasporas at Goldsmiths University and Kingston School of Art.

As Francesca Telling explains: Beginning first with meetings for women and non-binary people, and later extending to all genders; EAWAC brought together a range of diasporic experiences, including but not limited to

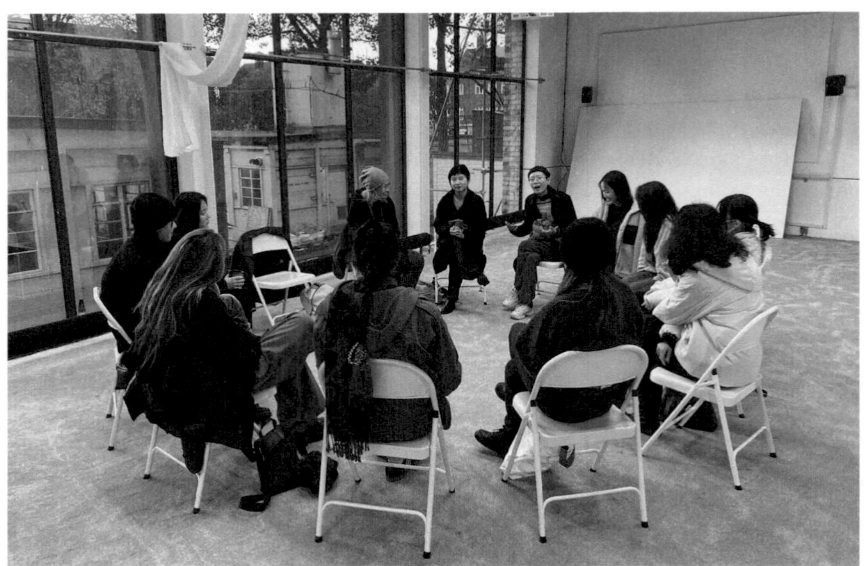

APR x EAWAC Meeting, Goldsmiths CCA, November 2021

international students, first and second generation British-born, heritages across East and Southeast Asia and mixed-heritage individuals. Where the presence of the ESEA diaspora in universities is predominantly made up by those on Tier 4 Visas - the meetings acknowledged vast differences among participants in precarity of educational and living conditions, migratory histories, understandings of politics and activism and experiences of race, language and culture. The specificity of colonial experiences within the ESEA diaspora was highlighted, recognizing that colonial and imperial relationships extend from both Euro-western power, and from within the ethno-cultural region itself. Amid this complexity, in coming together to share space and practices the importance of sharing food was highlighted as a unifying cultural experience; and friendships formed which defy the divisive fee structures and hostile conditions constructed by universities between home and international students. Overall, the sessions opened space to discuss the intersectional experiences of gender, race and nationality; and form connections through events ranging from meditation workshops, film screenings, potluck dinners and lunar new year celebrations.

These sessions enabled further cross-cultural curations to showcase the work of East and Southeast Asian students, including an *Out of Body* sound bar and meditation workshop led by Mi Zhang (Goldsmiths BA Fine Art, 3rd year) a British-Chinese student who wanted to explore 'Sound healing through

                                    De-/Anti-/Post-colonial Feminisms

the cleansing power of white crystal, all attentions on body, mind and soul.' In another, a film screening of *River is my Hometown* and subsequent conversation, artist River Cao shared research around the rebuilding of the Chinese landscape and the return of the revenants. She uses mourning as a method to create a series of self-narrative spaces to rethink the emotion of grief. Our *Take Up Space* sessions[22] enabled Korean student Siin Lee (Goldsmiths BA Fine Art, 3rd year) to develop the *Seeking Different Forms of Languages* movement-based workshop in which the residency space created a 'relaxing exploration to compose dialogues with body movements and random/non-random verbal sentences.' From this Siin developed *Receivers*, a collaborative performance work with performers Gigi Seetoo, Amber Harrison, Esio Richards and Iris Xu. *Receivers* was a journey to seek other forms of languages and communication that take place on individual and collective levels with performers responding to what Siin describes as the 'beats and rhythms that their own and other's bodies have within'. *Receivers* was first shown alongside Sandhaya Gurung, who explored her heritage through the lens of one specific cultural object, the Kukuri. The Kukuri artifact signifies the 200-year long relationship between colonial Britain and Sandhaya's homeland, Nepal. She portrayed both the appropriation and preservation of her culture through the Nepali knife as a facilitating object. Sandhaya also performed a military dance birthed from the relationship between Britain's colonial history and Nepal's passed down traditions, embodying this understandably confusing partnership within her interpretation and mimicking. The session also included Laiba Raja's reading performance of her short story *This Home is Haunted*, which engages with an array of themes pertaining to love, grief, mourning and healing. In Laiba's "sub sensorial understanding of the world" she employs the motif of the ghost a spectral figure that begins to haunt and linger in all corners of a grieving home in Pakistan. What is important to stress here is, despite the heavy burden of colonial histories that many of our students' process through their work and daily lives, we endeavour to centralise and celebrate the creation of work, through which students experiment and find methods to develop new critical articulations of these lived conditions.

What Does an Anti-Racist Classroom Look Like?
- co-written with Ali Eisa and JJ Chan

APR perpetually interrogates existing pedagogical structures; hungry for answers to change the potentially ineffective teaching patterns we have experienced as both learners and pedagogues. As bell hooks suggests: 'The classroom, with all its limitations, remains a location of possibility. In that field of possibility, we have the opportunity to labor for freedom, to demand of ourselves and our comrades, an openness of mind and heart that allows us to face reality even as we collectively

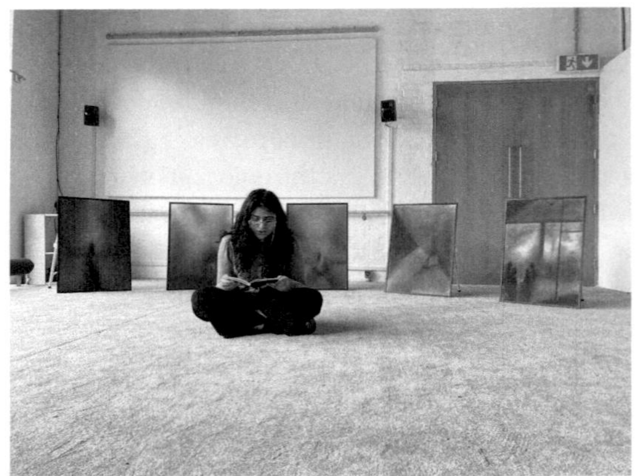

Laiba Raja reads *This Home is Haunted*, Goldsmiths CCA, 2021

imagine ways to move beyond boundaries, to transgress.'[23]

What does an anti-racist classroom look like? was developed by APR facilitators Ali Eisa and JJ Chan, in collaboration with Goldsmiths CCA and local schools. Ali with APR students, Warsha Ahmad (Kingston) and Sandhaya Gurung (Goldsmiths) first ran a two-hour workshop for teachers from Thomas Tallis School, in order to understand more deeply the classroom context and experiences of pupils, followed by a full day of workshops with year 7 students (age 11). Through this, Warsha and Sandhaya were able to explore the possibilities for embedding values from anti-racist approaches into physical learning environments, curriculums and promote emerging and alternative pedagogies for equity and justice. They learnt how to design creative activities and facilitate workshops for the first time. This project culminated in compiling a video resource on anti-racist education for pupils and teachers at local schools.

This work intersects with another APR workshop series: *Reimagining Crits*, which re-evaluates the presumed cornerstone of Art School curriculums, the 'crit'. In the context of ongoing industrial action at universities across the UK during the 2022-23 academic year, strikes affected many students' prescribed points of presentation and feedback across arts and practice-based courses, and alternative educational spaces were opened up by the radical potential of picket lines and teach-outs.

Francesca Telling devised these APR sessions asking: How can we envision these models differently by challenging the individualist and singular positioning that crits often assume? What could a non-hierarchical and caring crit look like? How can we make conversations about art more open and accessible to those who are marginalised by the conventional form these often take within art education? What are the frameworks of assessment and critique within institutional learning?[24]

                                        De-/Anti-/Post-colonial Feminisms

The resulting models featured somatic grounding exercises led by Abhaya Rajani, a sharing of tea and food, pre-and post crit meetings between APR facilitators and presenting artists, generous and flexible allocations of time, and the option to distribute facilitation, note-taking and translation responsibilities across staff and students in the group. More inclusive and accessible frameworks for participant feedback and contributions to conversation were established, including breakout groups, collaborative mind mapping, individual note-taking and the creation of informal social space around structured presentations. There was an emphasis on bodily and emotive responses, collective learning and consent; and a decentring of immediacy, teacher/student hierarchies and Western academicism. Overall, the agency of the presenting artist was prioritised, facilitating space for them to make choices around how and why they receive feedback - and which is sensitive to language barriers, neurodivergence, cultural difference, identity positions and experiences of marginalisation.

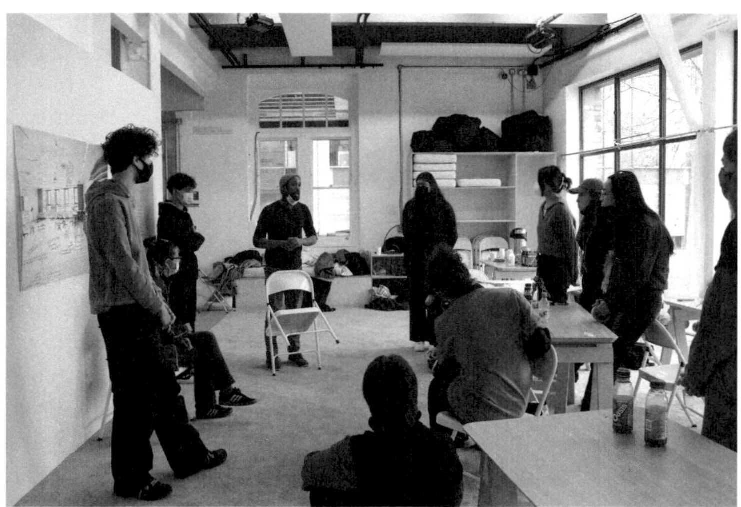

Ali Eisa runs What does an anti-racist classroom look like? Goldsmiths CCA, February 2022

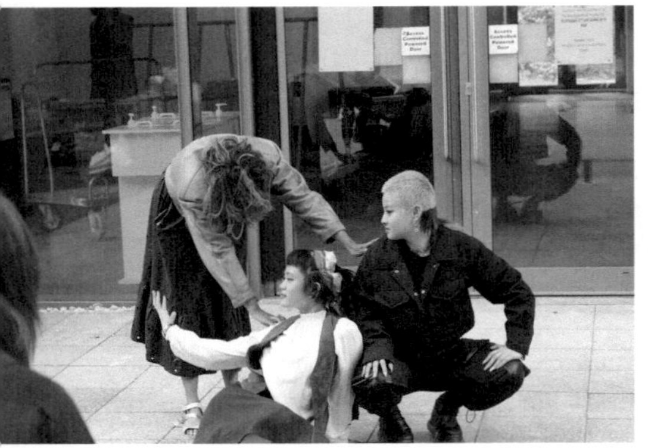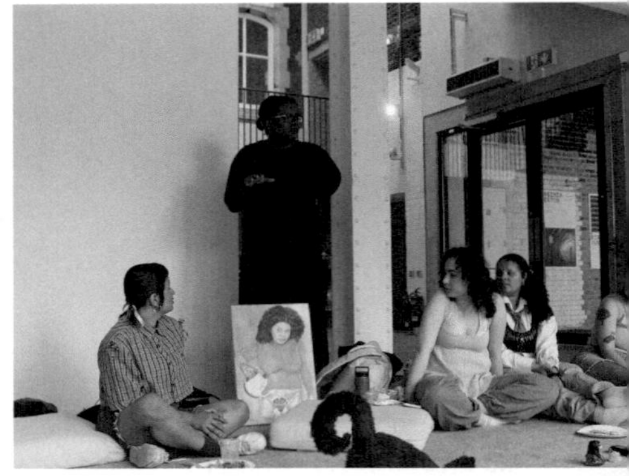

Shifting the Margins, performance workshop led by BA Fine Art and BA Fine Art and History of Art students, outside Goldsmiths CCA, June 2022, with Michelle Williams Gamaker, Xuan Yeo and Blue. Lori-Ann Burgess, from Floor Five Collective shares her work at the Shifting the Margins Symposium, June 2022

Shifting the Margins – co-written with Janna Graham and Laiba Raja

Shifting the Margins[25] was a year-long APR research project, initiated in the summer of 2022, embodying our insistence on the generative possibilities of institutional critique and institutional accountability and betterment. It was created in response to the disillusionment towards institutions, the lack of community or care it offered its students and the recurring experiences of marginalisation and racism. This context raised several questions for the students: Why does the future vision of the UK government, policymakers, university administrators and the careers office not align with the one we imagine for ourselves? Is there a space to plan for another idea of the university to emerge?

To respond to this, we set up an inter-departmental co-research group of staff and students, leading student-directed workshops and reflection sessions, as part of a peer-programming methodology.

As APR Facilitator Laiba Raja explains: This research project brought together students from BA Curating, BA Fine Art and BA Fine Art and History of Art, who began to question, examine and draw linkages between the highly atomised vision of the future proliferating within the Careers department of the university and feelings of isolation and marginalisation felt by these students. It aimed to bridge the gap between departments to create a sustained network of friendship, connections and solidarity. This project encouraged an experimental approach to make practice-based education better for its students. The *Shifting the Margins* toolkit with case studies and interviews, was collated to guide tutors, course leaders and departments within the institution, to not only critically examine their own roles in reinforcing anachronistic and Eurocentric

                                                   De-/Anti-/Post-colonial Feminisms

ways of teaching, but also actively move towards a more collective, community-rooted pedagogical practice.[26]

Students not only worked across departments, but also went on field trips to visit other Collectives, such as *The Shipwright* (a Queer Theatre company in Deptford), Floor Five Collective and artist graduates based at SET, Woolwich. The project hosted *School of the Damned*, an alternative art education programme, as well as working with artist Raju Rage on creative survival. Exploring co-produced work informed the development of a *Shifting the Margins* toolkit[26] to embed anti-racism in teaching and learning and create more inclusive pathways for BIPoC students into a future of professional practice. The aim was to share hopeful futures and make them tangible for students to draw on. While much of the co-researched insights documented in the resource could be transferrable to other institutions within the APR Network and beyond, the collective process – of exploring and making together, building strong bonds of friendship and allyship - enabled participating Goldsmiths students to truly engage with the process of learning from one another. They established strong methods of formulating their research in innovative and creative means and worked to build a community through the practice of collectivity.

Another Art School is Possible - cowritten with Ali Eisa, Francesca Telling, Laiba Raja,Abhaya Rajani, Alice Gale-Feeny, JJ Chan and Sarah Howe

This day-long pilot workshop took inspiration from the work of Columbian sociologist, Orlando Fals Borda's methods of Participatory Action Research (PAR)[27] which connect research to social justice movements and aimed to find collective solutions to the struggles of indigenous and working communities. PAR placed emphasis on the creation of artworks, as many communities had high levels of illiteracy, and by working visually and collectively, countered the dominance of Eurocentric, academic language-based communication and knowledge production. From an Arts perspective, we reminded students that we were working within a lineage, including *The BLK arts Group/Black Arts Movement* and more recently *Documenta fifteen*, curated by Indonesian collective Ruangrupa, a collaboration with collectives from the global majority.

Led by Ali Eisa and supported by the APR team, we asked participants across our network to reflect on our five years of APR output and to consider what is next? What should our collectivity look and feel like moving forward? Should APR continue growing into a larger project? What would more resources allow APR to do and not to do (or who would we become?) How can we address the gaps in what APR provides? What Art School is possible if APR has a say?

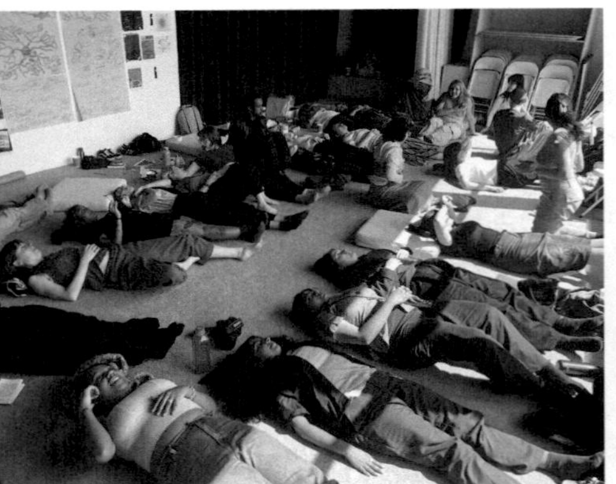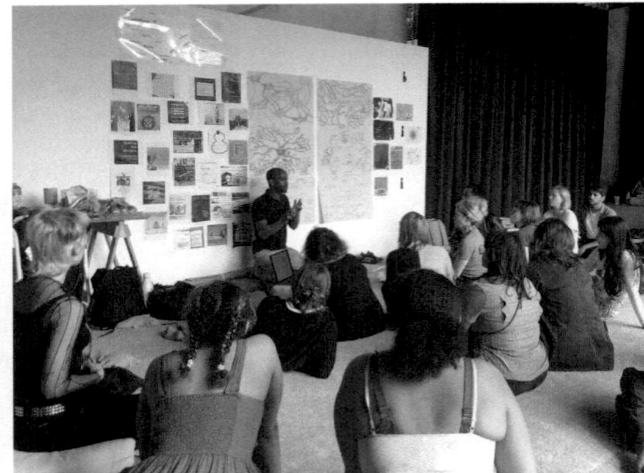

Left: Abhaya Rajani leads a grounding exercise, Another Art School is Possible, May 2023
Right: Ali Eisa leads a session for Another Art School is Possible, May 2023

To help students to work through this, APR Facilitator Alice Gale-Feeny introduced David Bohm's *On Dialogue* (1990), in particular his interest in communication, how groups relate and fragment in communities. Alice asked the students to consider how we actually produce a collective thought (noting the potential utopianism or resistance to having collective thoughts) by suggesting the process of how we arrive there '*is* where the work is'. Bohm proposes that when a dialogue is facilitated, the facilitator works themselves out of a job and becomes redundant, as the facilitated become active and autonomous. For Bohm, this is a marker of a 'successful' dialogue, and the facilitator should aim for this. Through all the APR projects, this possibility of 'redundancy' for our faciliators is key to how our students find greater agency to direct their own learning.

As with many of our sessions, the workshop functioned like a pulsing organ or a lung that expands and contracts. We worked on the floor, we encouraged students to work in groups, to work with those we have not met before, and bonds are built through informality. Abhaya Rajani offered a grounding exercise at the start of the session, to work within a more mindful and somatically aware space. On the ground, the pedagogical hierarchy dissolves, and paid educators, alumni and students share their experiences. The process is deeply intergenerational, with listening, drawing, mapping and reflecting processes as key to the work. Reflections that stemmed from *Another Art School is Possible* included Aya Adnan Mohammed from Middlesex sharing French Philosopher Édouard Glissant's notion of 'the right to opacity of everyone' from his book *Poetics of Relation* (1990), whereby it is important within dialogue to not have to be transparent at all times; and APR alumni Tara White, reflects 'Art making's inherent soft edges are still too radical for capitalist structures…. I think the state has a fear of artists, because of our adaptability and ability to shapeshift. Craft has a more

De-/Anti-/Post-colonial Feminisms

malleable interpretation and is often the default institutional understanding of creativity, whereby products can be categorised, are reproducible and marketable.' Abahaya Rajani shared that she had never heard about models of collectivity in her education, and that although collaboration was encouraged at the Royal College of Art (where she studied) – collectivity enables individuals to come together because they want to and with no pre-determined outcome in mind. Weitian Liu, currently studying a PhD in Advanced Practices (Visual Cultures) at Goldsmiths, made the distinction between two words that sound the same: *Course* – how the institution manages students and which involves collaboration and dialogue; and *Cause* – what is needed to have a collective endeavour or common cause. Weitan noted the contradiction between the Course and Cause – the Course brings students together, but the Cause is one that brings together students of different kinds, who have a real passion to work collectively. At APR we have necessarily had to analyse our structural conditions. Through *Causes and Courses* we situate our discussions organically, between the personal and structural situations we work within – our insistence on the felt and often intuitive space we work from, can make it hard to unpick and assess what we find from a quantitative viewpoint, but the appetite for our work increasingly shows there is a need for the methodologies we are developing.

Anti-Conclusion: An Ever-Evolving Survival Strategy,
Reflections and Suggestions – co-written with Ali Eisa and Sarah Howe
On reaching our fifth birthday, we have a strong sense of our pedagogic values, their histories and future possibilities. As Ali Eisa reflects: A conclusion suggests there might be a fixed or determined set of insights, practices or guides that APR's work would elaborate for others. However, its more in line with the embrace of multiplicity, difference and polyphony that APR has convened over the last few years to allow our approaches to art, learning and anti-racism to continue to be open, non-linear and subject to the particular realities of those who take up its call. Drawing on Stuart Hall's writings on identity as an 'unfinished conversation' and 'as always, in part, an invention; about "becoming" as well as "being"' – APR's approach to pedagogy is sensitive, relevant and caring towards culturally diverse and neurodivergent lived experiences only because it continues to open up safe spaces for students, staff, artist and allies to ask questions and demand changes for our spaces of making and learning to meaningfully reflect our different realities.

In 2022, Jo Addison invited Samia La Virgne and Zubair Shafiq to become APR associates with the aim of designing a tool to assess the current progress of APR. Zubair Shafiq was a Visiting Research Fellow at King's College London (KCL) and former Assistant Professor of Media Studies at the Islamia

University of Bahawalpur in Pakistan. Samia La Virgne's practice-based PhD research examined womanhood and the social stigma of blackness through the stereotypical representation of black women in the performing arts industry, on stage and screen, and the effects it has on black actresses, in the UK and US. Together, they explored the experiences of arts students, faculty, and alumni, presenting a video report based on the outcome of a survey and brought with them their expertise in film/TV and media. Some key recommendations they suggested for APR to make a sustainable impact and future in the HE and Arts sectors included the development of new toolkits, and in addition to our work within Fine Art departments, to expand APR work to include more Performing and Visual Arts, such as theatre and film programmes.[28] They also suggested the project's expansion to include other universities in the Midlands, such as Birmingham City University.[29]

Eschewing the parasite/host metaphor, APR began as a group which operated from the periphery, and in satellite contexts, such as MMU, this continues to be the case. MMU's APR facilitator Sarah Howe highlighted some key needs for working in a satellite capacity, but these points also can be applied to our network: more time for engagement and for making connections in planning activities; finding more support within and from institutions; dealing with the problem of overload and workloads; the difficulties of creating opportunities cross-institutions; and finding long-term financial support for APR initiatives.

We have understandably had to carve space within our respective universities on minimal resources - investing time, labour and energy to identify what is currently not fully addressed within HE. We can identify the value of APR's anti-racist work, but now would like to see it embedded across all practice-based courses in the UK, and are now considering, *what would it take to make this a reality?*

De-/Anti-/Post-colonial Feminisms

Notes

1. See APR's homepage https://aparticularreality.co.uk/, which includes a full version of our mission statement.

2. This text draws from multiple contributions and texts from our APR facilitators, including notes taken from peer observation, email and text exchanges responding to specific questions I have asked my colleagues. While this document is an analysis of our work authored by me, it is only made possible with my indebted thanks to our APR team.

3. Quotes interspersed in this essay are from *A Particular Reality: Art, Learning, Anti-Racism* [Available: https://www.aparticularreality.co.uk], a 10-minute film made by Francesca Telling, Amrit Sanghera and Alice Gale-Feeny in collaboration with APR staff and participants. The film is augmented by a script voiced by students, staff, alumni and collaborators, with a bespoke soundtrack made by Ratiba Ayadi ft. Silent Songstress. Jo Addison presented this film at the Advance HE Equality, Diversity and Inclusion conference, Manchester in March 2022.

4. The APR zine is available here to download: https://aparticularreality.co.uk/zine-edition-1/. The APR alumni who developed this resource are Mona Campbell, Paola Rafaella Kossakowska, Amrit Sanghera (Kingston) Janaki Mistry and Tara White (Goldsmiths).

5. This project was developed online with Zoe Watson, Harold Offeh and Michelle Williams Gamaker. Referencing the Hydra, a multi-headed creature from ancient Greek mythology, the project focuses on our understanding of art school in the age of Covid-19, asking "What would an intersectional art school look like?", a question has been repeatedly discussed in different APR programmes across our network. Intersectionality, as defined by Kimberlé Williams Crenshaw, is not intended as a theory but a prism for understanding certain kinds of problems and, as such, is 'a metaphor for understanding the ways that multiple forms of inequality or disadvantage sometimes compound themselves, and they create obstacles that are often not understood within conventional ways of thinking about anti-racism, feminism or whatever social justice advocacies we have'. https://youtu.be/ViDtnfQ9FHc

6. The support of Janna Graham, Course Leader in BA Curating and Director of Research Dr Nina Wakeford at Goldsmiths and Mark Harris and Andrea Stokes at Kingston has also been invaluable.

7. Jo Addison is Head of the Department of Fine Art at Kingston School of Art, Kingston University London.

8. *Art and Cultural Reciprocity*, talk delivered at the East Midlands Art Conference, 12 April 1986.

9. Gavin Jantjes was the first Black Senior Lecturer in Fine Art at Chelsea School of Art in the 1980s, and in a 2021 email between us, he also argued [*my emphasis added*]: '*That art schools are still not catering to their students' needs and almost deliberately unaware of discrimination, is a clear example of the cyclical nature I speak of.*...It's as if each generation has to work through its problems of inequality. The changes are so minimal that one has to magnify them to register them at all....You work hard only to realise that, at the point of exhaustion when you are so tired of fighting for change, you become aware that almost all your peers have moved ahead and achieved what they set out to do and you have spent your time, energy, and talent arguing for a principle. And the goal you had of becoming a recognised artist is as distant as when you first started.....The part that's sad is not the broad, cross-generational support for BLM, sexual equality or climate change et al but the fact that these have remained issues of dispute when history and facts gathered over the last 50 years show that they should not be.... *very few institutions teach how to recode the history they teach. The wretched of the earth [Fanon] have to do it all by themselves. To become the best, they have to shape an alternate history and, like Linton Kwesi Johnston, claim: "It is no mystery, we making history"*. In my day there [were] not a lot of tools with which to reshape history. Today it's a lot better. *So, my advice to those younger than me should be: "Go find the tools, do the research, trust your gut and don't be afraid to stand up for what you know to be true".*'

10. As an artist and academic, and a person of colour, my lived-experience of art school, studying at Middlesex University between 1998–2001, was, on the whole, a positive one. I was one of a handful of students of colour on the course, specifically South Asian, first-generation British Sri Lankan. With hindsight, I was, like most undergraduates from intersectional backgrounds working today, wrestling with my identity through my work, and that early desire to explore representation through race, gender, and sexuality has never gone away. When I undertook my postgraduate studies between 2005–2012 at Goldsmiths on the MA in Visual Anthropology and Fine Art PhD programmes, I continued my institutional journey with longer-term goals to expand my practice through teaching in HE. However, I began to feel the resistance of the institution during my employment as a Lecturer on the BA Fine Art Programmes at Kingston and Goldsmiths in 2014.

11. APR Zine Edition 1, October 2020.

12. APR Zine Edition 1, October 2020.

13. Penny Jane Burke, and Jackie McManus, *Art for a few: exclusions and misrecognitions in art and design higher education admissions*. Project Report. National Arts learning Network and HEFCE, London, 2009.

14. See Jemma Desai's *This Work isn't For Us*, a critical appraisal of historic "diversity' initiatives, an alternative policy document, and an embodied ethnography, assembling testimonies from arts workers navigating institutionally initiated gestures at "inclusion". https://heystacks.com/doc/337/this-work-isnt-for-us—by-jemma-desai

15. From Harold Offeh's speech, APR symposium, 2020. Our first APR Symposium: *Art/Learning/Anti-Racism - The Realities of Race and Difference in Art*, coordinated by Kingston's Amrit Sanghera, invited Dr Adesola Akinleye, Professor Kalwant Bhopal and Dr Harold Offeh. Available to watch here: https://aparticularreality.co.uk/art-learning-anti-racism/

16. See the co-authored article in Arts Professional by UK Artists 4 BLM, Jade Montserrat, Cecilia Wee, Michelle Williams Gamaker *"We need collectivity against structural and institutional racism in the cultural sector", June 2020* which discusses the glass ceiling for Culture Workers of colour within the sector. https://www.artsprofessional.co.uk/magazine/article/we-need-collectivity-against-structural-and-institutional-racism-cultural-sector

17. During the Q and A, Sterling shared this reflection with our students: 'I always want to make everyday paintings that have a sinister or a slapstick twist, because I feel like that's what marginalisation feels like. You're looking in the mirror every day and you're like "I am this; I will be treated like this". Which is, let's say, if you're the default or the norm in whatever society you live in you're not going to think of that. I will always remember when I was doing my BA a black photographer came in, and he was like, "OK everyone, raise your hand if you think about race every day?" – and it was only the black people that raised their hands. I thought it was interesting to see how it clouds your life.'

18. Working across painting, drawing, photography and moving image, Biswas's work demonstrates an acute commitment to addressing questions of identity, ideas of dislocation and belonging, underpinned by an interest in colonial histories and how this relates to gender, race and class. Biswas's tutor at Leeds University, art historian, Professor Griselda Pollock said it was Biswas 'who forced us all to acknowledge the Eurocentric limits of discourses within which we practice.' Pollock collaborated in Biswas' earliest film *Kali* (1984), in which Biswas dressed as the Hindu goddess and placed a covering over the face of Pollock, who embodied an icon of imperialism within the film. (Jahla, Kabir, *The Art Newspaper*, 2021)

19. Lucy also experimented with developing the unfamiliarity of familiar spaces by sharing her virtually created 'Tube compartment space' and invited participants to imagine the thoughts it evokes and how this experience can create multiple personal spaces within a generic interior.

20. See Robin DiAngelo *White Fragility: Why It's So Hard for White People to Talk About Racism*,

Boston: Beacon Press, 2018.

21. EAWAC members include artists who met at Chelsea, UAL: Zichen Wang, Qianlin Wang, Semin Hong, Annan Shao, Chuni Wu, Jiali Mai, Soyeon Kim and Lily Yang. East Asian Women Artist Community '(EAWAC) is organised by women of colour from the East Asian diaspora, coming together under the commonality of not wanting to exist in the given paradigm. Pursuing art careers in London, we have acknowledged significant under-representation of East Asian women artists – especially when contrasted with the escalating consumption and familiarisation of our culture. Through this community, we aim to actively navigate a common ground and dismantle the framework withholding us by resource sharing, cross-cultural learning, and regular discussions.' (EAWAC Mission Statement)

22. *Take Up Space* is a series initiated by Michelle Williams Gamaker, inviting APR's members to use our residency space at Goldsmiths CCA to make work, test out ideas, collaborate with others and hold conversations. This opportunity encourages those who identify as BIPoC and from other marginalised or intersectional backgrounds to 'take up space' where they do not often get to do so.

23. bell hooks, *Teaching to Transgress Education as the Practice of Freedom*, New York and London: Routledge, 1994, p.207.

24. Presenting artists include Amber Harrison, Judith Gao, Sharmain Forde, Zihan Mei, Xuan Yeo, Aya Adnan Mohammed.

25. *Shifting the Margins* is a collective research project by Janna Graham, Michelle Williams Gamaker, Francesca Telling, Ali Eisa, Laiba Raja, Alice Sun, Will Rose, Xuan Yeo, Lu Lei, Adrianna Whittingham, Emily Bianconi, Roisin Billeter, Danielle Menezes Heath, Alice Sutcliffe and Divya Kishore.

26. See APR's website.

27. Fal Borda's approach to research was influenced by revolutionary Marxist political movements in Latin America as well Paulo Freire's *Pedagogy of The Oppressed* (1968) and Augusto Boal's *Theatre of the Oppressed* (1970s). Multiple contributors have developed PAR, which is not a 'monolithic body of ideas and methods but rather a pluralistic orientation to knowledge making and social change.' See R. Chambers, 'PRA, PLA and Pluralism: Practice and Theory' in P. Reason and H. Bradbury (eds.), *The Sage Handbook of Action Research: Participative Inquiry and Practice*, London: Sage, 2008, pp. 297–318.

28. APR facilitator Sarah Howe reflects on the *Reimagining Crits* workshops for students based in Manchester that: 'The first two sessions highlighted issues with the current mode of review, working through possible alternatives that were then tried out. This proved to be an insightful experience in understanding some of the different concerns of the group at MMU had, to those who attended at Goldsmiths: predominantly how being on a Photography course rather than Fine Art Program shifted student expectations of the language used within a crit space.'

29. We are in extended dialogue with the Fine Art Department at Bath Spa University to join APR in 2024/25.

The Practice of Feminist Art Education

Leslie C. Sotomayor II

Theory as an Active Approach

In this chapter, I reflect on my journey as a Latin@/x and activist educator, drawing ideas from the work of Gloria Anzaldúa. Centered critically in an inquisitive decolonial unlearning that interweaves acknowledgements of mainstream education's continuation of colonial trauma, I am seeking to provide alternative spaces for acts of self-healing to combat the wounds of racism and sexism in the USA today. Because historically theorizing and knowledge building has been in the hands of dominant Anglo-American culture, and marginalized populations and black, indigenous and people of color (BIPOC) have been excluded, it is critical that spaces for theorizing all experiences and knowledges are created through curricula. By theorizing (making sense) of our own experiences, marginalized and BIPOC populations have the possibility to re-member ourselves, our historical contexts, and critically reflect on our social realities. We are then able to re-imagine ourselves in new ways. Marginalized BIPOC populations need a vehicle and path to rewrite histories and cross borders with new knowledge and methods for theorizing. We need tools to navigate the in-between spaces, and critically look at what's behind the situations and contexts in which we find ourselves. We can find new ways of 'forming our own categories and theoretical models for patterns we uncover'[1] in current educational systems, curricula and knowledge production. We need theorizing because it includes critical self-reflection on our historical contexts, myths/symbology and spirituality. The use of lived experiences and intuition can overcome feelings of not-belonging and provide the possibilities for transformations, creative acts,[2] and re-imagining as core characteristics to creating one's own story. In what follows, I share my reflections, approaches, and *visual plática*[3] (*testimonio*) interwoven with contextualizations of my own theorizing, fragments of my experiences and student manifestations as a means of witnessing an ongoing process in arts education.

In addition, I claim that the performative feminist writing practice of *autohistoria-teoría*, coined by Gloria Anzaldúa,[4] is a way to create self-knowledge, belonging, and bridge collaborative spaces through curating, education and art. In this vein, *autohistoria-teoría* is a way for a student to create personal meaning in their own performances (writing, art, curating, educating, etc.) and build a bridge to a new kind of collaborative work with the reader, where meaning can link the author's and reader's experiences and historical contexts.[5] In making meaning for oneself, the performative element of these public acts initiates social change within communities. Only when we send

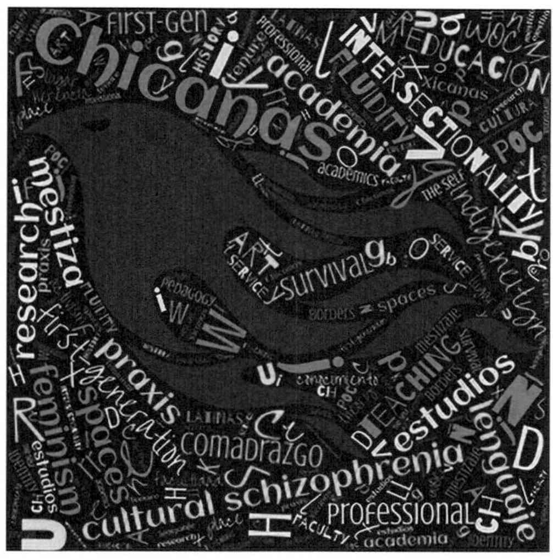

Image from *Visual Plática*, by Esther De Leon. '...for when I was younger, there were no other works known to me...that portrayed characters that looked like me...sounded like me...that spoke of my childhood.' Used with author's permission.

'our voices, visuals and visions outward into the world, we alter the walls and make them a framework for new windows and door.'[6] I situate the theorizing of my own lived experiences, the things that have changed and transformed me in some way, as foundational to trace through the lineage of testimonio work. Gloria Anzaldúa's theorizing of *autohistoria-teoría* and *conocimiento* serve as pivotal concepts from which I can reflect upon, process, create and evolve my own positionality.

My feminist writing practice includes performing my own visual *testimonio*. *Visual pláticas* or *testimonios* are a performative practice of *nepantla*, an act of living in-between worlds. Through *visual pláticas*, I offer images as text and as performance.[7] Gloria Anzaldúa emphasizes that our stories, *testimonios*, *autohistorias* are performances – a collaborative effort between the reader and writer and/or artist.[8] Writing performatively becomes a feminist/artist/act – an embodiment of the self through a visual text. Developing these visual *testimonios* is a decolonizing act that uses visual language to share testimonio where the artist/writer has engaged with *autohistoria-teoría* and is theorizing their own lived experiences.[9] Through the collaging of image and text, the maker/performer navigates tense, ambiguous, and shifting borderlands spaces.[10] In what follows, I present two iterations of my *visual pláticas* as expressions of my experiences as a Latina in the United States grappling between borders, as well as one of my student's works, Esther de Leon (see above). The following *visual plática* is based on my life experience juxtaposed with my experiences in mainstream college education.

First Day of College

Citizenship: American
Country of Origin: United States of America
Birth City & State: Secaucus, New Jersey
Birth Year: 1978
Relocation: Philadelphia
Relocation Year: 1987
College #1: 1995

Walking for the first time: disconnected. On another planet didn't quite belong.
Barely a year, failing out………discuss my situation. I have no recollection of what was
said as I sat in his office, feeling invisible, not belonging anywhere.

Child #1: Miscarriage 1996
Child #2: 1998
Child #3: 2002
Child #4: 2005
College #2: 2009
First Latina College Class: 2010
Bachelor's Degree #1: 2014
Bachelor's Degree #2: 2014
Bachelor's Degree #3: 2014
Child #5: Miscarriage 2015
Master's Degree: 2015
Child #6: 2016

PhD #1: 2020
PhD #2: 2020

During my first year as an adult learner pursuing my bachelor's degree, I needed
to take an elective. One of the only classes that would fit my tight schedule that was
hyphenated with motherhood was an Introduction to Women's Studies course.
I had no idea what the class was, or that there was even a field with this name.

Mother Birth Year: 1944
Father Birth Year: 1950
Marriage Year: 1975
Sibling Birth Year: 1980
English Language: 1984

For the first time, I was witnessing what a Latina could be other than a mother,
and I began to learn about my history as a Latina in the United States.
I felt I didn't belong in most of my other classes because the curriculum taught
excluded experiences and voices of people of color from education, art, and curating.
I became aware of the things **I did not possess**; knowledge of myself, my history,
art training, or a language and vocabulary to articulate myself through.
English is, after all, my second language.

Because the education I received in elementary through high school failed to include me, I grew up living in-between and feeling like I didn't belong anywhere.
People of color have been required to assimilate,
look,
speak,
act like their White neighbors,
educators,
artists,
curators
…….the whole picture isn't just about displacing whiteness although necessary
…..but also critically examining the layers of
whiteness as not only critical of white identities,
of {whiteness} as an institutionalized way
of thinking, educating, and moving in the world.
Eurocentric
White supremacy
ideology >>>>>>> permeates historical and contemporary institutionalized frameworks.
We witness
are complicit
enact >>>>>> within the realms
of White supremacy daily through

visual culture
legislation
politics
education
socioeconomic structures.

It leaks throughout our society and cultures in exponential forms. Unless we intentionally **interrogate** White superiority and recognize that is extends beyond a skin color, it stains the minds and perceptions of who we are and are not, we will reproduce these mindsets and power dynamics. White ideology is a consciousness of thinking, **a mindset** that can be housed in vessels **despite**
the color of skin
language
culture
religions
ethnicity
ancestral roots.

College courses failed to theorize and include experiences **like mine** in the art field— again, I was feeling an all too familiar feeling that I have felt throughout my whole life, **not belonging.** It was the first academic setting I had with other Latino/a students, where we became vulnerable with each other through our testimonios. Just as important, I know the value of sitting in the classroom seats, witnessing a Latina enter the room and open a window into testimonios, poetry, listening and sharing lived experiences that rarely are voiced in academia. Based on my experiences of not belonging to myself, my autohistoria-teoría is a process for self-empowerment.

Conocimiento and *Autohistoria-teorïa*: Components of *Testimonios*

I am positioning *testimonio* as an approach, a method, to conducting research and to bearing witness to learners' and my own experiences that is informed by Anzaldúa's idea of *autohistoria-teoria*.[11] The practice of *testimonio* has heavily informed studies by US-based scholars in areas such as critical race theory and Chicana/o and Latino/a studies. *Testimonio* is a first-person oral and/or written account drawing on self-reflective, narrative practices intended to be made public, an urgent call for action regarding something to which one bears witness, to bring to light a wrong.[12]

Although my theorizing is anchored in Gloria Anzaldúa's writings, with all that I glean from her, my own lived experiences are also informed by conversations I have with the learners I meet while facilitating learning environments on college campuses, local communities, and online. BIPOC and underrepresented populations have a strong sense of not belonging and a feeling of existing in-between home and college environments when they pursue their scholarship or research in higher education.[13] I argue they can bridge these experiences through engagement with Gloria Anzaldúa's theories of *conocimiento* and *autohistoria-teoría*.

In her essay 'now let us shift...the path of conocimiento...inner works...public acts' (2002), Anzaldúa offers a tentative definition of autohistoria as 'a term I use to describe the genre of writing about one's personal and collective history using fictive elements, a sort of fictionalized autobiography or memoir: and *autohistoria-teoría* [as] a personal essay that theorizes.'[14]

Another example of Anzaldúa's autohistoria is 'La Prieta', an essay that she shares about her experiences of vulnerability growing up.[15] She explains and reflects; theorizes about her lived experiences through her health issues, education, geographical location, language, sexuality and cultures. I view Anzaldúa's essay as a format or model for my own theorizing of self through my stories. Anzaldúa explains that *conocimiento* and *autohistoria-teoría* are catalysts for new paths to be forged through theoretical work, ways of understanding, creating knowledge, and awareness.[16] I posit that *conocimiento* and *autohistoria-teoría* initiate a re-creating and re-imagining of oneself in a new way, differently. In bridging historical contexts, myths/religion, and re-imagining through critical reflection, creativity and spirituality, *autohistoria-teoría* makes possible the rewriting of oneself.

Conocimiento is a key characteristic of *autohistoria-teoría*. I refer to Anzaldúa's *conocimiento* theory as "transformative acts" because in my experience, her theory evokes deep reflections that intensify when engaged, changing something within us. For Anzaldúa: '*conocimiento* is reached via creative acts – writing, art-making, dancing, healing, teaching, mediation, and spiritual activism – both mental and somatic (the body, too, is a form as well as site of creativity).'[17]

I describe the "acts" that comprise Anzaldúa's theory of *conocimiento* as "transformative" because each act is intended to bring about something new, different, and/or to shed light on something. I also use the phrase 'transformative acts' to avoid reproducing an ideology of hierarchy, as the use of steps or stages would suggest. *Conocimiento* is a transformation process, an ongoing healing

De-/Anti-/Post-colonial Feminisms

process, developing critical self-awareness. It is a form of resistance and spiritual activism. I define spiritual activism as a practice in our everyday lives that works towards all forms of systemic oppression and advocates for interconnectedness. A back and forth relationship that turns inward, critically reflecting on the self, and turns outward focusing on activism. Spiritual activism is the inner work while public acts provide interconnectedness.[18] The latter is essential to the power of creative acts as a manifestation of spiritual activism, enabling new perspectives to come about, to reimagine and reconstruct, exposing layers and realities that did not exist before.[19]

Anzaldúa explains that by connecting and theorizing personal experiences with social realities and 'by making certain personal experiences the subject of this study, I also blur the private/public borders.'[20] Through the process of connecting and theorizing personal experiences, *autohistoria-teoría* is "fused" together facilitating a re-construction of oneself through agency. Anzaldúa critically engages with the concept of *conocimiento* as a form of resistance to traditional modes of knowing. She also refers to *conocimiento* as her lived practice of spiritual inquiry. For Anzaldúa, 'spirituality is a symbology system... Through spirituality we seek balance and harmony with our environment.'[21] *Conocimiento*, as spiritual inquiry, is 'driven by the desire to understand, know, *y saber* [and know] how human and other beings know. Beneath your desire for knowledge writhes the hunger to understand and love yourself.'[22]

The holistic experience through the path of conocimiento emerges 'from opening all your senses, consciously inhabiting your body and decoding its symptoms.'[23] The unquenchable thirst for knowing oneself and longing for our true selves to emerge from the depths of our being through intuitive and spiritual awakening is fundamental. Creative expression is an inherent characteristic of *conocimiento*: 'through creative engagements, you embed your experiences in a larger frame of reference, connecting your personal struggles with those of other beings on the planet, with the struggles of the Earth itself.'[24] By holistic practice, Anzaldúa positions all aspects of one's life in relationship to each other and to other people.

Deep-diving into Anzaldúa's conocimiento theory, I posit that transformative acts are crucial to avoid perpetuating a top-down hierarchy or reproducing a Eurocentric White supremacist framework of knowledge. To restructure the relationship between the educator and learners as one of transparent and open communication, a radical positionality is mandatory. Anzaldúa's *conocimiento* theory underlies what I call seven recursive transformative acts: (a) *arrebato/susto*, (b) *nepantla*, (c) *Coatlicue*, (d) reframing, (e) *autohistoria-teoría*, (d) renewal, and (f) *nepantlera*. Although the transformative acts are not linear, there is a core catalyst beginning with the stages of fear and the rupture leading to *nepantla*, a realm of in-between-ness, where the things that were once felt or were thought to be stable, all of sudden are not. Various stages can occur concurrently and what is learned or made aware is called *conocimientos* or awareness/knowledge.[25]

Nepantla and *Testimonios*

Anzaldúa theorizes the meaning of the native Nahuatl word *nepantla* at length when discussing the transformational recursive stages of *conocimiento*. *Nepantla,* a word from the native southern Mexican people meaning for the "space between two bodies of water, the space between two worlds."[26] *Nepantla* is a tumultuous place that is in transition as one transforms. *Nepantla*, being the second stage in the *conocimiento* process, occurs after a shock, a *susto* (fear) that shakes you down to your core. It is only then that, '*éste arrebato*, the earthquake, jerks you from the familiar and safe terrain and catapults you into *nepantla*, the second stage.'[27] When a person is in the process of crossing from one physical, geographical, emotional, or spiritual location into another, the crossing creates an in-between space, a gap. In the in-between space of *nepantla*, many things may be experienced: healing, awakening of the consciousness, acceptance of self, negotiations and contradictions.

In *nepantla*, a person may choose to become a *nepantlera*, spiritual activists who are 'agents of awakening, inspire and challenge others to deeper awareness, greater *conocimiento*; they serve as reminders of each other's search for wholeness of being.'[28] It is important to note that the seven transformative recursive stages as theorized by Anzaldúa are not static or lineal, but rather fluid and 'all seven are present within each stage, they occur concurrently, chronologically or not.'[29] The transformational recursive stages 'zigzag' through the stages with no discrimination to time and no exclusivity to one stage but rather crossing in-between more than one at all times.

Visual pláticas or *testimonios* are a performative practice of *nepantla*, an act of living in-between worlds. *Nepantla* is always about the gap, the place in-between thresholds that are crossed over, back and forth and borders that one must navigate throughout life. I borrow from Kavitha Koshy's (2006) theory of *nepantlera*-activism in transnational spaces[30] as she develops this concept for nepantleras as intentionally situating self within transnational spaces and working towards transforming them into collaborative critically-reflective environments while also respecting how other people occupy different standpoints and spaces. As curators and/or *nepantleras* in various environments, we are mediators, finding commonalities and initiating meaningful dialogues.[31] In the visual plática that follows, *Falling*, I reflect on my own feelings of not belonging.

Curator/*Curadora* Pillars

Reframing and naming life narratives is an act of germinating a vision, a conjuring of one's self that can transform experiences of hurt/pain/feeling undervalued into stories of empowerment. Because some life stories are not part of dominant culture discourse, underrepresented people often feel a strong sense of not belonging. It is possible for curators and learners to change their experience of this historical devaluation and sense of not belonging. I believe that through creative acts/art and re-framing our stories as a form of *curando* – the Spanish word for healing – it is possible to empower and reconcile one's whole self.

Anzaldúa names *la facultad* as the inner psychic knowing practiced with daily rituals from indigenous communities or *curanderas*, like *chamanas*, artists, spiritual activists and *nepantleras.* Anzaldúa describes *curanderas* as 'liminal people, at the thresholds of form, forever betwixt and between.'[32] For *curanderas*, realities shift. *Curanderas* are able to travel to other worlds inhabiting spiritual and physical

　　　　　　　　　　　　　　　　　　　　De-/Anti-/Post-colonial Feminisms

Falling

Explored feelings of not belonging
                        one image in my mind: It looks like a solid wall.

            Seeds from a tree fall….root…. ground….. branches

Seeds fall from branches above earth
                        blooms forming fruits
                        roots of our culture
            branches, white, dominant
            reject language experiences roots heritage.

Underrepresented people in the United States have historically been
                        marginalized
                        oppressed
                        enslaved
                        deemed inferior
making it difficult to blossom in society and culture.
Generations of trees do not flower. Wrapped thick layers of flesh. cut open growing inside
becoming visible inwardly___ cannot be seen from the outside.

Inward transformations enacting a spiritual manifestation activate participation,
interconnected, a living, visual metaphor for
                        spiritual practice
                        awareness
                        connection
                        curating new-ness
                                bodies
                                pollinating
                                germinating seeds
                                transformation
naked eye, not visible, needs be process and cyclical.

realms that often are 'unseen by those whose awareness focuses entirely on the ordinary reality of daily life.'[33] *Curanderas*, for example, may use material objects, prayers, specific mantras or phrases mingled with anything from nature, to herbs in the process of healing a person and restoring a soul or spirit. The back and forth crossings for a *chamana* or *curandera* is the 'method of deriving knowledge and power to perform these activities.'[34] Like the back and forth crossings into various transformative acts in the *conocimiento* process, the *chamanería* journey is a tearing and re-constructing 'incorporating a wider vision.'[35]

Curanderismo are traditional healers, a spiritual practice carried through cultural lineages through a holistic practice of the mind, body and soul. According to Aztec ritual practices, for example, Coatlicue and other female deities were often consulted and honored for their 'extraordinary generative powers.'[36] In a similar way, I situate *curadora*/curator as a type of healer or a facilitator for a healing process that requires a back and forth crossing into other realms much like a *nepantlera*. Through Anzaldúa's theories of *conocimiento* and *autohistoria-teoría*, I situate the *curadora/curator* as a healer, emphasizing the curatorial practice through creative acts towards healing and transformations of self and others.

Using Anzaldúa's theories of *autohistoria-teoría* and *conocimiento* for curating art educational spaces provided a method to address learners' deep sense of not belonging.[37] Curating educational spaces bear the possibility of transformation and healing because *la curadora*, the healer, is creating or conjuring an environment that is intentional in facilitating dialogues, curiosities, and for learners to engage as they are. The curators is merely a guide and curator. The environments that are curated invite learners to participate as they feel led. This process is organic, an offering that is intimate and extended to each other in the given environment. There is no telling what may occur. A connectionist faculty, Anzaldúa explains, is required 'to show the deep common ground and interwoven kinship among all things and people. This faculty, one of less-structured thoughts, less-rigid categorizations and thinner boundaries, allows us to picture-via reverie, dreaming, and artistic creativity – similarities instead of solid divisions.'[38] Anzaldúa's connectionist theory blurs the boundaries of difference by focusing on the similarities that connect individuals. Curating educational spaces makes accessible 'linkage making strategies and our healing of broken limbs.'[39] Healing is facilitated by the *curadora*, who is also a *nepantlera*, a crosser, a mediator in the educational space offering perspectives and creating new perspectives with learners. New ways of learning and knowledge are created through the inscribing of various forms in creative expressions/creative acts.[40] Feminist curating of educational spaces does not entail a regurgitation of information, a traditional banking system of education.[41] This approach does not support a monologue, but rather conversations with creative acts through which individual and collective lived experiences, histories, and various contexts can be shared.

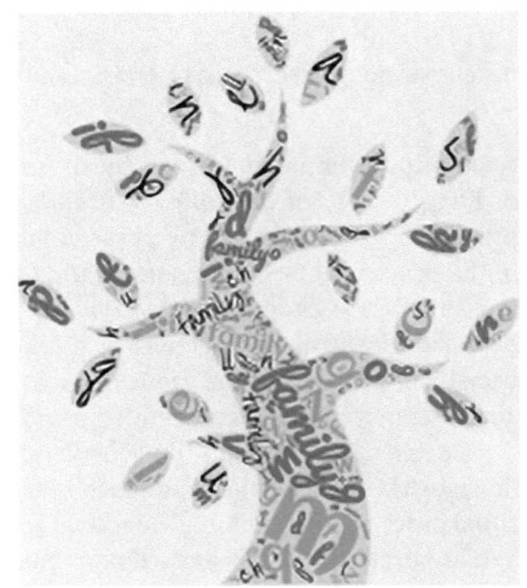

Chingona State of Mind

by Esther De Leon

'I had to learn on my own

much of my own mother's experiences of us were not something I wished to imitate or emulate...

my only resources to other parenting were Dad....

I resolved to parent in a different way.'

Used with permission.

De-/Anti-/Post-colonial Feminisms

For example, Esther's digital work was created during a Women's and Gender Studies, Women of Color (WOC) course that I created and facilitated. Through critical reflective readings and conversations, the learner may choose to engage in how they feel comfortable and how and what they want to share. Often, teaching in this way is hard emotionally for both the learner and the facilitator. It is vulnerable and intentional work, engaging with traumatic experiences in our educational pasts and present.

Often the academic canon appears to only focus on the thoughts, knowledge and concepts of over-represented dominant White males. As a *curadora* (healer, curator), I curate with the intention of holistic learning to be created together in educational spaces. I define holistic learning and curating as an activation that intentionally integrates intellectual, emotional, spiritual, imaginative and embodied experiences. In other words, the whole self. I curate class art exhibits highlighting the works of Latina American, American and Caribbean artists. For example, well known artists such as Ana Mendieta (*Sileuta* Series), Claudia Bernardi (*ser mujer es resistir*), and Josefina Aguilar (*muñeca* series) were shown and discussed in conjunction with lesser known BIPOC artists: for example, Nayda Cuevas[42]; Esther Ortiz[43]; Natalia Anciso[44]; Celeste de Luna[45]; Consuelo Jimenez Underwood[46]; Carmen Argote[47]; Margarita Cabrera[48]; Elia Alba[49]; Marco Sanchez[50]; Sheila Lorenzo de la Peña[51]; Liliana Wilson[52] and Antonio Howard.[53] We discuss as a class, how, when, and why artists of color and women artists are not part of mainstream art but often tokenized and segregated. If I do not see myself represented in my local arts venue, how is that internalized invisibility, pain and not-belonging felt? If I do not see others, diverse from me represented, how am I to expand my knowledge of others?

I curate art exhibitions specifically for students in a way that agitates against narrow definitions of multiculturalism and encourages critical self reflection about responsibilities and accountability of institutions as collectives.[54] Much research has been executed on the ideas post-1980s about multiculturalism and diversity and its integration into curriculum. Lucy Lippard (1990),[55] Andrea O'Reilly Herrera (2011),[56] Reilly (2017),[57] Desai (2020)[58], and many others have established that there is a blatant difference between incorporating diversity as a recipe for color *versus* an actual integration of diversity. Introspective investigating by learners prompts their own thoughts of their values, perspectives, and beliefs as they have been influenced by these institutions.[59]

For creative acts to activate healing, an individual has to work through the transformative acts of *conocimiento* for themselves rather than taking in knowledge from the outside-in and internalizing it as if it was a third person/neutral experience.[60] Again, I am reminded of the connection between the Banyan wasps and the curating of new perspectives and changing academic canons, as pollinating and germinating seeds towards transformations from the inside. Curating educational spaces requires the facilitation of creative acts as possible new ways for enacting a healing process and connectionist theories. The curation should be taking-into-account a holistic framework of the mind, body, spirit and soul. I want to mirror through curating Anzaldúa's imagery of *curanderismo* as 'indigenous healing practice or shamanism, mixed with beliefs, rituals, and specific practices, and the shamanic journey where one is able to shape shift (in Náhuatl, *nagual*) and travel to other realities.'[61] Anzaldúa explains that the role of the shaman (often also considered a poet) is 'to preserve and create cultural or group identity by mediating between the cultural heritage of the past and the present everyday situations people find themselves in.'[62] Transformation is a matter of the heart, it is not something that can be measured within the classroom experience; directly challenging colonizing frames of theorizing and teaching.

Curating curriculum begins with the self, as educator. By actively listening to ourselves and to each other we can develop empathy and initiate a process of healing for ourselves as individuals. As Anzaldúa states, when we change ourselves, we change the world. The very act of writing within 'suppressed knowledge' and 'marginalization' is an embodied practice of decolonizing. I found that as a decolonial feminist facilitator, I must be on my own journey of self-awareness, consciousness, self-empowered, to develop myself as a critical self-reflective person. Writing about decolonization and writing within decolonization are two very different acts. This difference is significant and extends beyond producing different results. Writing about something is informational, a self-help of sorts, a guide to structuring something fixed, that is replicable. But writing within is an approach and action that will vary depending on individuals and their experiences. It is not fixed but fluid. Writing within is a way to approach a situation that is directly impacting or influencing the individual – not as advice or steps but as an embodied way of doing. For Anzaldúa actual doing writing within these curricular landscapes and boundaries is an embodiment of the experience and work of decolonizing. As Keating explains:-

> In *Borderlands/La Frontera*, for example, her theories of mestiza consciousness, border thinking, and la facultad decolonize western epistemologies by moving partially outside Enlightenment based frameworks. Anzaldúa does not simply write about 'suppressed knowledges and marginalized subjectivities'; she writes from within them, and it's this shift from writing about to writing within that makes her work so innovatively decolonizing.[63]

I have observed in my teaching that when students are aware of their history and share their experiences, they become vulnerable, and through the shared vulnerability can develop empathy. For example, they can see the humanity in each other no matter what their differences are, which can lead to self-empowerment, healing process, and a sense of belonging in the world and to one's self.

Curatorial pillars for empowerment can guide both students and educators through possible ways of how to reframe socially-inscribed narratives – past, present and future – toward a sense of belonging to self in the world.[64] Reframing embodied narratives of not belonging is needed to enrich society and curate education in which all can thrive.[65] This involves:

A)   Activating a call for awakening: underrepresented populations, histories, community engagement and testimonios: No representation is representation.

B)   Openness/Vulnerability: environments geared towards developing community and a sense of belonging through empathy, sharing, and intimacy. Prioritizing similarities versus differences.

   De-/Anti-/Post-colonial Feminisms

C) Curating: empowerment through reframing socially inscribed narratives: past/present/future as a holistic practice for and from the self.

D) Connections/Interconnections: Connecting lived experiences from individual to collective.

E) Belonging to Self: transformation through self-reflection and creative acts.

F) Healing Through our wounds: Process of healing from traumas through a holistic, spiritual activist process.

Throughout the book *Bridging: How Gloria Anzaldúa's Life and Work Transformed Our Own*,[66] scholars share how vulnerability, exposing, and sharing their wounds, their pain, they too were able to enter a process of healing. The invitation that awaits us is to cross into the difficult terrain of becoming vulnerable with self and others as a beginning into a reclusive process of healing and transformation impacting each other. Anzaldúa's inner-most work of critically self-reflecting always crosses outside of herself as she made connections with others, whether through verbal sharing, art or embodiment through writing, music, audio, etc.[67] For example, Esther De Leon, in *Chingona State of Mind,* illustrates the place of in-between-ness, vulnerability and finding strength through knowledge building, finding place within self.

Keating coined the term 'risking the personal' to explain Anzaldúa's concept of using our lived experiences through critical self-reflection, awareness, and inner work towards healing and transformation.[68] Students writing, sharing and reflecting on their own and others' *testimonio* is an example, of the possibilities for healing as students become vulnerable with each other. For example, during the course of the semester one of the students that shared about having to say goodby to her grandfather as he fell critically ill and passed away shortly after. She shared her experiences and news in coping with her grandfather's loss, which to her also felt like losing a part of her Mexican culture and Spanish language. Students in the class were able to share in empathy with her.

Healing Through Our Wounds

Wounds may be caused by many things; society, culture, tradition, racism and/or systemic oppression. Wounds, or pain may cause us to either recognize or be aware of something that was not visible prior. To choose the use of pain 'as a conduit to recognizing another's suffering, even that of the one who inflicted the pain' is a choice to enter into a spiritual practice. Anzaldúa explains healing of our wounds as a 'spiritual practice of conocimiento' that is a 'port you moor to in all storms.'[69] Entering our wounds means acknowledging our vulnerability, but to stay in the wound as a victim is to allow *desconocimiento*, a negative energy that is disempowering because it does not move towards transformation. However, by transforming our wounds through healing they can become strengths. To 'heal the traumas of racism and other systemic *desconocimientos.*'[70] To reach or heal through the wound, is believing that aside from love, 'pain might open this closed passage by reaching through the wound to connect' with self and others.[71]

Healing is an on-going process of the soul, mind, spirit to focus all energy towards wholeness. Wholeness of self is the process of healing, '[t]here is never any resolution, just the process of healing.'[72] As Anzaldúa explains, 'healing as taking back the scattered energy and soul loss wrought by woundings.'[73] In taking back our energy, fragments and pieces of ourselves we work through the transformative acts of *conocimiento* in the struggle to put ourselves back together. We embrace, sit, resist, and challenge our pain, our wounds. We touch them, pick at them, let them scab over – they bleed, are sutured up – again. It is in *conocimiento*'s recursiveness that we are continuously dying and being reborn, taking our fragmented parts and, like Coatlicue, resurrecting. But as we rebuild ourselves, we are not putting ourselves together in the way we were once before because we have transformed through the process and we become different. The diligent work of re-newing our whole selves changes us in some way. In the rebuilding we take the fragments that have changed through *conocimiento* and rebuild ourselves in a new way. Curating feminist educational spaces allows for lived experiences to connect with others, historical and relevant contexts, and an active theorizing emerges creating new pools of knowledge. As one of the transformative acts of the conocimiento process, Anzaldúa invokes Coyolxauhqui as a symbol of the 'ongoing process of making and unmaking' and 'putting the pieces together in a new way.'[74]

Healing through our wounds is for our individual selves, our community, and the starting point 'to begin to heal the world.'[75] By changing the narratives that exist through our own pain, we embody new, positive, life-changing beliefs. Healing empowers us to 'share strategies on peaceful coexistence' and *conocimiento* through compassion and empathy, enabling us to 'extend our hand to others, *con el corazón con razón en la mano.*'[76]

Our wounds from colonialism, discrimination, or trauma, individually or collectively, has caused our fragmentation and it is against this that we need a holism of the body, spirit and mind. Like the *Coyolxauhqui* imperative, taking the fragments of our life and putting ourselves together is healing through our wounds in search of 'inner completeness.'[77] Vallone (2014) writes that the healing of wounds does not stop at wholeness, but also needs reparation. Vallone explains that consciousness awareness is only part of the process towards wholeness, because public acknowledgment and taking responsibility is just as important. She writes, it is '[n]ot just healing, but having the wounds acknowledged publicly.'[78] By taking responsibility and presenting these wounds through art/visual platicas for public acknowledgment, Vallone is connecting Anzaldúa's (2015) pivotal argument about the world's interconnectedness – we are all impacted by each other. Akin to a Shaman, who works with the wound, not against it, to find a way to reveal and heal on a spiritual level; healing through our wounds is a radical holistic act in theorizing our lived experiences and challenging dominant, often negative, societal views.[79]

Notes

1. Gloria Anzaldúa, *Making Face, Making Soul: Haciendo Caras: Creative and Critical Perspectives by Feminists of Color* (1st Edition), San Francisco, CA: Aunt Lute Books, 1990, p. xxv.

2. Creative acts: I define the creative acts as deep, meaningful, embodied experiences that are woven into our mind, body, soul, and spirit manifesting through a creative vessel. For example, painting, music, writing, dance I consider as some forms of creative acts.

3. *Visual plátíca*: I define as the creative feminist practice of visual text and imagery on paper or Word document as a visual expression that may integrate imagery, letters, fonts, colour, symbols or anything that the author deems necessary on the page.

4. G. Anzaldúa and A. Keating, *A light in the Dark: Luz en lo Oscuro: Rewriting Identity, Spirituality, Reality*, Durham, NC: Duke University Press, 2015.

5. G. Anzaldúa and A. Keating, *The Gloria Anzaldúa Reader*, Durham, NC: Duke University Press, 2009.

6. G. Anzaldúa, *Making Face, Making Soul / Hacienda Caras*, 1990, p. xxv.

7. Leslie Sotomayor and C. García, 'Nepantlando: A Borderlands Approach to Curating, Art Practice, and Teaching' in M. Sharma and A. Alexander (eds.), *The Routledge Companion to Decolonizing Art, Craft, and Visual Culture Education*, New York and London: Routledge, 2023.

8. G. Anzaldúa, *Borderlands: La Frontera: The New Mestiza,* (2nd ed.), San Francisco, CA: Aunt Lute Books, 1999.

9. Y. J. Lin, Y. Wei, E. Hajesmaeili, X. Zúñiga, I. Bailey, V. Hicks, and L. Sotomayor II 'Precarity in Conversation', *Visual Culture and Gender*, vol. 16 (2021), pp. 41-51.

10. Examples and theorizing of *visual platícas* may be found in: C.S.. Garcia and L. Sotomayor, '*Nepantlando*: A Borderlands Approach to Curating, Art Practice, and Teaching' in M. Sharma and A. Alexander (eds.), *Routledge Companion to Decolonizing Art, Craft and Visual Culture Education*, 2023.

11. Kathryn Blackmer Reyes and Julia E. Curry Rodríguez, '*Testimonio:* Origins, Terms, and Resources', *Equity and Excellence in Education,* vol. 45 no. 3 (2012), *Chicana/Latina Testimonios: Methodologies, Pedagogies and Political Urgency*, pp. 525-538.

12. Ibid. p. 526.

13. T. L. Strayhorn, *College students' Sense of Belonging: A Key to Educational Success for All Students*, New York and London: Routledge, 2012.

14. G. Anzaldúa, *The Gloria Anzaldúa Reader,* 2021, p. 578.

15. Ibid. pp. 38-50.

16. G. Anzaldúa, *Light in the Dark/Luz en lo Oscuro*, 2015, p. 20

17. G. Anzaldúa and A. Keating, *The Gloria Anzaldúa Reader*, 2009, p. 542.

18. G. Anzaldúa, *Light in the Dark/Luz en lo Oscuro*, 2015.

19. A. Keating, *Teaching Transformation: Transcultural Classroom Dialogues,* New York, NY: Springer, 2007.

20. G. Anzaldúa, *Light in the Dark/Luz en lo Oscuro*, 2015, p.6.

21. Ibid. pp. 38-39.

22. Ibid. p. 121.

23. Ibid. p. 120.

24. Ibid. p. 119.

25. Ibid. p. 201.

26. Ibid. p. 237.

27. Ibid p. 122.

28. G. Anzaldúa, *Making Face, Making Soul/ Hacienda Caras*, 1990, p. 293

29. G. Anzaldúa, *Light in the Dark/ Luz en lo Oscuro*, 2015, p. 124.

30. K. Koshy. 'Nepantlera-activism in the transnational moment: In dialogue with Gloria Anzaldúa's theorizing of nepantla', *Human Architecture: Journal of the Sociology of Self-Knowledge*, vol. 4 no. 3 (2006), pp. 147-161.

31. K. Zaytoun, "'Now let us shift' the subject: Tracing the path and post humanist implications of La Naguala/The Shapeshifter in the works of Gloria Anzaldúa', *MELUS*, vol. 40 no. 4 (2015), pp. 69–88.

32. G. Anzaldúa, *Light in the Dark/Luz en lo Oscuro*, 2015, p. 31.

33. Ibid. p. 32.

34. Ibid. p. 33.

35. Ibid. p. 33.

36. C.F. Klein, 'A New Interpretation of the Aztec Statue Called Coatlicue,'Snakes-Her-Skirt'', *Ethnohistory*, vol. 55 no. 2 (2008), p. 243.

37. J. Mendez-Negrete, 'Pedagogical Conocimientos: Self and Other in Interaction', *National Association for Chicana and Chicago Studies Annual Conference 2013. Proceedings special issue "Rio Bravo: A Journal of the Borderlands"*, 2013, pp. 226-250. https://scholarworks.sjsu.edu/naccs/Tejas_Foco/Tejas/14/

38. G. Anzaldúa and A. Keating (eds.), *This Bridge We Call Home: Radical Visions for Transformation*, New York and London: Routledge, 2013, pp. 567-568.

39. G. Anzaldúa, *Making Face, Making Soul: Haciendo Caras*, 1990, p. xvi.

40. Ibid. p. 24.

41. P. Freire, *Pedagogy of the Oppressed*, New York: Seabury Press, 1970.

42. Nayda Cuevas https://www.naydacuevasart.com/

43. Esther Ortiz https://www.erieartsandculture.org/blog/esther-ortiz

44. Natalia Anciso https://artsinoakland.org/articles/natalia-anciso/

45. Celeste de Luna https://www.celestedeluna.com/

46. Consuelo Jimenez Underwood http://www.consuelojunderwood.com/

47. Carmen Argote https://carmenargote.com/

48. Margarita Cabrera https://americanart.si.edu/artist/margarita-cabrera-30256

49. Elia Alba https://www.eliaalba.net/about/biography

50. Marco Sanchez https://www.marcoprintsanchez.com/contact

51. Sheila Lorenzo de la Peña with Carolyn Brown Treadon 'Evolution of a Virtual Art Therapy Open Studio' in *Virtual Art Therapy*, New York and London: Routledge, 2022.

52. Liliana Wilson https://esperanzacenter.org/artists/liliana-wilson/

53. Antonio Howard https://www.antoniohoward.com/

54. L. Sotomayor, 'Uncrating Josefina Aguilar: Autohistoria and Autohistoria-Teoría in Feminist Curating of a Muñecas Series', *Studies in Art Education A Journal of Issues and Research*, vol. 60, no. 2 (2019), pp.132-143.

55. Lucy Lippard *Mixed Blessings: New Art in a Multicultural America*, New York: New Press, 1990.

56. Andrea O'Reilly Herrera, *Cuban Artists Across the Diaspora: Setting the Tent Against the House*, Austin, TX: University of Texas Press, 2011.

57. M. Reilly and L.R.Lippard (2018), *Curatorial Activism: Towards an Ethics of Curating*, London: Thames and Hudson, 2018.

58. D. Desai, 'Educating for Social Change through Art: A Personal Reckoning', *Studies in Art Education*, vol. 61 no. 1 (2020), pp. 10-23.

59. A. Keating, *Teaching Transformation: Transcultural Classroom Dialogues*, New York, NY: Springer, 2007.

60. G. Anzaldúa, *Light in the Dark/Luz en lo Oscuro*, 2015.

61. Ibid. p. 215.

62. Ibid. p. 121.

63. Ibid. p. xxix.

64. L. Sotomayor, *Teaching In/Between: Curating Educational spaces through Conocimiento and Autohistoria-teoría*, Vernon Press, 2022.

65. T.L Strayhorn, *College students' Sense of Belonging: A Key to Educational Success for All Students,* 2012.

66. A. Keating and G. González-López. *Bridging: How Gloria Anzaldúa's L:ife and Work Transformed Our Own*, Austin, TX: University of Texas Press, 2011.

67. Ibid. p. 13.

68. Ibid. p. 2.

69. G. Anzaldúa and A. Keating, *Light in the Dark: Luz en lo Oscuro,* p. 154

70. Ibid. p. 154.

71. Ibid. p. 153.

72. Ibid. p. 20.

73. Ibid. p. 89.

74. Ibid. p. 20.

75. Ibid. p. 21.

76. Ibid. p. 20.

77. G. Anzaldúa,'Introduction: Reading Gloria Anzaldúa, Reading Ourselves... Complex Intimacies, Intricate Connections', *The Gloria Anzaldúa Reader*, 2009, pp. 1-16 and p. 320.

78. M. Vallone, 'The Wound as Bridge: The Path of Conocimiento in Gloria Anzaldúa's Work'. *E-rea Revue électronique d'études sur le monde anglophone*, vol 12 no. 1 (2014), p. 32.

79. E. Facio and L. Irene (eds.), *Fleshing the Spirit: Spirituality and activism in Chicana, Latina, and Indigenous Women's Lives,* Tucson, AZ: University of Arizona Press, 2014.

About the Contributors

Dalida María Benfield, PhD, is an artist-researcher, filmmaker and theorist. Her practice is focused on decolonial feminist re-arrangements of the geo-politics of knowledge. She is the co-founder and Research and Program Director of the Center for Arts, Design + Social Research (Boston, US), an international platform supporting socially engaged arts research and popular education. Her work, often collectively produced, includes films and video installations, experimental writing, curatorial projects and activist pedagogical interventions. She has co-initiated numerous autonomous cultural, educational and research organizations and programmes, such as Video Machete (1994-2007); the Women's International Information Project (1998-2002); and the Institute of (im)Possible Subjects (2013-present). She was also an original member of the Escuela Popular Norteña, a popular education collective co-founded in 1990 by María C. Lugones and Geoff Bryce.

Katy Deepwell is the editor of KT press and Professor of Contemporary Art, Theory and Criticism at Middlesex University. She was founding editor of *n.paradoxa: international feminist art journal* (1998-2017) and KT press, as well as The-Feminist-Art-Observatory at www.ktpress.co.uk. Her recent books include: *50 Feminist Art Manifestos*, KT press, 2022 and *Feminist Art Activisms and Artivisms*, Amsterdam:Valiz, 2020.

Ayanna Dozier, PhD, is a Brooklyn-based filmmaker-artist and writer working with performance, experimental film, installation, and analog photography. Recent exhibitions include: Hauser and Wirth (Los Angeles, CA), BRIC (Brooklyn, NY), Microscope Gallery (New York, NY), Block Museum (Chicago, IL), MoCA, Arlington (Arlington, VA), and The Shed (New York, NY). She was a 2022 Wave Hill Winter Workspace Resident (Bronx, NY), a 2018-2019 Helena Rubinstein Fellow in Critical Studies at the Whitney Independent Studies Program, and a Joan Tisch Teaching Fellow from 2017-2022 at Whitney Museum of American Art (New York, NY). Her film work is in the permanent collection of the Whitney Museum of American Art. She is the author of Janet Jackson's *The Velvet Rope* (2020) and is an assistant professor in film at University of Massachusetts, Amherst.

Michelle Williams Gamaker is an artist working in moving image, often in dialogue with film history. Through an interrogation of cinema and its artifice, she recasts characters as fictional activists, proposing critical alternatives to colonial and imperialist storytelling in early twentieth-century British and Hollywood studio films. Her exhibition, *Our Mountains Are Painted on Glass*, premiered her film *Thieves* at South London Gallery in 2023. *The Bang Straws* was exhibited at The London Open 2022, Whitechapel Gallery and several film festivals. Williams Gamaker is joint-winner of Film London's Jarman Award 2020. She is also a recipient of the FLAMIN Production Award 2022 and the British Academy's Wolfson Fellowship to research 'Narrative Reparations: On Fictional Activism, Fictional Revenge and Fictional Healing'. She is a Reader in BA Fine Art at Goldsmiths and a Trustee of Gasworks, London.

Co-contributors to A Particular Reality (APR)

JJ Chan is an artist working across sculpture, moving image and writing. Through storytelling and world-building, their work (re)searches for an alternative space beyond aggressively progressive capitalist time, seeking new worlds from the ashes of the present. They are Senior Lecturer in Fine Art at Kingston University London.

Ali Eisa is an artist and co-founder of Lloyd Corporation, a collaborative project taking inspiration from informal and local economies with artist Sebastian Lloyd Rees. Ali develops and facilitates participatory projects focusing on issues of human rights, empowerment and access for people from highly marginalised backgrounds. Ali is a Lecturer in BA Fine Art, Goldsmiths University and Programme leader for A Particular Reality.

Alice Gale-Feeny is an artist and writer who makes performance via dance, sculpture, video and facilitation. Recent and forthcoming projects include: contributor to *Diffracting New Materialisms*, Palgrave Macmillan (2023); 'JOAN' in *WRONG WRITING* anthology (2023); *Performance Exchange*, Seventeen Gallery, London (2021). Alice is a Lecturer in BA Fine Art at Kingston University, London.

Sarah Howe is an artist working across expanded portraiture and self-portraiture, to produce moving images, photography and written prose combined in large-scale multimedia installations. The works engage with individuals and communities to develop frameworks for presenting visual and spoken narratives, around themes of identity, empathy and health. Sarah is a Lecturer in Photography at Manchester Metropolitan University.

Laiba Raja is an artist, writer and designer. Her research is rooted in the exploration between translation and language, using visual and material cultures of the subcontinent. She is also a part of Aurat March, a prominent Women's Movement and community of resistance in Lahore, Pakistan. She graduated from the BA Fine Art programme at Goldsmiths University in 2022.

Abhaya Rajani is a dalit queer feminist artist and educator based in London. She is invested in constructing a dialogue within safe spaces to develop anti-caste consciousness through films, workshops, durational performances, participatory research, translations and text. She is a co-founder of Godhadi collective and Rakhan Productions. Abhaya is a 2021-22 recipient of the Stanley Picker Fellowship, currently working as an APR Fellow and visiting lecturer, BA Fine Art, Kingston School of Art.

Francesca Telling is an artist and creative learning facilitator. Her practice traverses photography, sculpture and writing to investigate how social histories are recorded in objects and images, building speculative archival explorations of grief and cultural loss through the use of outmoded technologies, traditional processes and found ephemera.

Fatima Hussain is an independent artist-curator and an academic researcher based in Pakistan. She is Assistant Professor at the National College of Arts (NCA) in Pakistan. She is a co-investigator in a GCRF-UKRI-funded 'The Culture and Conflict' project that is based at the London School of Economics and Political Science (LSE) and Middlesex University. In Pakistan, she co-directs Laajverd (founded in 2008), an interdisciplinary collective that works at the intersection of culture, art and architecture, and Second Practice (founded in 2018), which focuses on designing and carrying out collaborative practice-based artistic research. Fatima is interested in transdisciplinary methodologies to think across fields and geographical boundaries. Her art and academic practice are particularly concerned with critical inquiry into geographies appropriated by hegemonic conceptualizations of space that impact the way creative practice is represented in postcolonial contexts. Fatima has presented projects at the 17th Istanbul Biennale (2022), Karachi Biennale (2022), Karachi Biennale (2017), University of Toronto (2013), SAVAC (2013), Independent Curators International NY (2012), Zahoor ul Akhlaq Gallery (2011), SPILL Festival London (2010), Flux Deptford X (2009), The Guild NY (2009),and Aicon Gallery London (2008), among others.

 De-/Anti-/Post-colonial Feminisms

Aarti Kawlra is an anthropologist and currently an Affiliate Fellow at the French Institute, Pondicherry (IFP) India and Academic Director of the 'Humanities Across Borders' program (https://humanitiesacrossborders.org/) of the International Institute for Asian Studies Leiden (IIAS), The Netherlands. She was the co-principal investigator of the ICSSR sponsored project 'Craft in the discourse of caste-based education in twentieth century South India', at the Madras Institute of Development Studies (MIDS) Chennai. Her publications include the article 'Recipes for Re-enchantment: Natural Dyes and Dyeing in India' in *Cloth and India: Towards Recent Histories 1947-2015*, Marg (2016); the monograph *We Who Wove with Lotus Thread: Summoning Community in South India*, Hyderabad: Orient Blackswan, 2018; and the book chapters 'Reconstituting Craft in the Idiom of Education for the Masses' in Milind Brahme, M. Suresh Babu and Thomas Muller (eds.), *Inclusive Education in India: Concepts, Methods and Practice*, New Delhi: Mosaic Books, 2018; 'Between Culture and Technology: Theme Saris and the Graphic Representation of Heritage in Tamil Nadu, India' in Ayami Nakatani (ed.), *Fashionable Traditions: Asian Handmade Textiles in Motion,* London: Lexington Books, 2020; and 'Narrating Indigo: Telling and Re-telling Subjectivities of Craft in India' in Chandan Bose and Mira Mohsini (eds.), *Encountering Craft,* Routledge, 2023. She is the co-editor of the Humanities Across Borders Methodologies Book Series, Amsterdam University Press. She is a member of the board of the Knowledge House of Craft, an international network and association for those who create and maintain craft knowledge.

Shanna Ketchum-Heap of Birds is a citizen of the Diné/Navajo Nation. In 2022, she completed her PhD at Middlesex University, London, focused on contemporary Native American/Indigenous visual artists and theatre and performance studies. Recent essays were published in *Artforum International, Wired Italia,* and *Art Review* magazine and in Tony Fisher and Eve Katsouraki (eds.), *Beyond Failure: New Essays on the Cultural History of Failure in Theatre and Performance.* Routledge, 2018. See https://dinehwriter.art/ She has lectured at Artists Space in NYC, the Walker Art Center in Minneapolis, Nanyang University in Singapore, and Skype/Zoom lectures for the Barcelona Facultat De Geografia; Història Universitat De Barcelona; Museu D'art Contemporani De Barcelona (MACBA) and Shape: A Virtual Artist Residency, sponsored by Vinegar Projects: An Artists-Run Space. Ketchum-Heap of Birds also curated *Suffer, Dance, Stand: Native Survival* with Edgar Heap of Birds, Douglas Miles, and Warren Realrider in 2022 at OK #1 in Tulsa, Oklahoma. Dr. Ketchum-Heap of Birds is currently on the board of Spiderwoman Theater Company (the longest running Native American feminist theater group in the USA).

Sharlene Khan is a South African visual artist and scholar whose multi-media works focus on the socio-political realities of a post-apartheid society and the intersectionality of race-gender-class. She holds a PhD (Arts) from Goldsmiths and is Associate Professor at the Department of Fine Arts, Wits School of the Arts, University of the Witwatersrand, Johannesburg. She has exhibited in the UK, Italy, France, Germany, South Africa, India, South Korea and Greece. Her writings have appeared in *Art South Africa, Artthrob, Springerin, Manifesta journal, Contemporary-And, The Conversation Africa, Imbizo: International Journal of African Literary and African Studies, Agenda* and *The Palgrave Handbook of Race and the Arts in Education.* She is a recipient of the Rockefeller Bellagio Visual Arts residency (2009), the Canon Collins/Commonwealth Scholarship (2011), the African Humanities Postdoctoral Fellowship (2017), the National Institute for Humanities and Social Sciences Award for Visual Arts (2018) and was runner-up winner in the

Videokunst Preis Bremen video art award (2015). Her catalogues include: *What I look like, What I feel like* (2009), *I Make Art* (2017) and *When the moon waxes red... Negotiating Subjective Terrain as an 'Inside-Outsider', an 'Outside-Insider'* (2019).

Dr Neelam Raina has a BA (Hons) History, MA Textiles, MA Design, and her PhD is in Design and Development. She is currently Associate Professor of Design and Development, Faculty of Arts and Creative Industries, Department of Design, Middlesex University and an expert in post-conflict reconstruction and sustainable livelihoods. She is also Principal Investigator in a GCRF-UKRI funded 'The Culture and Conflict' project for a section of the grant based at Middlesex University in collaboration with London School of Economics and Political Science (LSE). She has been a keen advocate for Afghanistan since the fall of Kabul and is the Director Public Affairs of the All Party Parliamentary Group on Afghan Women and Girls for the UK government. Dr Raina has edited *Creative Economies of Culture in South Asia: Craftspeople and performers* (Routledge: forthcoming, 2024). In addition to academic publications, Raina contributes to key policy documents through evidence presented in UK Parliament as part of her advocacy and activism around gender, justice and security in South Asia.

Leslie C. Sotomayor II is an artist, curator, and holds a dual PhD in Art Education and Women's, Gender, and Sexuality Studies. Currently she is a Visiting Assistant Professor at Texas Tech University in Women's and Gender Studies. She focuses on Gloria Anzaldúa's theory of *conocimiento* and *autohistoria-teoría*, a feminist writing practice of theorizing one's experiences as transformative acts, to guide her teaching methodology and create curriculum for empowerment and transformation in curating art/educational spaces/ communities that decolonize White hegemonic canons. Sotomayor has completed artworks, installations and curated numerous art exhibitions including: *Let's Pretend* (2021), *Entre Mundos/Traveling In-Between* (2018), *Hilos Rojos* (2017), a solo traveling exhibition in Cuba, and *Borrandofronteras/Erasingborders* (2015), a Cuban and Cuban-American Collaborative Art Exhibition and Cultural Exchange. Sotomayor has numerous publications about her research and work in the United States and Cuba engaging in *testimonio*, social change, and decolonizing curatorial projects, visual arts studio practice, research and scholarship in Chicana/Latina Studies: *The Journal of Mujeres Activas en Letras y Cambio Social, Artizien: Art and Teaching Journal, Studies in Art Education, Art Education*, and *Visual Arts Research*. Her recent book is *Teaching In/between: Curating Educational Spaces with Autohistoria-teoría and Conocimiento,* Wilmington: Vernon Press, 2022.

Madina Tlostanova is a feminist verbal artist and Professor of Postcolonial fFminisms at the Department of Thematic Studies (Gender studies division) at Linköping University, Sweden. She focuses on decolonial thought, postsocialist human condition and art, feminisms of the Global South, critical future studies. She has authored fourteen scholarly books and around 300 articles and book chapters translated into several languages. Her most recent books include *What Does it Mean to be Post-Soviet? Decolonial Art from the Ruins of the Soviet Empire*, Durham: Duke University Press, 2018; co-authored with Tony Fry, *A New Political Imagination. Making the Case.* Routledge, 2020; co-edited with Redi Koobak and Suruchi Thapar-Björkert, *Postcolonial and Postsocialist Dialogues. Intersectons, Opacities, Challenges in Feminist Theorizing and Practice*, Routledge, 2021 and, the most recent experimental monograph, *Narratives of Unsettlement. Being Out-of-joint as a Generative Human Condition*, Routledge, 2023.

                    De-/Anti-/Post-colonial Feminisms

Françoise Vergès is a French political scientist, activist, historian, film producer and public educator. She grew up on the island of La Réunion, and worked for many years as a journalist and editor in the women's liberation movement in France. Recent publications include: *A Feminist Theory of Violence*, London: Pluto, 2022, *A Decolonial Feminism,* Pluto, 2021, and *A Programme of Absolute Disorder*, Pluto, forthcoming 2024. She is the Chair of Global South(s), Collège d'études mondiales in Paris, Fondation Maison des Sciences de l'Homme, Paris. Her other books include: *De la violence coloniale dans l'espace public* (2021); published in English as *The Wombs of Women; Capitalism, Race, Feminism,* Durham: Duke University Press, 2020; and *Aimé Césaire, Resolutely Black: Conversations with Francoise Verges*, Hoboken: Wiley, 2019; *Monsters and Revolutionaries. Colonial family romance and "Métissage"*, Durham: Duke University Press, 1999. She writes on slavery, colonialism, imperialism, decolonial feminism and a new politics of dispossession and racialization. She is the curator of "L'Atelier," a regular collective workshop among artists and scholars, and other events. She is an activist in the global anti-racist struggle. She holds a PhD in Political Science from the University of California, Berkeley.